Samuel Beckett

Waiting for Godot

Endgame

EDITED BY PETER BOXALL

Consultant editor: Nicolas Tredell

ICON BOOKS

Published in 2000 by Icon Books Ltd.,
Grange Road, Duxford, Cambridge CB2 4QF
e-mail: info@iconbooks.co.uk
www.iconbooks.co.uk

Distributed in the UK, Europe, Canada, South Africa and Asia by the
Penguin Group: Penguin Books Ltd., 27 Wrights Lane, London W8 5TZ

Published in Australia in 2000 by Allen & Unwin Pty. Ltd.,
PO Box 8500, 9 Atchison Street, St. Leonards, NSW 2065

Consultant editor: Nicolas Tredell
Managing editor: Duncan Heath
Series devised by: Christopher Cox
Cover design: Simon Flynn
Typesetting: Wayzgoose

ISBN 1 84046 082 2

Printed and bound in Great Britain by
Cox & Wyman Ltd., Reading

Contents

INTRODUCTION 5

Places the plays in the context of Beckett's writing life, and introduces the critical approaches to be considered in the Guide.

CHAPTER ONE 9

First Responses to *Waiting for Godot* and *Endgame*

This chapter covers a range of initial responses to *Waiting for Godot* and *Endgame*, and is split into two sections.

1. Nothing Happens Twice: Reviews and Early Journalism
This section looks at a range of reactions to the first performances of the plays, and considers the scope and the nature of their initial impact. It includes extracts from reviews by critics such as Kenneth Tynan, Harold Hobson, Patrick Kavanagh, Jacques Lemarchand and Vivian Mercier.

2. Presence, Negativity and the Human Condition: First Essays
Moving on from early journalism and reviews, this section looks in more detail at two of the first full-length essayistic responses to the plays. The section reads Martin Esslin's humanist reading of the plays as examples of the 'Theatre of the Absurd', against Adorno's Marxist reading of *Endgame* as a critique of post-war European culture.

CHAPTER TWO 51

Humanising the Void

This chapter traces the development of a liberal humanist reading of the plays, from the sixties to the present day, and is split into two sections.

1. New Criticism and Esslin's Three Categories
This section looks at Martin Esslin's influential introduction to his 1965 collection of essays. It discusses and lays out the three modes of critical enquiry that Esslin suggests are valid responses to Beckett's writing.

2. Kenner, Cohn and the Liberal Humanist Beckett
This section traces the development of humanist readings of the plays as they have developed from Esslin's work onwards, focusing particularly on the work of Ruby Cohn (with extracts from *Samuel Beckett: The Comic Gamut*) and Hugh Kenner (with extracts from *A Reader's Guide to Samuel Beckett* and *Samuel Beckett: A Critical Study*).

CHAPTER THREE   94

Beckett and the Emergence of Theory

This chapter traces the development of other theoretical approaches, as they have grown up alongside the more dominant liberal humanist paradigm discussed in chapter two, and is split into three sections.

1. Beckett, Derrida and the Resistance to Theory
This section considers the relative paucity of theoretical approaches to Beckett, focusing on Derrida's discussion of his own reluctance to embark on a reading of Beckett's work.

2. Beckett, Iser and Reader Response
This section looks back to the seventies, and discusses the emergence of a 'reader response' approach to Waiting for Godot. It includes extracts from Wolfgang Iser's The Implied Reader, and from his essay entitled 'Counter-sensical Comedy and Audience Response in Beckett's Waiting for Godot'.

3. Beckett, Post-structuralism and Feminism
This section looks at the emergence in the late eighties of post-structuralist and deconstructive-feminist readings of Waiting for Godot and Endgame. It includes extracts from Steven Connor's essay entitled 'The Doubling of Presence in Waiting for Godot and Endgame', and from Mary Bryden's essay entitled 'Gender in Transition'.

CHAPTER FOUR   137

Political Criticism

This chapter discusses the growth of an overtly political criticism, as it has developed from Adorno's Marxist reading of Endgame. It includes extracts from Ernst Fischer's seventies Marxist work, Art Against Ideology, from Werner Huber's consideration of the relation between Beckett and Bertolt Brecht, and from Declan Kiberd's reading of Godot and Endgame as post-colonial texts in Inventing Ireland.

NOTES   168

SELECT BIBLIOGRAPHY   178

ACKNOWLEDGEMENTS   185

INDEX   186

INTRODUCTION

SAMUEL BECKETT wrote the two plays for which he is best known, *Waiting for Godot* and *Endgame*, in the middle phase of his writing career. *Waiting for Godot* was written in French, as *En attendant Godot*, between October 1948 and January 1949, in the midst of a frantic burst of activity that produced two plays, three novels and several short stories.[1] The first draft of *Endgame* was also written in French, as *Fin de partie*, in 1955, after his frenzy of prose writing had come to a close with *The Unnamable* (which was published in French in 1953). The impact that these plays had, both on Beckett's career, and on post-war European culture, was enormous. The success of the first productions of *Godot* in 1953 took Beckett from obscurity to notoriety and, in its total disregard for existing conventions, threw the dramatic world into an excited, confused consternation. With the first productions of *Fin de partie* in London in 1958, Beckett emerged as a playwright of extraordinary radicalism and extreme dramatic precision, whose vision of life in the twentieth century became, for many, definitive. His starkly vivid stage images articulated a post-war experience that had previously been inarticulable, and in doing so gave birth to a new drama.

The critical response to *Godot* and *Endgame* has reflected both the cultural importance of the plays and their originality. Whilst the general recognition of the drama's importance has been testified to by the vast quantity of critical work it has produced in a relatively short period of time, the originality of the plays is reflected in the uncertainty and confusion with which they were first received by the critical community. The boldness with which *Godot* undermined dramatic conventions caused a huge sensation, and the play commanded a great deal of attention, but the very newness that so distinguished it made it very hard to interpret, or even to describe. It seemed to their first audiences that both *Godot* and *Endgame* achieved their effects by the stubborn refusal to meet all expectations; the apparatuses of drama, such as plot, setting, catastrophe, were all abandoned, and with them went the conventions that allowed the critic to pass educated and sound judgement. None of the criteria by which good drama was measured appeared to be met in these plays, and yet here they were, looking good. In the very early reviews, critics responded to this undermining of established theatrical codes in two ways – they either dismissed the plays as trivial nonsense, or they saw them as a profoundly challenging dramatic development that required critics and dramatists alike to rethink the conventions that had sustained theatre thus far. For those critics in the latter category, however, it was not immediately clear how to proceed with the interpretation of an art whose power was perceived to lie in its uninterpretability, its radical denial of the processes by which theatre becomes meaningful. What seemed to be required was a critical or elucidatory language that could somehow interpret the plays' uninterpretability, that could cast light on the plays' meaninglessness in ways that made it appear meaningful, without reconstructing the very critical and dramatic conventions whose denial constituted their meaning. The struggle to create such a language – to preserve the impact of the plays' meaninglessness whilst exploring what such meaninglessness might mean – has characterised the development of Beckett studies over the last five decades. As literary theory has grown and mutated throughout this period, *Godot* and *Endgame* have been subject to a wide range of analytical approaches, which have sought a means of giving critical expression to Beckett's dramatic negativity. The agonistic and difficult dialogue between Beckett and literary criticism that has ensued has helped us to understand Beckett's plays; it has also helped us to understand criticism.

This Guide traces the relationship between the plays and their critical reception as it has evolved over these decades. In doing so, it does not follow a strictly chronological order. Rather, it takes its organising principle from the theoretical and political battles that have surrounded the plays from the fifties to the nineties. The first chapter addresses the political gulf that opened in Beckett's critical reception in the fifties, after the first productions of *Waiting for Godot* and *Endgame*. Reading a range of contemporary reviews, and focusing on two of the earliest major essays on Beckett's drama by Martin Esslin and Theodor Adorno, this chapter explores the initial rift between a liberal humanist and a Marxist reading of the plays. For Martin Esslin, the plays are an essentially affirmative and redemptive vision of a struggling but persisting humanity, naked and noble, seen in its truest light. For Adorno, on the contrary, they offer no such comforting representation of a fundamental humanity; on the contrary, they demonstrate the collapse of a culture that allowed such ideological structures as humanism to persist. *Endgame* dramatises the deterioration of culture, after the atrocities of the twentieth century, to a bomb-site in which none of the myths that have sustained Western civilisation are left standing. All that emerges from the play's ruins is a mute critique of the social processes that have led to such destruction, which is mute because there is no longer a cultural language left intact with which to articulate resistance or protest. Beckett's drama was beyond the interpretive powers of theory or philosophy, because what it dramatised was the failure of such discourses to be able to express the depravity of contemporary conditions, which is expressible only in the desolate spaces of Beckett's stage.

This early opposition between a critical approach that read Beckett's representation of meaninglessness, or 'absurdity', as being ultimately recuperable in the figure of a transcendent humanity and one that saw his negativity as a powerful and unparaphrasable critique of the collapse of post-war European culture, has proved extremely durable in Beckett studies. Indeed, this opposition provides the framework for the remaining chapters of the book. The second, third and fourth chapters trace different critical strands as they develop from the initial divergence in critical opinion. The second chapter focuses on the development of a liberal humanist paradigm as it progresses from Esslin's early appropriation of Beckett's drama as an example of the 'Theatre of the Absurd'. This paradigm, which has remained extremely influential from the sixties to the present day, regards the plays as apolitical representations of the 'human condition'. Drawing on a formalist critical method that has affinities with New Criticism and early structuralism, the critics represented in this chapter pay particular attention to the formal qualities of Beckett's drama. It is in the beauty and symmetry of the shapes that Beckett makes on stage that the redeeming quality of his vision can be found. He may give expression to a humanity that has become detached from metaphysical and theological roots, but the sheer, ineffable beauty and grace of the dramatic structures with which he expresses humanity in crisis provides the drama with its own meaning and its own epiphany. The third chapter traces a number of theoretical approaches, as they have grown up alongside the more dominant liberal humanist paradigm, from the reader response approach to Beckett's drama adopted by Wolfgang Iser in the seventies to the deconstructive and feminist approaches by Steven Connor and Mary Bryden developed in the eighties and nineties. Where the liberal humanists had recast Beckett's representation of absurdity as positive and life-affirming by focusing on the stage as the physical space in which an essential humanity asserts itself, these theorists suggested that his drama undermined the certainty of 'presence' on the stage. Moving away from the suggestion that Beckett dramatises a 'human' predicament, critics such as Connor and Bryden regard Beckett's stage as a site on which meaning, identity and subjecthood, were put radically into question. For these critics Beckett's negativity is not contained within his humanism, but allows him to explore the ongoing dynamics of language and representation, to dramatise the limits at which representation topples into nothingness. In doing so, Beckett's stage becomes a space in which subjects live out the eternal process of the invention and projection of selfhood. The fourth chapter traces the evolution of a more engaged political criticism, as it has developed from Adorno's influential early essay. It explores readings of the political possibilities of Beckett's drama, from Ernst Fischer's 1966 essay on *Endgame* to nineties readings of the drama as a post-colonial aesthetic by critics such as Declan Kiberd. Where the previous two strands of critical development cast Beckett's drama as being largely apolitical, the critics represented here read his drama as being deeply engaged with a culturally specific set of political concerns.

In tracing the uneasy relationship between *Godot* and *Endgame* and the critical approaches that have sought to account for them, this Guide has a twofold purpose. Its first aim is to offer a range of readings of the plays that is as wide, inclusive and revealing as possible. Its second aim is to show how Beckett's drama reflects critically upon critical establishments themselves, as they have developed their own theoretical and ideological agendas. One of the values of Beckett's plays is that, in their characteristically impoverished surplus, they exceed the moment of their own reception, and move beyond the grasp of the culture to which they speak. It is this capacity for Beckett's writing to resist critical inclusion, to draw attention instead to the fabric of the critical garment it disdains, that is perhaps one of its more precious characteristics. The critics in this Guide have preserved this capacity – they have had no choice.

CHAPTER ONE

First Responses to *Waiting for Godot* and *Endgame*

1. Nothing Happens Twice: Reviews and Early Journalism

THAT THE critic has a hard time with Beckett's texts has become one of the sustaining myths of the Beckettian critical industry. When trying to approach the drama critically, one is likely to meet with a kind of pitying mockery, both from a knowing Beckett audience who have ruled effective criticism out of court and from the plays themselves, which contain sometimes elaborate structures of resistance to elucidation and explication. A critic of Beckett's drama risks being lampooned in the same way that Winnie lampoons her would-be critic in the play *Happy Days*. Winnie, who is inexplicably buried in a mound throughout the performance, narrates an incident in which an ignorant, 'coarse' observer lumbers his way on to the stage to ask 'What's she doing? . . . What's the idea? . . . stuck up to her diddies in the bleeding ground . . . What does it mean? . . . What's it meant to mean?'.[1] Critics have taken the hint, and the notion that it is somehow inappropriate to demand significance from a Beckett play has hardened into an orthodoxy. Mindful of the famous exchange of insults in *Godot*, which culminates in Estragon's withering parting shot 'Crritic!' (*CDW* 70), critics have sheltered themselves from such opprobrium by seeking to develop a mode of analysis that falls short of critique. 'We cannot, of course, say what this play means' quickly became a refrain in interpretations of Beckett's plays.

It is clear, however, that critics have sought, and continue to seek, for meaning in Beckett's writing – that, after all, is one of the functions of criticism. This contradiction, between a critical method that seeks to avoid saying what the plays mean, and the need for critics to explain and interpret the works that they approach, can be found running through Beckett criticism from the fifties to the nineties. The earliest reviews and essays on *Waiting for Godot* and *Endgame* deal explicitly and sometimes tortuously with this problem. *Godot* appeared to initial audiences to depict the absurdity and meaninglessness of life: it seemed to be a play that dramatised the collapse of meaning, language and belief. How can one approach this total collapse, this extreme statement of the inadequacy of the stories and myths that we construct to protect ourselves from the brute absurdity of physical existence, with a coherent critical language? Surely, such a devastating revelation of the falsity of our value systems and codes of belief, if it has any real power, would undermine any critical language that sought to evaluate it or codify it. This problem is faced time and time again by the first reviewers of *Godot*. The language of explanation and judgement tends to give way to an inarticulate expression of the power of the performance, coupled with an emphasis on the incapacity of criticism to articulate the means by which the performance achieved such power. Jacques Lemarchand, reviewing the first ever performance of *En attendant Godot* in the tiny Théâtre de Babylone in Paris, exemplifies this prostration of criticism before an art it can admire, but cannot paraphrase:

■ I do not quite know how to begin describing this play by Samuel Beckett, *Waiting for Godot* (directed by Roger Blin, now playing at the Théâtre de Babylone). I have seen this play and seen it again, I have read and reread it; it still has the power to move me. I should like to communicate this feeling, to make it contagious. At the same time I am faced with the difficulty of fulfilling the primary duty of the critic, which, as everyone knows, is to explain and narrate a play to people who have neither seen it nor read it. I have experienced this difficulty many times before; the sensation is infinitely agreeable. One feels it each time one is called upon to describe a work that is beautiful, but of an unusual beauty; new, but genuinely new; traditional, but of an eminent tradition; clever, but with a cleverness the most clever professors are unable to teach; and finally, intelligent, but with that clear intelligence that is non-negotiable in the schools.[2] □

The power of the play, Lemarchand insists, is such that it exceeds description, and cannot be transcribed or translated by the critic. In fact, Lemarchand stresses in the same review that the resistance of the play to his critique of it is such that he would 'be extremely sorry if anyone should say to himself after reading [the review], "I see what it's about . . ."'.[3]

This reticence, amongst the first reviewers of *Godot*, to impinge on what appeared to be the almost sacred territory of the play, is not merely critical sheepishness, or reluctance to fall into the trap that Beckett sets for the unwary critic. It is a symptom of the kind of challenge that the play represented to the dramatic community. This challenge asserted itself in two related ways. Firstly, *Godot* slipped through the nets of critical explication because of its originality. In this it has much in common with most 'legitimately' new plays. For dramatic works to come fully into being, some critics argue, they have to operate within an accepted theatrical convention. Once we have agreed that the play in front of us is Jacobean, Elizabethan, naturalist, realist or expressionist, then we can settle into the performance, knowing that the stage will come to mean in certain pre-established ways. We understand, often unconsciously, how an aside works, how a soliloquy works, how plot and characters develop together over the duration of the performance, within what we have tacitly accepted as the dominant convention. Conventions, however, are historical constructs that change over time, and which adapt to historical contingencies. As changing social conditions demand or produce new forms of expression, plays periodically arrive that do not conform to the dominant convention, but which challenge or undermine it in important ways. These plays, precisely because they exceed the accepted boundaries of drama, and use the stage in unpredictable ways, cannot easily be incorporated into their contemporary critical discourses. As they break through the frontiers of dramatic knowledge and understanding, they prove unsettling and baffling to their commentators, but in time a new convention is established to accommodate the new play, and drama as a whole has changed, even progressed, as a result.[4] That *Godot* exceeded the known dramatic conventions of its time in this way, and that this excess was partly responsible for the critical reluctance or inability to say what it meant, is noted by many of its early reviewers. Lemarchand comments, in the review quoted above, that '*Waiting for Godot* is a profoundly original work: because of this it will necessarily be a disconcerting one'.[5] Similarly, in a review of the first (1955) English performance of *Godot*, in the London Arts Theatre Club, Kenneth Tynan writes: '*Waiting for Godot* frankly jettisons everything by which we recognise theatre . . . It forced me to re-examine the rules which have hitherto governed the drama; and, having done so, to pronounce them not elastic enough.'[6] Adjectives such as 'startling', 'extraordinary' and 'baffling' abound in reviews (both complimentary and damning) that cannot incorporate the event of *Waiting for Godot* into the system of expectations and requirements that contained twentieth-century Western theatre.

But *Godot* also presented a second sort of challenge to its critics, which is not reducible to its rejection of established theatrical conventions. This challenge is related to the play's negativity. What makes critics most uneasy is not simply that Beckett seeks to develop a new convention, or to use the stage in surprising and innovative ways, but that he threatens to abandon convention and theatricality altogether. Beckett's theatre seemed unique, and uniquely threatening, to most of his fifties' critics, because what he appeared to represent on the stage was 'nothing'. Harold Hobson speaks for many bemused contemporary critics when he comments, in his review of the 1955 performance in London, that 'in the course of the play, nothing happens'. There is no 'dramatic progress', no 'theatrical tension'.[7] The action, such as it is, is continually threatening to yield to the long, awkward silences that the audience can feel gathering behind the dialogue just as Pozzo's nightfall collects behind the tranquil twilight sky. What Beckett presented to the audience in Godot was theatre that was only just theatre, on the very brink of becoming the opposite of theatre. The stage was only fitfully controlled by the script. There was little effort to draw anyone into the collective conviction that the stage represented 'A country road' at 'Evening' (CDW 11) – it most often appeared to represent nothing other than itself. It frequently felt as if the audience had wandered into the theatre during a break in the rehearsal. As Jean Anouilh commented in a review of the 1953 performance, quoting the play itself, 'Nothing happens, nobody comes, nobody goes, it's awful.'[8] It is this representation of dramatic negativity that distinguished Beckett's theatre most clearly from other playwrights who experimented with similar ideas. It was not new for a dramatist to present the audience with the notion that the stories which make life meaningful have no essential truth value – the 'absurdity' of life had been dramatised before by Sartre and other proponents of Parisian existentialism. Where Beckett's work was shockingly original was in its adoption of a new dramatic form that directly articulated this sense of a loss of meaning. Rather than expressing the terror of existential angst from within a stable and recognisable theatrical convention, Beckett caused the stage to become the *site* of meaning's desertion. As Vladimir and Estragon wait passively on the stage for Godot to arrive and confer meaning on their waiting, Beckett abandoned every theatrical principle and undermined every expectation. Even Vladimir and Estragon's stability as characters is given no guarantee. Vladimir may be heavier than Estragon, he may be lighter (CDW 13). Vladimir may actually be called Mister Albert, Estragon's name may be Catullus (CDW 47). Beckett presents us with a situation in which 'nothing is certain' (CDW 16), and in doing so he takes dramatic form beyond its own limits, kicks out every prop that holds the dramatic space in shape, and presents us with a stage that is perpetually falling into the void left by its relentless negation of its own meaning. He does not adopt a strange convention, he negates the very idea of convention itself.

In order to respond to the challenge that this form of aesthetic negativity represented, critics were faced with the problem of generating an interpretative language or methodology that could incorporate it and examine it without destroying it. It appeared to many that this new play questioned some of the most basic assumptions that underlay not only drama, but also life in the world, and that it was extremely important to understand how it did so, and what kinds of answer there may be to *Godot*'s questions. To interrogate a dramatic practice whose primary quality was a lack of all quality, however, is rather like grasping water. For Theodor Adorno, one of Beckett's earliest critics, the 'criterion of a philosophy whose hour is struck' was that it 'proved equal to the challenge' of interpreting Beckett's drama.[9] The first and, in the English-speaking critical community, the most enduringly influential means of bringing Beckett's drama into interpretability was to convert negativity into positivity. An early stirring of this drive towards positivity is hinted at in Vivian Mercier's much-quoted article on *Godot* in 1956. In 'The Uneventful Event', Mercier comments that:

■ [Beckett] has achieved a theoretical impossibility – a play in which nothing happens, that yet keeps audiences glued to their seats. What's more, since the second act is a subtly different reprise of the first, he has written a play in which nothing happens, twice.[10] □

This witticism, playful as it is, suggests a mode of approaching Beckettian negativity that quickly became virtually orthodox. It grasps the positivity that inhabits the linguistic denotation of nothingness, and employs it as a means of concretising the non-events of the play. 'Nothing happens' is not a purely negative statement, but can be read as suggesting that something happened – the thing that happened was 'nothing'. The substantiality of nothing as a Beckettian event is given more weight by the fact that it happens twice. Finally, we see what happens in this enigmatic play – nothing happens – and now all we have to do is approach this event as if it was any other dramatic occurrence.

This thought figure re-emerges time and time again, and in various guises. The meaning of the play, for example, could be said to be its meaninglessness. If you take lack of meaning as a positive quality, then it is possible to progress beyond the aporia, or unsolvable intellectual problem, presented to the critic by an act of signification that refuses to signify. By performing such a conversion, it was even possible for critics to read the representation of meaninglessness as something reassuring and life-affirming. What Beckett achieves in *Godot*, some argued, is the removal of all the distracting baggage of everyday life, to reveal to the audience an essential truth about humanity. He depicts the naked human deprived of all comforting myths, awaiting validation from a higher source. The nothingness that is discovered beneath the sound and fury of life in the world is an emptiness that is intensely spiritual, and that helps us to understand, in a 'deep' sense, what it is to be human. In this respect, *Godot* appeared to be a profoundly Christian play. For G. S. Fraser, rather than conveying a sense of 'blank despair', the 'message of *Waiting for Godot* is perhaps something nearer a message of religious consolation':

■ Audiences do not leave the theatre, after seeing his play, feeling that life has been deprived of meaning. They feel rather that a new light has been cast on life's meaning, at several deep levels.

What sort of light, however? That is what so far has eluded critics of the play as performed. Mr. Beckett is rumoured to have instructed his English producer not, by any manner of means, to tell the actors what the theme of the play was. Yet unless Mr. Beckett whispered his central secret in the producer's ear, the warning was probably unnecessary. The elusiveness of the core has, indeed, led some critics to contend that there is no core; that the whole startling effect of the play on the stage depended on the excellent production and acting and on Mr. Beckett's own mastery of the mechanics of stage craft. The play, on this theory, would resemble the machine recently invented by an ingenious Californian, which works perfectly, with the minimum of friction, but does no 'work,' performs no function. Or, to put this with more dignity, the theory might be that Mr. Beckett in *Waiting for Godot* dramatises the notion of emptiness. This, or something like this, was the reaction of Jean Anouilh to the first performance of *En attendant Godot* in Paris. 'Nothing happens. Nobody comes, nobody goes, it's awful! But,' Anouilh added, 'I think the evening at the Babylone is as important as the première of Pirandello, put on in Paris by Piteoff in 1923.' And from what we know of Mr. Beckett's other work, we might assume that to dramatise emptiness, to have his much ado literally about nothing, may have been his conscious intention. Yet, with a play even more than a poem, we have to consider not the author's conscious intention – what the author, in a conversation, may say about 'life' – but the whole complex significance, the valid levels of meaning, of a coherent structure. What *Waiting for Godot* essentially is is a prolonged and sustained metaphor about the nature of human life. It is a metaphor which makes a particular appeal to the mood of liberal uncertainty which is the prevailing mood of modern Western Europe; and which makes (to judge by the play's failure in Miami) much less appeal to the strenuous and pragmatic temper of the contemporary American mind. It is also a play by an Irishman, by a friend and disciple of James Joyce; a play, therefore, by a man whose imagination (in the sense in which Mr. Eliot used this phrase of Joyce himself) is orthodox. In other words, we should consider where Mr. Beckett springs from and what he is reacting against in his roots. Even at his most nihilistic he will come under Mr. Eliot's category of the Christian blasphemer.

The fundamental imagery of *Waiting for Godot* is Christian; for at the depth of experience into which Beckett is probing, there is no other source of imagery for him to draw on. His heroes are two tramps, who have come from nowhere in particular and have nowhere in particular to go. Their life is a state of apparently fruitless expectation. They receive messages, through a little boy, from the local landowner, Godot, who is always going to come in person to-morrow, but never does come. Their attitude towards Godot is one partly of hope, partly of fear. The orthodoxy of this symbolism, from a Christian point of view, is obvious. The tramps, with their rags and their misery, represent the fallen state of man. The squalor of their surroundings, their lack of a 'stake in the world,' represents the idea that here in this world we can build no abiding city. The ambiguity of their attitude towards Godot, their mingled hope and fear, the doubtful tone of the boy's messages, represents the state of tension and uncertainty in which the average Christian must live in this world, avoiding presumption, and also avoiding despair. Yet the two tramps, Didi and Gogo, as they call each other, represent something far higher than the other two characters in the play, the masterful and ridiculous Pozzo and his terrifying slave, Lucky. Didi and Gogo stand for the contemplative life, Pozzo and Lucky stand for the life of practical action taken, mistakenly, as an end in itself. Pozzo's blindness and Lucky's dumbness in the second act rub this point in. The so-called practical man, the man of action, has to be set on his feet and put on his way by the contemplative man. He depends – as becomes clear, in the first act, from Pozzo's genuine though absurd gratitude for the chance of a little conversation – on the contemplative man for such moments of insight, of spiritual communication, as occur in his life. The mere and pure man of action, the comic caricature of the Nietzschean superman, Pozzo, is like an actor who does not properly exist without his audience; but his audience are also, in a sense, his judges. Pozzo and Lucky, in fact, have the same sort of function in *Waiting for Godot* as Vanity Fair in *The Pilgrim's Progress*. But they are, as it were, a perambulating Vanity Fair; Didi and Gogo are static pilgrims. It is worth noting, also, that Didi and Gogo are bound to each other by something that it is not absurd to call charity. They treat each other with consideration and compunction (their odd relationship, always tugging away from each other, but always drawn together again, is among other things an emblem of marriage). Pozzo and Lucky are drawn together by hate and fear. Their lot is increasing misery; but if Didi and Gogo are not obviously any better off at the end of the play than they were at the beginning, neither are they any worse off. Their state remains one of expectation.

   Waiting for Godot – one might sum up these remarks – is thus a modern morality play, on permanent Christian themes.[11] □

Thus, Fraser takes what appeared to contemporary audiences to be the defining thematic characteristics of the play – amorality, impermanence, despair, meaninglessness – and conjures them into their opposites – moral pedagogy, permanent Christian values, hope, and the promise of redemption from the 'squalor' and 'misery' of our 'fallen world'. Gogo and Didi wait for salvation from the doubt-ridden condition of living, in a barren limbo in which the meaning of our lives is hidden from us, but even during this uncertain wait the play maintains a moral structure that, precisely because it persists in such a sparse universe, becomes all the more enduring. It is Estragon and Vladimir's 'charity', their fundamental humanity, that sets them aside from Pozzo and Lucky, and forms the moral fabric of the play.

Whilst Christian interpretations of *Godot* maintained some currency over the following two decades,[12] the majority of critics resisted such an unconditional reading of *Godot* as a 'modern morality play'. The structure that Fraser's reading relies on, however, in which an essential and potentially redemptive humanity is seen to lie beneath a patina of trivial social meaning structures, is duplicated by many critics who reject an overt Christian thematic. The 'human condition' came to be widely viewed as the substance of this insubstantial play. Gogo and Didi may appear to be on the verge of fading out, as the play fails to provide the dramatic conditions for their continued existence, but this flickering of the reality effect does not threaten to reveal the void. Rather, it opens on to the wide expanses of humanity itself. Gogo and Didi are not on the brink of becoming nobody at all, because they promise to become 'everyman'. By the steady removal of all individual qualities, the play arrives at a picture of an all-encompassing generality. This representation of a denuded but stubbornly persistent species, no qualities and all essence, was enthusiastically welcomed, not least because it offered a model of 'universal' theatre that crossed national and political divides. For many critics, Beckett's drama was regarded as diametrically opposed to the politically committed Irish theatre that preceded it. Here was an Irish dramatist who rose above the parochial nationalist squabbles that dominated his country's productions for the stage, to forge a drama that spoke of issues that were more fundamental and permanent than cultural and political controversies. Patrick Kavanagh speaks for many critics, when, in 1956, he makes a clear distinction between Beckett's universal theatre, and those less powerful dramatists who become engaged in local concerns.

■ To those of us who cannot abide the theatre with its flatulent pieties, its contrivances and its lies, *Waiting for Godot* is a wonderful play, a great comedy. I do not set out to interpret *Godot*, merely to say why I like it, which is probably the only valid criticism.

Take a play like *The Bishop's Bonfire*, which was well received in Dublin. There you have the old unhappy Shibboleths paraded, the theme of 'Ireland' as a moral reality, and the last refuge of the weak, the theme that our failure to ramble out into the flowery lanes of liberty which O'Casey is always talking about, is due to forces outside ourselves. In O'Casey's case the restrictions of religion are the villain of the melodrama.[13]

All of us who are sincere know that if we are unhappy, trying to forget our futility in pubs it is due to no exterior cause, but to what is now popularly called the human condition. Society everywhere today and its beliefs are pastiche; there is no overall purpose, no large umbrella of serenity.

This world-wide emotion has seeped through national boudoirs. It flowed into Ireland many years ago, but the 'Ireland' writers continued as if nothing had happened. Now and again one noticed their discomfiture; why, they seemed to be asking themselves, was no one giving them any heed?

These 'Ireland' writers, who are still writing, of course, could not see that the writers of Ireland were no longer Corkery and O'Connor and the others, but Auden and George Barker – anyone anywhere who at least appreciated, if he could not cure, their misfortune. Saying this is liable to make one the worst in the world, for a national literature, being based on a convention, not born of the unpredictable individual and his problem, is a vulnerable racket and is protected by fierce wild men. A national literature is the only thing some men have got, and men will not relinquish their hold on the only thing that gives them a reason for living.

It is because of this awareness of the peculiar sickness of society and a possible remedy suggested that I like Beckett's play. The remedy is that Beckett has put despair and futility on the stage for us to laugh at them. And we do laugh.

I am not going to say that *Godot* is a great illuminating, hope-creating masterpiece like *King Lear*, but then, that is the present condition of humanity. Beckett is an honest writer. Academic writers and painters are always ready to offer the large illuminating symbol; they give us gods and heroes, and they write and paint as if society were a solid, unified Victorian lie.

I know that I am not being very direct in my statements about *Waiting for Godot*, but that is part of this play's importance; it both holds a mirror up to life and keeps reminding you, if you are interested in sincerity, that the reason that you couldn't endure the theatre hitherto was that it was tenth-rate escapism, not your dish at all.[14] □

Kavanagh here contrasts Beckett's modernist and internationalist vision of futility and despair, which is located at the level of an individual struggle against a 'world-wide' existential crisis, with a myopic nationalist literature, which is stupidly preoccupied with local beliefs and commitments that have already been shown to be trivial and illusory. Influentially pitting Beckett against the nationalist myth-makers of the Celtic revival, Kavanagh suggests that Beckett is unafraid of the harsh realties of the twentieth-century human condition, and is able to tell it how it is, without cowering in the shelter of national identity or political struggle. Collective problems and identifications give way in Beckett to an almost joyful recognition of chronic isolation. But for Kavanagh, crucially, Beckett's representation of isolation, futility and despair, is a humanist, affirmative vision, rather than a negative one. In putting futility on the stage, he recognises a human quality and is able to confront it: by making it funny, he is able to make us face it, and even almost like it. Beckett's emptiness becomes a positive comment on humanity in crisis. His comedy is its remedy.

This positivisation of Beckett's vision, coupled with an emphasis on the redemptive quality of his humour, proved more problematic for critics, however, with the appearance of Beckett's second published play, *Endgame*. This was partly due to differences between the texts themselves, and partly to the history of their performance. The textual differences between the two plays were immediately clear to contemporary reviewers. Where *Godot* takes place on an open road, waiting for the arrival of a saviour, *Endgame* unfolds in a cramped, internal stage space, in which history and nature have ended, and the saviour has already failed to appear. If, in *Godot*, 'Hope deferred maketh the something sick' (*CDW* 12), it seemed to be the temporary sickness of anxiety and unknowingness, and the deferral of hope held out the promise of cure in eventual arrival. In *Endgame*, there is no such uncertainty about the outcome of history, and sickness is a permanent condition. The evens chance of redemption in *Godot* has failed to pay off and the protagonists, Hamm and Clov, have lost their stake money. Many critics thought of *Godot* and *Endgame* as two parts of the same play. *Endgame* is where Gogo and Didi finally end up, after a lifetime of baffled hope, or Hamm is actually Godot himself, cruelly indifferent to the sufferings of those who depend upon his mercy and his help. However you look at it, critics claimed, *Endgame* is *Godot* wound down, defeated and unremittingly bleak. The dialogue no longer canters, but doggedly trudges, grinding out its inevitable, toneless 'tale of woe'. This shared sense that *Endgame* strenuously resisted the critical conversion of negativity into something honestly life-affirming was further emphasised by the style of the first French-language production in London and the English-language productions in London and New York. Where the 1955 performance of *Godot*, directed by Peter Hall at the Arts Theatre Club, had been played for laughs, both Roger Blin's London performance of *Fin de partie* and the New York and London performances of *Endgame* (directed by Alan Schneider and George Devine respectively) were played with a weight and gravitas that stifled the comedy of the latter play.[15] The effect of this downplaying of the comic elements in the play was exacerbated by reports that Beckett was involved with Blin's, Schneider's and Devine's productions, and wanted them to be played as flat and straight as possible. It also emerged that Beckett was unhappy with Peter Hall's upbeat performance of *Waiting for Godot*, and preferred even this 'lighter' play to be performed in a deadpan monotone. Even for many of Beckett's most vocal supporters, this rejection of any basis for hope or affirmation cast doubt on Beckett's stature as a dramatist, and put *Endgame* beyond the acceptable boundaries of theatre. Kenneth Tynan, whose enthusiastic review of *Godot* in the *Observer* was very influential,[16] exemplified such a response in his 1957 review of *Fin de partie*:

■ As produced in London, *Waiting for Godot* made Beckett's world valid and persuasive. Though deserted by God, the tramps survived, and did so with gaiety, dignity and a moving interdependence; a human affirmation was made. I had heard, and discounted, rumours that Beckett disliked the London production. Those rumours I now believed. The new play, directed by Roger Blin under the author's supervision, makes it clear that his purpose is neither to move nor to help us. For him, man is a pigmy who connives at his own inevitable degradation. There, says Beckett, stamping on the face of mankind: there, that is how life is. And when protest is absent, the step from 'how life is' to 'how life should be' is horrifyingly short.

Before going any further, I ought to explain what I think the play is about. I take it to be an analysis of the power-complex. The hero, a sightless old despot robed in scarlet, has more than a passing affinity with Francis Bacon's paintings of shrieking cardinals. He lives in a womb-shaped cell, attended by Clov, his shambling slave, on whose eyes he is totally dependent. His throne is flanked by two dust-bins, wombs within the womb, inhabited by his parents, Nagg and Nell. Eventually Nell dies, whereupon the tyrant asks Clov to see what Nagg is up to. 'Il pleure,' says Clov. 'Donc,' says the Boss, 'il vit.'[17] The curtain falls on a symbolic stalemate: King (Nagg) versus King and Knight (Boss and Clov). The boss is imprisoned for ever in the womb. He can never escape from his father.

Schopenhauer once said: 'The will is the strong blind man who carries on his shoulders the lame man who can see.' Beckett reverses the positions. It is the lame man, Clov – representing perception and imagination – who is bowed down by the blind bully of naked will. The play is an allegory about authority, an attempt to dramatise the neurosis that makes men love power. So far, so good. I part company with Beckett only when he insists that the problem is insoluble, that this is a deterministic world. 'Quelque chose suit son cours':[18] and there is nothing we can do about it. My interpretation may be incomplete, but it illuminates at least one of the play's facets. The blind irascible hero, Hamm, is working on an interminable novel: does this not bring to mind the 'cantankerous Irishman' by whom Beckett was once employed? Hamm stands for many things: for the Church, the State, and even Godot himself; for all the forms of capricious authority. One of them may perhaps be Joyce.

When I read the play, I enjoyed long stretches of it – laconic exchanges that seemed to satirise despair, vaudeville non-sequiturs that savagely parodied logic. Within the dark framework I even discerned glimmers of hope. I now see that I was wrong. Last week's production, portentously stylised, piled on the agony until I thought my skull would split. Little variation, either of pace or emphasis, was permitted: a cosmic comedy was delivered as if its author had been Racine. . . . I suddenly realised that Beckett wanted his private fantasy to be accepted as objective truth. And that nothing less would satisfy him. For a short time I am prepared to listen in any theatre to any message, however antipathetic. But when it is not only disagreeable but forced down my throat, I demur. . . .

This kind of facile pessimism is dismaying in an author of Beckett's stature. It is not only the projection of a personal sickness, but a conclusion reached on inadequate evidence. I am ready to believe that the world is a stifling, constricting place – but not if my informant is an Egyptian mummy.[19] □

Tynan's frustration with *Endgame* – his reluctance to accept an art form that refused either to 'move' or to 'help' us – was typical of the response that the play received from English-speaking journalists. There were some more enthusiastic reviews, which tended to come from critics who managed to find hope and affirmation in *Endgame* as they had done in *Godot*. For Harold Hobson in the *Sunday Times*, for example, the play filled those audience members who were neither 'philistines' nor 'half-wits' with a 'profound and sombre and paradoxical joy'. Where Tynan complains that *Endgame* couldn't help us, Hobson claims that 'its representation is among the greatest of the services that the English Stage Company has rendered to the British public'.[20] But most critics failed to distil tidings of comfort and joy from the play, and for many this failure cast doubt on the artistic legitimacy of both *Godot* and *Endgame*. In Tynan's review there is a sense that he feels that he has been duped[21] – *Endgame* reveals a recalcitrant, pathological negativity in Beckett's drama that remains beyond the pale of theatre and of criticism, and that suggests that even the critic of *Godot* was foolish to attempt to bring Beckett back into the fold. In recognising this excess, Tynan drew attention to a gap between the dominant critical discourse and Beckett's aesthetic practice, which had yet to be closed by critics who attempted to read his negativity as positive and affirming. The criteria that liberal humanist critics applied to their objects did not seem to be appropriate to Beckett's drama. Art should move us; art should console us; art should tell us something essential and permanent about the human condition; art has a moral responsibility to help us cope with the world as it is; if it cannot change the world, it must at least make it beautiful. These prerequisites had seemed to be met, albeit in peculiar fashion, in *Godot*, but *Endgame's* apparent representation of absolute despair without 'protest' undermined all of the qualities by which art was recognisable.

By proving more resistant than *Godot* to critical domestication, *Endgame* brought relations between Beckett and his critics to a point of crisis, and to an ultimatum. Either Beckett's work had to be rejected as inartistic, or the rules that governed the appreciation and understanding of art had to evolve to incorporate a form of expression that, for philistines, half-wits, and connoisseurs alike, may fail to tell us that the world and those who live on it are redeemable. The challenge that Beckett posed to the critical community was still, at the end of the fifties, alive, well and unanswered.

2. Presence, Negativity and the Human Condition: First Essays

The first fuller-length critical responses to *Waiting for Godot* and *Endgame*, in the late fifties and early sixties, were focused on developing a means of interpreting Beckett's theatre that could move beyond the boundary marked out by Tynan's rejection of *Endgame*. This work took two directions, whose divergent paths can be traced through the following forty years, and the remaining chapters of this book. The first of these, pioneered most influentially by Martin Esslin, sought to expand an existing liberal humanist critical discourse to incorporate Beckett's work, by sketching the contours of a new dramatic convention that would render its senselessness into sense. For Esslin, the difficulty posed by the drama arose because such a convention had not yet been clarified, rather than because it undermined any of the fundamental tenets of the brand of Anglo-American New Criticism that was hegemonic in fifties English culture. He suggested that Beckett was part of a larger body of dramatists, such as Adamov, Ionesco, Genet and Pinter, who were responding to twentieth-century European history by developing a recognisably distinct dramatic form, which he dubbed the 'Theatre of the Absurd'. In order to make this new form of theatre available to the mainstream, Esslin set out to 'provide a framework of reference that will show the works of the Theatre of the Absurd within their own convention'.[22] In doing so, the 'frustration and indignation'[23] that humanist critics such as

Tynan felt could be overcome, and the plays' 'relevance and force can emerge'.[24] The second direction taken by critics in the late fifties was charted originally by Theodor Adorno. Adorno suggested, *contra* Esslin, that an entirely new discourse was required for the interpretation of Beckett's drama, which was able to articulate its radical senselessness without absorbing it into the very bourgeois humanist ideology that it strenuously resisted. The negativity of Beckett's work, and its indifference to the demands made upon it by his critics, was not something that criticism had to overcome, but was itself the very meaning that had to be interpreted. For Adorno, 'Understanding it can mean only understanding its unintelligibility, concretely reconstructing the meaning of the fact that it has no meaning.'[25] Meaninglessness cannot be converted into meaning by the critic, but has to be examined in the condition and the moment of its meaninglessness. Its resistance to meaning, to ideology, and to interpretation has to be preserved within the act of interpretation itself. Where Esslin introduced a critical practice of elucidation, positivisation and humanisation that sought to understand and accommodate Beckett, Adorno laid the foundations of a hermeneutic method that saw in Beckett's negative resistance to all forms of containment his political and aesthetic promise.

Esslin's theorisation of a convention that could accommodate the new absurdist theatre turned around what he saw as a radical new departure in the use of the stage itself. What makes absurdist theatre strange and difficult is the fact that, in such plays, the stage seems to emerge from the control of the script – the reality effect, and all the other dramatic apparatuses that are conventionally used to draw the stage into a plot or dramatic situation are abandoned, allowing the stage to appear as a bare physical space that fails to become meaningful in any discernible theatrical or artistic way. For Esslin, this privileging of the space of the stage as a physical reality is the meaning and the promise of absurdist theatre, rather than a block to its interpretation, and when this is realised and properly accounted for, the plays are allowed to come into clear critical focus. This naked, but undeniably present space expresses the only fundamental truth available to our understanding – that we are here, in the world. All else, in Beckett's drama as in twentieth-century life, is revealed to be fake. For Esslin, as for Robbe-Grillet, another of Beckett's influential early critics, Beckett's theatre is best understood as a theatre of existential human presence, in which the superficial metaphysical, social and ideological meaning structures are seen to collapse around the brute physical existence of the characters on stage, who are stripped of all the illusions and myths that adorn their beings, and protect them from the void. In Beckett's drama, the particular and contingent features of life in the world dissolve to present us with a concrete image of the universal reality of human existence, common to all cultures, reducible to none.

■ The human condition, Heidegger says, is to be there. Probably it is the theatre, more than any other mode of representing reality, which reproduces this situation most naturally. The dramatic character is on stage, that is his primary quality: he is there.

Samuel Beckett's encounter with this requirement afforded a priori, an exceptional interest: at last we would see Beckett's man, we would see Man.[26] □

It is the intention to expose this existentialist reality lying at the heart of being-in-the-world that motivates Beckett's seemingly baffling experiments with logic and reason. It is true that language, dialogue and plot fail, but these do not collapse around an unapproachable and uninterpretable negativity. Rather they disintegrate to reveal the concrete architecture of the stage, which is itself interpretable as an analogue for the condition of humanity.

■ If Beckett's plays are concerned with expressing the difficulty of finding meaning in a world subject to incessant change, his use of language probes the limitations of language both as a means of communication and as a vehicle for the expression of valid statements, an instrument of thought. When Gessner asked him about the contradiction between his writing and his obvious conviction that language could not convey meaning, Beckett replied, *'Que voulez-vous, Monsieur? C'est les mots; on n'a rien d'autre.'* But in fact his use of the dramatic medium shows that he has tried to find means of expression beyond language. On the stage – witness his two mime-plays[27] – one can dispense with word altogether, or at least one can reveal the reality behind the words, as when the actions of the characters contradict their verbal expression. 'Let's go,' say the two tramps at the end of each act of *Waiting for Godot*, but the stage directions inform us that 'they don't move'. On the stage, language can be put into a contrapuntal relationship with action, the facts behind the language can be revealed. Hence the importance of mime, knockabout comedy, and silence in Beckett's plays – Krapp's eating of bananas, the pratfalls of Vladimir and Estragon, the variety turn with Lucky's hat, Clov's immobility at the close of *Endgame*, which puts his verbally expressed desire to leave in question. Beckett's use of the stage is an attempt to reduce the gap between the limitations of language and the intuition of being, the sense of the human situation he seeks to express in spite of his strong feeling that words are inadequate to formulate it. The concreteness and the three dimensional nature of the stage can be used to add new resources to language as an instrument of thought and exploration of being.[28] □

By exploiting the physical presence of the stage to its maximum potential, Beckett is able to dramatise the collapse of metaphysical meaning structures around the naked truth of 'being there'. The myths of national and personal identity, the construction of a stable system of beliefs that help to make sense of our being in the world, all such narratives prove themselves to be woefully inadequate in the face of the horrifying actuality of existence.

Thus for Esslin, it is the physical action of waiting in *Waiting for Godot*, rather than the question of who or what Godot represents, that should be thought of as the focal point of the play. In the following extract, Esslin draws on Beckett's own critical exposition of Proust's novel *A La Recherche du Temps Perdu*, to emphasise the illusoriness of 'identity', and other narrative structures that graft meaning onto our existence in the world. As Vladimir and Estragon wait for Godot to arrive to liberate them from brute existence into the paradise of significance, the concrete space in which they are waiting reveals the true nature of being in time:

■ Whether Godot is meant to suggest the intervention of a supernatural agency, or whether he stands for a mythical human being whose arrival is expected to change the station, or both of these possibilities combined, his exact nature is of secondary importance. The subject of the play is not Godot but waiting, the act of waiting as an essential and characteristic aspect of the human condition. Throughout our lives we always wait for something, and Godot simply represents the objective of our waiting – an event, a thing, a person, death. Moreover, it is in the act of waiting that we experience the flow of time in its purest, most evident form. If we are active, we tend to forget the passage of time, we pass the time, but if we are merely passively waiting, we are confronted with the action of time itself. As Beckett points out in his analysis of Proust, 'There is no escape from the hours and the days. Neither from tomorrow, nor from yesterday because yesterday has deformed us or been deformed by us. . . . Yesterday is not a milestone that has been passed, but a daystone on the beaten track of the years, and irremediably part of us, within us, heavy and dangerous. We are not merely more weary because of yesterday, we are other, no longer what we were before the calamity of yesterday'.[29] The flow of time confronts us with the basic problem of being – the problem of the nature of the self, which, being subject to constant change in time, is in constant flux and therefore ever outside our grasp – 'personality, whose permanent reality can only be apprehended as a retrospective hypothesis. The individual is the seat of a constant process of decantation, sluggish, pale and monochrome, to the vessel containing the fluid of past time, agitated and multi-coloured by the phenomena of its hours.'[30]

Being subject to this process of time flowing through us and changing us in doing so, we are, at no single moment in our lives, identical
with ourselves. Hence, 'we are disappointed at the nullity of what we
please to call attainment. But what is attainment? The identification of
the subject with the object of his desire. The subject has died – and
perhaps many times on the way.'[31] If Godot is the object of Vladimir's
and Estragon's desire, he seems naturally ever beyond their reach. It is
significant that the boy who acts as go-between fails to recognise the
pair from day to day. The French version explicitly states that the boy
who appears in the second act is the same boy as the one in the first
act, yet the boy denies that he has ever seen the two tramps before and
insists that this is the first time he has acted as Godot's messenger. As
the boy leaves, Vladimir tries to impress it upon him: 'You're sure you
saw me, eh, you won't come and tell me tomorrow that you never saw
me before?' The boy does not reply, and we know that he will again
fail to recognise them. Can we ever be sure that the human beings we
meet are the same today as they were yesterday? When Pozzo and
Lucky first appear, neither Vladimir nor Estragon seems to recognise
them; Estragon even takes Pozzo for Godot. But after they have gone,
Vladimir comments that they have changed since their last appearance. Estragon insists that he didn't know them.

VLADIMIR: Yes you do know them.

ESTRAGON: No, I don't know them.

VLADIMIR: We know them, I tell you. You forget everything.
[*Pause. To himself*.] Unless they're not the same . . .

ESTRAGON: Why didn't they recognize us, then?

VLADIMIR: That means nothing. I too pretended not to recognize
them. And then nobody ever recognizes us. (*CDW* 47)

In the second act, when Pozzo and Lucky reappear, cruelly deformed
by the action of time, Vladimir and Estragon again have their doubts
whether they are the same people they met on the previous day. Nor
does Pozzo remember them: 'I don't remember having met anyone
yesterday. But tomorrow I won't remember having met anyone today'
(*CDW* 82).

Waiting is to experience the action of time, which is constant
change. And yet, as nothing real ever happens, that change is itself an
illusion. The ceaseless activity of time is self-defeating, purposeless,
and therefore null and void. The more things change the more they are
the same. That is the terrible stability of the world. 'The tears of the
world are a constant quantity. For each one who begins to weep,

somewhere else another stops' (*CDW* 33). One day is like another, and when we die we might never have existed. As Pozzo exclaims in his great final outburst:

> Have you not done tormenting me with your accursed time! . . . One day, is that not enough for you, one day like any other day, one day he went dumb, one day I went blind, one day we'll go deaf, one day we were born, one day we shall die, the same day, the same second, . . . They give birth astride a grave, the light gleams an instant, then it's night once more. (*CDW* 83)

And Vladimir, shortly afterwards, agrees: 'Astride of a grave and a difficult birth. Down in the hole, lingeringly, the gravedigger puts on the forceps' (*CDW* 84).

Still Vladimir and Estragon live in hope: they wait for Godot, whose coming will bring the flow of time to a stop. 'Tonight perhaps we shall sleep in his place, in the warmth, dry, our bellies full, on the straw. It is worth waiting for that, is it not?'[32] This passage, omitted in the English version, clearly suggests the peace, the rest from waiting, the sense of having arrived in a haven, that Godot represents to the two tramps. They are hoping to be saved from the evanescence and instability of the illusion of time, and to find peace and permanence outside of it. They will no longer be tramps, homeless wanderers, but will have arrived home.[33] □

To hope for a metaphysical solution to the continual agony of being in time, however, is, for Esslin, a form of Sartrean 'bad faith'. Rejecting Christian and other theological interpretations of the play, he suggests that the only form of salvation available to Estragon and Vladimir is the recognition that no Godot will ever come to transmute existence into meaning. The promise of the play is found in the moments when Vladimir and Estragon come closest to comprehending the naked actuality of existence, shorn of all illusions and all comforting myths. It is when this truth is understood that the play opens out onto the vast vistas of existential freedom.

■ That *Waiting for Godot* is concerned with the hope of salvation through the workings of grace seems clearly established both from Beckett's own evidence and from the text itself. Does this, however, mean that it is a Christian, or even that it is a religious play? There have been a number of very ingenious interpretations in this sense. Vladimir's and Estragon's waiting is explained as signifying their steadfast faith and hope, while Vladimir's kindness to his friend, and the two tramps' mutual interdependence are seen as symbols of

Christian charity. But these religious interpretations seem to overlook a number of essential features of the play – its constant stress on the uncertainty of the appointment with Godot, Godot's unreliability and irrationality, and the repeated demonstration of the futility of the hopes pinned upon him. The act of *Waiting for Godot* is shown as essentially *absurd*. Admittedly it might be a case of *'Credere quia absurdum est'*, yet it might even more forcibly be taken as a demonstration of the proposition *'Absurdum est credere.'*

There is one feature of the play that leads one to assume there is a better solution to the tramps' predicament, which they themselves both prefer to *Waiting for Godot* – that is, suicide. 'We should have thought of it a million years ago, in the nineties. . . . Hand in hand from the top of the Eiffel Tower, among the first. We were respectable in those days. Now it's too late. They wouldn't even let us up' (*CDW* 12). Suicide remains their favourite solution, unattainable owing to their own incompetence and their lack of the practical tools to achieve it. It is precisely their disappointment at their failure to succeed in their attempts at suicide that Vladimir and Estragon rationalise by waiting, or pretending to wait, for Godot. 'I'm curious to hear what he has to offer. Then we'll take it or leave it' (*CDW* 18). Estragon, far less convinced of Godot's promises than Vladimir, is anxious to reassure himself that they are not tied to Godot.

> ESTRAGON: I'm asking you if we are tied.
>
> VLADIMIR: Tied?
>
> ESTRAGON: Ti-ed.
>
> VLADIMIR: How do you mean tied?
>
> ESTRAGON: Down.
>
> VLADIMIR: But to whom? By whom?
>
> ESTRAGON: To your man.
>
> VLADIMIR: To Godot? Tied to Godot? What an idea! No question of it. [*Pause.*] For the moment. (*CDW* 20–21)

When, later, Vladimir falls into some sort of complacency about their waiting – 'We have kept our appointment . . . We are not saints, but we have kept our appointment. How many people can boast as much?' – Estragon immediately punctures it by retorting, 'Billions.' And Vladimir is quite ready to admit that they are waiting only from irrational habit. 'All I know is that the hours are long . . . and constrain us to beguile them with proceedings . . . which may at first sight seem to be reasonable, until they become a habit. You may say it is to prevent our reason from foundering. No doubt. But has it not long been straying in the night without end of abyssal depths?' (*CDW* 75).

In support of the Christian interpretation, it might be argued that Vladimir and Estragon, who are *Waiting for Godot*, are shown as clearly superior to Pozzo and Lucky, who have no appointment, no objective, and are wholly egocentric, wholly wrapped up in their sadomasochistic relationship. Is it not their faith that puts the two tramps on a higher plane?[34]

It is evident that, in fact, Pozzo is naïvely over-confident and self-centred. 'Do I look like a man that can be made to suffer?' (*CDW* 34) he boasts. Even when he gives a soulful and melancholy description of the sunset and the sudden falling of the night, we know that he doesn't believe the night will ever fall on him – he is merely giving a performance; he is not concerned with the meaning of what he recites, but only with its effect on the audience. Hence he is taken completely unawares when night does fall on him and he goes blind. Likewise Lucky, in accepting Pozzo as his master and in teaching him his ideas, seems to have been naïvely convinced of the power of reason, beauty and truth. Estragon and Vladimir are clearly superior to both Pozzo and Lucky – not because they pin their faith on Godot, but because they are less naïve. They do not believe in action, wealth or reason. They are aware that all we do in this life is as nothing when seen against the senseless action of time, which is itself an illusion. They are aware that suicide would be the best solution. They are thus superior to Pozzo and Lucky because they are less self-centred and have fewer illusions. In fact, as a Jungian psychologist, Eva Metman, has pointed out in a remarkable study of Beckett's plays, 'Godot's function seems to be to keep his dependants unconscious.'[35] In this view, the hope, the habit of hoping, that Godot might come after all is the last illusion that keeps Vladimir and Estragon from facing the human condition and themselves in the harsh light of fully conscious awareness. As Dr Metman observes, it is at the very moment, toward the end of the play, when Vladimir is about to realise that he has been dreaming, and must wake up and face the world as it is, that Godot's messenger arrives, rekindles his hopes, and plunges him back into the passivity of illusion.

For a brief moment, Vladimir is aware of the full horror of the human condition: 'The air is full of our cries. . . . But habit is a great deadener.' He looks at Estragon, who is asleep, and reflects, 'At me too someone is looking, of me too someone is saying, he is sleeping, he knows nothing, let him sleep on. . . . I can't go on!' (*CDW* 84–85) The routine of *Waiting for Godot* stands for habit, which prevents us from reaching the painful but fruitful awareness of the full reality of being.

Again we find Beckett's own commentary on this aspect of *Waiting for Godot* in his essay on Proust: 'Habit is the ballast that chains the dog to his vomit. Breathing is habit. Life is habit. Or rather life is a succession of habits, since the individual is a succession of individuals. . . . Habit then is the generic term for the countless treaties concluded between the countless subjects that constitute the individual and their countless correlative objects. The periods of transition that separate consecutive adaptations . . . represent the perilous zones on the life of the individual, dangerous, precarious, painful, mysterious, and fertile, when for a moment the *boredom of living* is replaced by the *suffering of being*.'[36] 'The suffering of being: that is the free play of every faculty. Because the pernicious devotion of habit paralyses our attention, drugs those handmaidens of perception whose co-operation is not absolutely essential.'[37]

Vladimir's and Estragon's pastimes are, as they repeatedly indicate, designed to stop them from thinking. 'We're in no danger of thinking any more. . . . Thinking is not the worst . . . What is terrible is to *have* thought' (*CDW* 60).

Vladimir and Estragon talk incessantly. Why? They hint at it in what is probably the most lyrical, the most perfectly phrased passage of the play:

VLADIMIR: You are right, we're inexhaustible.

ESTRAGON: It's so we won't think.

VLADIMIR: We have that excuse.

ESTRAGON: It's so we won't hear.

VLADIMIR: We have our reasons.

ESTRAGON: All the dead voices.

VLADIMIR: They make a noise like wings.

ESTRAGON: Like leaves.

VLADIMIR: Like sand.

ESTRAGON: Like leaves.

[*Silence.*]

VLADIMIR: They all speak together.

ESTRAGON: Each one to itself.

[*Silence.*]

VLADIMIR: Rather they whisper.

ESTRAGON: They rustle.

VLADIMIR: They murmur.

ESTRAGON: They rustle.

[*Silence.*]

VLADIMIR: What do they say?

ESTRAGON: They talk about their lives.

VLADIMIR: To have lived is not enough for them.

ETSRAGON: They have to talk about it.

VLADIMIR: To be dead is not enough for them.

ESTRAGON: It is not sufficient.

[*Silence.*]

VLADIMIR: They make a noise like feathers.

ESTRAGON: Like leaves.

VLADIMIR: Like ashes.

ESTRAGON: Like leaves.

[*Long silence.*] (*CDW* 58)

This passage, in which the cross-talk of Irish music-hall comedians is miraculously transmuted into poetry, contains the key to much of Beckett's work. Surely these rustling, murmuring voices of the past are the voices we hear in the three novels of his trilogy; they are the voices that explore the mystery of being and the self to the limits of anguish and suffering. Vladimir and Estragon are trying to escape hearing them. The long silence that follows their evocation is broken by Vladimir, '*in anguish*', with the cry 'Say anything at all!' after which the two relapse into their wait for Godot.

The hope of salvation may be merely an evasion of the suffering and anguish that spring from facing the reality of the human condition. There is here a truly astonishing parallel between the Existentialist philosophy of Jean-Paul Sartre and the creative intuition of Beckett, who has never consciously expressed Existentialist views. If, for Beckett as for Sartre, man has the duty of facing the human condition as a recognition that at the root of our being there is nothingness, liberty, and the need of constantly creating ourselves in a succession of choices, then Godot might well become an image of what Sartre calls 'bad faith' – 'The first act of bad faith consists in evading what one cannot evade, in evading what one is.'[38] □

Esslin's method in his interpretation of Godot is extended to incorporate *Endgame* also. The sense, felt by critics such as Tynan and Robbe-Grillet, that *Endgame* pushes further than Godot, and thus cannot be analysed with the same critical tool, is not shared by Esslin. *Endgame*, like Godot, is a play in which immediate presence is pitched against illusory narrative structures, and a deep sense of the meaning of being is salvaged from the collapse of all the trivial meanings that make up social being. In the following extract, Esslin suggests some means of approaching the play – it is a monodrama set in the inside of one character's mind, it is a partly auto-biographical account of Beckett's relationship with Joyce – before stressing, in a familiar reluctance to say specifically what the play means, that no single interpretation can be applied to it. The play is a dramatisation of a 'situation that has deepened into a universal significance', and this significance has been achieved by a process of 'contraction', which has freed it from 'all elements of a naturalistic social setting and plot'.

■ The suggestion that *Endgame* may . . . be a monodrama has much to be said for it. The enclosed space with the two tiny windows through which Clov observes the outside world; the dustbins that hold the suppressed and despised parents, and whose lids Clov is ordered to press down when they become obnoxious; Hamm, blind and emotional; Clov, performing the function of the sense for him – all these might well represent different aspects of a single personality, repressed memories in the subconscious mind, the emotional and the intellectual selves. Is Clov then the intellect, bound to serve the emotions, instincts, and appetites, and trying to free himself from such disorderly and tyrannical masters, yet doomed to die when its connection with the animal side is severed? Is the death of the outside world the gradual receding of the links to reality that takes place in the process of ageing and dying? Is *Endgame* a monodrama depicting the dissolution of a personality in the hour of death?

It would be wrong to assume that these questions can be definitely answered. *Endgame* certainly was not planned as a sustained allegory of this type. But there are indications that there is an element of mono-drama in the play. Hamm describes a memory that is strangely reminiscent of the situation in *Endgame*: 'I once knew a madman who thought the end of the world had come. He was a painter – an[d] engraver . . . I used to go and see him, in the asylum. I'd take him by the hand and drag him to the window. Look! There! All that rising corn! And there! Look! The sails of the herring fleet! All that loveli-ness! . . . He'd snatch away his hand and go back into his corner. Appalled. All he had seen was ashes . . . He alone had been spared. Forgotten . . . It appears the case is . . . was not so . . . so unusual' (*CDW* 113). Hamm's own world represents the delusions of the mad painter.

Moreover, what is the significance of the picture mentioned in the stage directions? 'Hanging near the door, its face to the wall, a picture' (*CDW* 92). Is that picture a memory? Is the story a lucid moment in the consciousness of that very painter whose dying hours we witness from behind the scenes of his mind?

Beckett's plays can be interpreted on many levels. *Endgame* may well be a monodrama on one level and a morality play about the death of a rich man on another. But the peculiar psychological reality of Beckett's characters has often been noticed. Pozzo and Lucky have been interpreted as body and mind; Vladimir and Estragon have been seen as so complementary that they might be the two halves of a single personality, the conscious and the subconscious mind. Each of these three pairs – Pozzo–Lucky; Vladimir–Estragon; Hamm–Clov – is linked by a relationship of mutual interdependence, wanting to leave each other, at war with each other, and yet dependent on each other. '*Nec tecum, nec sine te.*' This is a frequent situation among people – married couples, for example – but it is also an image of the interrelatedness of the elements within a single personality, particularly if the personality is in conflict with itself.

In Beckett's first play, *Eleutheria*, the basic situation was, superficially, analogous to the relationship between Clov and Hamm. The young hero of that play wanted to leave his family; in the end he succeeded in getting away. In *Endgame*, however, that situation has been deepened into a truly universal significance; it has been concentrated and immeasurably enriched precisely by having been freed from all elements of a naturalistic social setting and external plot. The process of contraction, which Beckett described as the essence of the artistic tendency in his essay on Proust, has here been carried out triumphantly. Instead of merely exploring a surface, a play like *Endgame* has become a shaft driven deep down into the core of being; that is why it exists on a multitude of levels, revealing new ones as it is more closely studied. What at first sight may have appeared as obscurity or lack of definition is later recognised as the very hallmark of the density of texture, the tremendous concentration of a work that springs from a truly creative imagination, as distinct from a merely imitative one.

The force of these considerations is brought out with particular clarity when we are confronted by an attempt to interpret a play like *Endgame* as a mere exercise in conscious or subconscious autobiography. In an extremely ingenious essay[39] Lionel Abel has worked out the theory that in the characters of Hamm and Pozzo Beckett may have portrayed his literary master, James Joyce, while Lucky and Clov stand for Beckett himself. *Endgame* then becomes an allegory of the relationship between the domineering, nearly blind Joyce and his adoring disciple, who felt himself crushed by his master's overpowering literary influence. Superficially the parallels are striking: Hamm is presented as being at work on an interminable story, Lucky is being made to perform a set piece of thinking, which, Mr Abel argues, is in fact a parody of Joyce's style. Yet on closer study this theory surely becomes untenable; not because there may not be a certain amount of truth in it (every writer is bound to use elements of his own experience of life in his work) but because, far from illuminating the full content of a play like *Endgame*, such an interpretation reduces it to a trivial level. If *Endgame* really were nothing but a thinly disguised account of the literary, or even the human, relationship between the two particular individuals, it could not possibly produce the impact it has had on audiences utterly ignorant of these particular, very private circumstances. Yet *Endgame* undoubtedly has a very deep and direct impact, which can spring only from its touching a chord in the minds of a very large number of human beings. The problems of the relationship between a literary master and his pupil would be very unlikely to elicit such a response; very few people in the audience would feel directly involved. Admittedly, a play that presented the conflict between Joyce and Beckett openly, or thinly disguised, might arouse the curiosity of audiences who are always eager for autobiographical revelations. But this is just what *Endgame* does not do. If it nevertheless arouses profound emotion in its audience, this can be due only to the fact that it is felt to deal with a conflict of a far more universal nature. Once that is seen, it becomes clear that, while it is fascinating to argue about the aptness of such autobiographical elements, such a discussion leaves the central problem of understanding the play and exploring its many-layered meanings still to be tackled.

[. . .]

The experience expressed in Beckett plays is of a far more profound and fundamental nature than mere autobiography. They reveal his experience of temporality and evanescence; his sense of the tragic difficulty of becoming aware of one's own self in the merciless process of renovation and destruction that occurs with change in time; of the difficulty of communication between human beings; of the unending quest for reality in a world in which everything is uncertain and the borderline between dream and waking is ever shifting; of the tragic nature of all love relationships and the self-deception of friendship (of which Beckett speaks in the essay on Proust), and so on. In *Endgame* we are also certainly confronted with a very powerful sense of deadness, of leaden heaviness and hopelessness that is experienced in states of deep depression: the world outside goes dead for the victim of such states, but inside his mind there is ceaseless argument between parts of his personality that have become autonomous entities.

This is not to say that Beckett gives a clinical description of pathological states. His creative intuition explores the elements of experience and shows to what extent all human beings carry the seeds of such depression and disintegration within the deeper layers of their personality. If the prisoners of San Quentin responded to *Waiting for Godot*, it was because they were confronted with their own experience of time, waiting, hope, and despair; because they recognised the truth about their own human relationships in the sadomasochistic interdependence of Pozzo and Lucky and in the bickering hate–love between Vladimir and Estragon.[40] This is also the key to the wide success of Beckett's plays: to be confronted with concrete projections of the deepest fears and anxieties, which have been only vaguely experienced at a half-conscious level, constitutes a process of catharsis and liberation analogous to the therapeutic effect in psychoanalysis of confronting the subconscious contents of the mind. This is the moment of release from deadening habit, through facing up to the suffering of existence, that Vladimir almost attains in *Waiting for Godot*. This also, probably, is the release that could occur if Clov had the courage to break his bondage to Hamm and venture out into the world, which may not, after all, be so dead as it appeared from within the claustrophobic confines of Hamm's realm. This, in fact, seems to be hinted at by the strange episode of the little boy whom Clov observes in the last stage of *Endgame*. Is this boy a symbol of life outside the closed circuit of withdrawal from reality?

[. . .]

It may well be that the sighting of this little boy – undoubtedly a climactic event in the play – stands for redemption from the illusion and evanescence of time through the recognition, and acceptance, of a higher reality: the little boy contemplates his own navel;[41] that is, he fixes his attention on the great emptiness of nirvana, nothingness, of which Democritus the Aberdite has said, in one of Beckett's favourite quotations, 'Nothing is more real than nothing'.[42]

There is a moment of illumination, shortly before he himself dies, in which Murphy, having played a *game of chess*, experiences a strange sensation: '. . . and Murphy began to see nothing, that colourlessness which is such a rare post-natal treat, being the absence . . . not of *percipere* but of *percipi*. His other senses also found themselves at peace, an unexpected pleasure. Not the numb peace of their own suspension, but the positive peace that comes when the somethings give way, or perhaps simply add up, to the Nothing, than which in the guffaw of the Aberdite naught is more real. Time did not cease, that would be asking too much, but the wheel of rounds and pauses did, as Murphy with his head among the armies [i.e. of the chessmen] continued to

suck in, through all the posterns of his withered soul, the accide\
One-and-Only, conveniently called Nothing.'[43]

Does Hamm, who has shut himself off from the world and killed
the rest of mankind by holding on to his material possessions –
Hamm, blind, sensual, egocentric – then die when Clov, the rational
part of the self, perceives the true reality of the illusoriness of the
material world, the redemption and resurrection, the liberation from
the wheels of time that lies in union with the 'accidentless One-and-
Only, conveniently called Nothing'? Or is the discovery of the little
boy merely a symbol of the coming of death – union with nothingness
in a different, more concrete sense? Or does the reappearance of life in
the outside world indicate that the period of loss of contact with the
world has come to an end, that the crisis has passed and that a disintegrating personality is about to find a way back to integration, 'the
solemn change towards merciless reality in Hamm and ruthless acceptance of freedom in Clov', as the Jungian analyst Dr Metman puts it?[44]

There is no need to try to pursue these alternatives any further; to
decide in favour of one would only impair the stimulating coexistence
of these and other possible implications.

[. . .]

Waiting for Godot and *Endgame*, the plays Beckett wrote in French, are
dramatic statements of the human situation itself. They lack both characters and plot in the conventional sense because they tackle their
subject matter at a level where neither characters nor plot exist.
Characters presuppose that human nature, the diversity of personality
and individuality, is real and matters: plot can only exist on the
assumption that events in time are significant. These are precisely the
assumptions that the two plays put in question. Hamm and Clov,
Pozzo and Lucky, Vladimir and Estragon, Nagg and Nell are not characters but the embodiments of basic human attitudes, rather like the
personified virtues and vices in medieval mystery plays or Spanish
autos sacramentales. And what passes in these plays are not *events* with a
definite beginning and a definite end, but types of *situation* that will
forever repeat themselves. That is why the pattern of Act I of *Waiting for
Godot* is repeated with variations in Act II; that is why we do not see
Clov actually leave Hamm at the close of *Endgame* but leave the two
frozen in a position of stalemate. Both plays repeat the pattern of the
old German students' song Vladimir sings at the beginning of act II of
Waiting for Godot, about the dog that came into a kitchen and stole some
bread and was killed by the cook and buried by its fellow-dogs, who
put a tombstone on its grave which told the story of the dog that came
into the kitchen and stole some bread – and so on *ad infinitum*. In
Endgame and *Waiting for Godot*, Beckett is concerned with probing down

to a depth in which individuality and definite events no longer appear, and only basic patterns emerge.[45] □

Esslin's reading of *Waiting for Godot* and *Endgame*, and his formulation of the Theatre of the Absurd, provided an interpretative convention that has remained extremely influential up to the present day. Fairly quickly after Esslin's categorisation of Beckett's plays in terms of a brand of populist existentialism and a formulaic dramatic nihilism, both audiences and critics became much more comfortable with the drama: the period of the plays' challenge to comprehension and interpretation seemed, as Esslin predicted, to come fairly quickly to a close. Pierre Marcabu commented wryly, in 1961, that within a short space of time *Godot* had become 'a game whose rules are completely unmysterious'. The initial threat that the play presented was quickly defused by those critics who protect their hermeneutic ideologies by 'drawing some of the teeth out of dangerous plays'.[46] For the majority of critics, less scathing than Marcabu, the plays remained extremely powerful, but it was generally agreed that their power had been more or less successfully contained within the dramatic and interpretative boundaries sketched out by Esslin. The critical formula that Esslin introduced in *The Theatre of the Absurd*, however, rests on fundamental contradictions that are not explicitly addressed, and he leaves many questions unanswered as a consequence. Perhaps the clearest contradiction that emerges from Esslin's account is that between value and valuelessness. Beckett's stage is a space in which all the processes that impute value to our presence in the world are exposed as being spurious and groundless, yet this process of exposure is itself highly valuable. Vladimir and Estragon are deemed by Esslin to be engaged in a recognition of the essential truth that the world is without meaning, but he describes this recognition, in the above extract, as the 'painful but fruitful awareness of the full reality of being'. The means by which such an awareness could bear fruit in Beckett's universe is not closely examined, beyond a reference to a crude existentialist category of absolute freedom. The moment at which it is discovered that we are not held in the world by an overarching system of signification is 'fruitful', because it is a moment of catharsis and liberation, in which we realise that we are free. Within the terms of Esslin's argument, however, it is difficult to see how such freedom could redeem the value and the fruitfulness that he imputes to it. For Esslin, Vladimir and Estragon are not free from anything, nor are they free to do anything. Even the political value that Sartre attaches to existential freedom is absent in Esslin's model, as the freedom that Beckett's characters win is the freedom to recognise that all action is futile and senseless.[47] The abstract concept of freedom that Esslin privileges as the 'illuminating' and 'inspiring' content of the plays belongs to the very system of 'metaphysical meaning structures' that

Beckett is in the business of debunking – outside such a system, it loses the value that Esslin seeks to claim for it. Many of the contradictions that run throughout Esslin's argument grow from this underlying problem. For example, the emphasis upon the instability of personal identity, and the illusoriness of the myths that tell us who we are, is made to coexist with an equal emphasis upon the sacred freedom of the individual. The category of individualism is regarded both as the myth that Beckett is rejecting in his drama, and as the privileged bearer of truth that emerges intact from it. Beckettian freedom both liberates you from who you are, and allows you to become who you are.

These contradictions are caused by Esslin's untheorised deployment of his sustaining distinction between social being and extra-social being, referred to earlier in this chapter. Without explicitly recognising the fact, Esslin's argument rests on the liberal humanist assumption that there are some universal values that attain their significance not from any of the social value systems that he is so keen to disparage, but from the force of their own self-evident rectitude. These values are not social, political or ideological, but are rather transcendent truths that do not need to refer to any epistemological authority for their validation. Thus, Esslin's argument abruptly brings a radical nihilism, which questions the validity of all truth and meaning, up against a stout defence of the validity of a stock of values that he deems to be unquestionable. He does not consider that the integrity of his nihilism is compromised and undermined by his privileging of such values, because he deems them to be natural rather than cultural. But for many critics, to place a selection of values beyond the range of the deconstructive power of art is itself an ideological move – the values that Esslin privileges in the name of an apolitical universalism are those that underpin the Western bourgeois ideology that he is implicitly protecting. As Eagleton has commented, one of the functions of ideology is to disguise its own ideological quality by presenting itself as natural,[48] and it is this naturalisation of the values of Western liberal humanism that accounts for Esslin's silent distinction between ideological and extra-ideological being. The universal reality that Esslin discovers in Beckett's drama, in which an individual confronts a confusing and irredeemable world with honesty, bravery and poetry, is a cornerstone of the Western bourgeois ideology in which his critique is steeped: the world may be bleak and difficult, but there is nothing we can do about it, so we must keep on going with humour and humility, stoically accepting the *status quo* as the given and immutable condition of humanity. For some critics, Esslin's interpretation of Beckett's drama thus succeeded in transforming a powerful critique of Western humanism into a defence of its most basic tenets. Beckett appeared as an apologist for Western decadence, and an advocate of a passive, stoical stance in the face of cultural unfreedom. He seemed to substitute a delight in the faithful representation of an unchanging, essential human condition, for any form of commitment to particular cultural realities, a substitution that was only conceivable for those who did not have to fight for their most basic rights. P.J. Murphy comments, in *Reconstructing Beckett*, that the result of Esslin's influential analysis 'is a bourgeoisification of Beckett which renders innocuous some of his potentially most radical comments about art and its relationship to life'.[49] The long history of criticism that casts Beckett's drama as a defender of decadent Western complacency has its beginning, for critics such as Murphy, in *The Theatre of the Absurd*. The challenge that *Waiting for Godot* and *Endgame* presented to the critical community was not so much responded to by Esslin, as annulled.

Adorno's influential essay, 'Trying to Understand *Endgame*', written in 1958, approaches the challenge of interpreting Beckett's drama in a very different way. Many of the assumptions that underpin and sustain Esslin's critique are explicitly rejected in this essay, which suggests that a mode of critique is required that can gain access to Beckett's negativity, without compromising the work's outright rejection of existing interpretative agendas. Adorno seeks to negotiate here between two critical approaches, which he deems equally unsatisfactory: the approach, adopted by 'the cultural spokespersons of authentic expression'[50] such as Esslin, which enthusiastically welcomes Beckett into a dominant critical ideology; and the approach, adopted in different ways by defenders of socialist realism such as Georg Lukács[51] and by liberal critics such as Kenneth Tynan, which rejects Beckett's work because, in its decadent abstraction, it does not conform to prescribed notions of how responsible, committed art should be. It is necessary, Adorno suggests, to understand the unique standpoint of Beckett's aesthetic, which refuses to cooperate either with the demand that a work of art should be directly politically committed, or with the avowedly apolitical[52] criteria by which Western humanist critics judge the authentic work of art. The reason that the challenge of interpreting Beckett's drama is so difficult and so urgent, is that it gives both bourgeois and formulaic socialist critical institutions the slip, and gestures beyond them towards an entirely different aesthetic that has yet to be critically articulated.

The means of grasping Beckett's negativity, and making it available for interpretation, that has been practised by most of the critics represented in this chapter so far, is rejected by Adorno as inadequate. It is neither sufficient nor even possible to take Beckett's representation of meaninglessness as the meaning of his work, and then to progress as if it was a positive quality. Adorno is emphatic that:

■ Drama cannot simply take negative meaning, or the absence of meaning, as its content without everything that is peculiar to it being affected to the point of turning into its opposite. The essence of drama was constituted by that meaning. Were drama to try and survive meaning aesthetically, it would become inadequate to its substance and be degraded to a clattering machinery for the demonstration of worldviews.[53] □

Here, Adorno's reading can be seen to be in direct opposition to Esslin's. Where Esslin suggests that something positive emerges intact from Beckett's dramatisation of meaningless, Adorno insists that there has to be something suspicious and inartistic about a form of dramatic expression that claims to represent a collapse of value systems without itself collapsing around the meaninglessness that it seeks to represent. Esslin's quiet distinction between trivial, social meaning and deep, universal meaning is rejected by Adorno. In fact, for Adorno, what distinguishes Beckett's drama is its move away from such a distinction, which he claims is commonly found in existentialist thought. Beckett's drama does not try to survive the collapse of meaning that is its content – for Adorno there is precisely not a stock of universal, unideological values that is salvaged from the wreckage of Beckett's drama, and elevated to the status of fundamental truth. Neither does the death of illusory meaning give way to a 'new kind of consciousness, which faces the mystery and terror of the human condition in the exhilaration of a new-found freedom',[54] as it does for Esslin. The difficulty of Beckett's drama, and its originality, stems from its rejection of a universally meaningful category that acts as a crutch to support the drama, and as a cement to plug the gap that opens between meaning and meaninglessness.

The creed of universal meaning that has emerged from absurdist and existentialist drama before Beckett, Adorno suggests, is that of the 'irreducibility of individual existence'.[55] The meaning that supports both Esslin's and Robbe-Grillet's critiques, the Heidegerrian certainty of 'being there' on the physical stage when time, narrative and language fail, is the backbone of an existentialist philosophy that Adorno claims is exploded in Beckett's drama, rather than given its definitive shape. Presence on the stage does not act as the guarantor of being for Adorno, as it does for so many of Beckett's critics. On the contrary, the categories of subjectivity and objectivity, concretion and abstraction, being and nothingness, are seen in their irreconciled disparity, and in a state of irredeemable alienation, rather than represented as being reconciled within the figure of a 'new kind of consciousness'. Being who you are, in the liberating reality of the moment, is simply not an option, for Adorno, in Beckett's dramatic universe. What the existentialist emphasis on individual existence failed to account for is the fact that individuality is produced by the very processes it is pitted against. It is difficult to see how you can use existence as a sealed refuge against ideology, when ideology at least partly produces existence. *Endgame* destroyed the illusion, touted by the existentialists, that existence could be used as a fail-safe defence against history, because in the play 'the individual himself is revealed to be a historical category'. Where Esslin leans heavily on the figure of transcendent 'being' as the content and the truth of Beckett's drama, Adorno is insistent that such a comforting quality is not to be found in the plays, because being is revealed to be an outcome of capitalist development, rather than something that can posit itself in a space outside social processes. Transcendent 'Being', in Beckett's drama, does not have the authority to articulate itself without reference to social being.

■ If individual experience in its narrowness and contingency has interpreted itself as a figure of Being, it has received the authority to do so only by asserting itself to be the fundamental characteristic of Being. But this is precisely what is false. The immediacy of individuation was deceptive; the carrier of individual experience is mediated, conditioned. *Endgame* assumes that the individual's claim to autonomy and being has lost its credibility.[56] □

Whilst Adorno rejects outright the notion that any kind of universal, positive 'message' emerges from Beckett's drama, however, this does not mean that his work is politically redundant, nor that the search for forms of artistic resistance to ideological control is necessarily futile. The individual for Adorno is 'both the outcome of the capitalist process of alienation and a defiant protest against it',[57] and the articulation of this protest is what the drama strives for above all else. It is not that there is no impulse towards protest against forms of unfreedom, but rather that Beckett's drama does not offer an existing discourse in which to couch such protest. The predicament in twentieth-century Europe is such that there are no modes of direct expression available in which to articulate dissent from a society that exercises 'virtually unmediated control' – to grant the individual the power to do so (as critics such as Esslin tend to do) is just another form of false consciousness. *Endgame* is a response to the decline of culture in a period of rampantly triumphant capitalism. The situation depicted on the stage is one in which dialogue, language and philosophy have degenerated into clichés and tautologies that offer no way out of the claustrophobic confines of the ruined shelter. One reason that *Endgame* is so powerful is because it is able to depict the reification of culture so ruthlessly, and in doing so the possibility of leaving a space for culture to speak with any authenticity or any truth is precisely what is squeezed out. But at the same time as it confronts us with a culture that has 'gone kaputt', *Endgame* presents us with a voiceless reflection on such a catastrophe – a dramatic urge towards a condemnation of what has become of culture, which cannot find a voice and whose only mode of expression is silence. This silent verdict on twentieth-century culture cannot be mediated or paraphrased by philosophy or by theory, because it is the inability of these discourses to deal with the depravity of post-Second World War culture that is the focal point of the play. For Adorno, the intriguing double movement of *Endgame* is that it both dismisses culture as being terminally closed in upon itself, unable to find a way out of its own corruption in order to reflect upon itself as bankrupt, and *at the same time* 'surges beyond' the confines of such bankruptcy towards an enigmatic, silent negativity that is all that is left of the subject in revolt.

It is the challenge of interpreting and understanding this double movement that Adorno suggests is the test for a philosophy 'whose hour has struck'. The following extract, which forms the introduction to 'Trying to Understand *Endgame*', formulates the distinction between existentialist philosophy and Beckett's drama, and gestures towards a means of interpreting the play that can understand the limits and the nature of its revolt.

■ Beckett's oeuvre has many things in common with Parisian existentialism. It is shot through with reminiscences of the categories of absurdity, situation, and decision or the failure to decide, the way medieval ruins permeate Kafka's monstrous house in the suburbs. Now and then the windows fly open and one sees the black, starless sky of something like philosophical anthropology. But whereas in Sartre the form – that of the *pièce à thèse* – is somewhat traditional, by no means daring, and aimed at effect, in Beckett the form overtakes what is expressed and changes it. The impulses are raised to the level of the most advanced artistic techniques, those of Joyce and Kafka. For Beckett absurdity is no longer an 'existential situation' diluted to an idea and then illustrated. In him literary method surrenders to absurdity without preconceived intentions. Absurdity is relieved of the doctrinal universality which in existentialism, the creed of the irreducibility of individual existence, linked it to the Western pathos of the universal and lasting. Beckett thereby dismisses existential conformity, the notion that one ought to be what one is, and with it easy comprehensibility of presentation. What philosophy Beckett provides, he himself reduces to cultural trash, like the innumerable allusions and cultural tidbits he employs, following the tradition of the Anglo-Saxon avant-garde and especially of Joyce and Eliot. For Beckett, culture swarms and crawls, the way the intestinal convolutions of *Jugendstil* ornamentation swarmed and crawled for the avant-garde before him: modernism as what is obsolete in modernity. Language, regressing, demolishes that obsolete material. In Beckett, this kind of objectivity annihilates the meaning that culture once was, along with its rudiments. And so culture begins to fluoresce. In this Beckett is carrying to its conclusion a tendency present in the modern novel. Reflection, which the cultural criterion of aesthetic immanence proscribed as abstract, is juxtaposed with pure presentation; the Flaubertian principle of a completely self-contained subject matter is undermined. The less events can be presumed to be inherently meaning-ful, the more the idea of aesthetic substance as the unity of what appears and what was intended becomes an illusion. Beckett rids him-self of this illusion by coupling the two moments in their disparity. Thought becomes both a means to produce meaning in the work, a meaning which cannot be rendered in tangible form, and a means to express the absence of meaning. Applied to the drama, the word 'meaning' is ambiguous. It covers the metaphysical content that is rep-resented objectively in the complexion of the artefact; the intention of the whole as a complex of meaning that is the inherent meaning of the drama; and finally the meaning of the words and sentences spoken by the characters and their meaning in sequence, the dialogic meaning. But these equivocations point to something shared. In Beckett's *Endgame* that common ground becomes a continuum. Historically, this continuum is supported by a change in the a priori of the drama: the fact that there is no longer any substantive, affirmative metaphysical meaning that could provide dramatic form with its law and its epiphany. That, however, disrupts the dramatic form down to its lin-guistic infrastructure. Drama cannot simply take negative meaning, or the absence of meaning, as its content without everything peculiar to it being affected to the point of turning into its opposite. The essence of drama was constituted by that meaning. Were drama to try to survive meaning aesthetically, it would become inadequate to its substance and be degraded to a clattering machinery for the demonstration of worldviews, as is often the case with existentialist plays. The explosion of the metaphysical meaning, which was the only thing guaranteeing the unity of the aesthetic structure, causes the latter to crumble with a necessity and stringency in no way unequal to that of the traditional canon of dramatic form. Unequivocal aesthetic meaning and its subjec-tivisation in concrete, tangible intention was a surrogate for the transcendent meaningfulness whose very denial constitutes aesthetic content. Through its own organised meaninglessness, dramatic action must model itself on what has transpired with the truth content of drama in general. Nor does this kind of construction of the meaning-less stop at the linguistic molecules; if they, and the connections between them, were rationally meaningful, they would necessarily be synthesised into the overall coherence of meaning that the drama as a whole negates. Hence interpretation of *Endgame* cannot pursue the chimerical aim of expressing the play's meaning in a form mediated by philosophy. Understanding it can only mean understanding its unintelligibility, concretely reconstructing the meaning of the fact that it has no meaning. Split off, thought no longer presumes, as the Idea once did, to be the meaning of the work, a transcendence produced and vouched for by the work's immanence. Instead, thought transforms itself into a kind of second-order material, the way the philosophical ideas in Thomas Mann's *Magic Mountain* and *Doctor Faustus* have their fate as material does, a fate that takes the place of the sensuous immediacy that dwindles in the self-reflexive work of art. Until now this transformation of thought into material has largely been involuntary, the plight of works that compulsively mistook themselves for the Idea they could not attain; Beckett accepts the challenge and uses thoughts *sans phrase* as clichés, fragmentary materials in the *monologue intérieur* that spirit has become, the reified residues of culture. Pre-Beckettian existentialism exploited philosophy as a literary subject as though it were Schiller in the flesh. Now Beckett, more cultured than any of them, hands it the bill: philosophy, spirit itself, declares itself to be dead inventory, the dream-like leavings of the world of experience, and the poetic process declares itself to be a process of wastage. *Dégoût*, a productive artistic force since Baudelaire, becomes insatiable in Beckett's historically mediated impulses. Anything that no longer works becomes canonical, thus rescuing from the shadowlands of methodology a motif from the pre-history of existentialism, Husserl's universal world-annihilation. Adherents of totalitarianism like Lukács, who wax indignant about the decadence of this truly *terrible simplificateur*, are not ill-advised by the interest of their bosses. What they hate in Beckett is what they betrayed. Only the nausea of satiety, the *taedium* of the spirit, wants something completely different; ordained health has to be satisfied with the nourishment offered, homely fare. Beckett's *dégoût* refuses to be coerced. Exhorted to play along, he responds with parody, parody both of philosophy, which spits out his dialogues, and of forms. Existentialism itself is parodied; nothing remains of its invariant categories but bare existence. The play's opposition to ontology, which outlines something somehow First and Eternal, is unmistakable in the following piece of dialogue, which involuntarily caricatures Goethe's dictum about *das alte Wahre* what is old and true, a notion that deteriorates to bourgeois sentiment:

HAMM: Do you remember your father?

CLOV [W*early*]: Same answer. [*Pause.*] You've asked me these questions millions of times.

HAMM: I love the old questions. [*With fervour.*] Ah the old questions, the old answers, there's nothing like them! (*CDW* 110)

Thoughts are dragged along and distorted, like the residues of waking life in dreams, *homo homini sapienti sat*. This is why interpreting Beckett, something he declines to concern himself with, is so awkward. Beckett shrugs his shoulders at the possibility of philosophy today, at the very possibility of theory. The irrationality of bourgeois society in its late phase rebels at letting itself be understood; those were the good old days, when a critique of the political economy of this society could be written that judged it in terms of its own *ratio*. For since then the society has thrown its *ratio* on the scrap heap and replaced it with virtually unmediated control. Hence interpretation inevitably lags behind Beckett. His dramatic work, precisely by virtue of its restriction to an exploded facticity, surges out beyond facticity and in its enigmatic character calls for interpretation. One could almost say that the criterion of a philosophy whose hour is struck is that it proves equal to this challenge.

French existentialism had tackled the problem of history. In Beckett, history swallows up existentialism. In *Endgame*, a historical moment unfolds, namely the experience captured in the title of one of the culture industry's cheap novels, *Kaputt*. After the Second World War, everything, including a resurrected culture, has been destroyed without realising it; humankind continues to vegetate, creeping along after events that even the survivors cannot really survive, on a rubbish heap that has made reflection on one's own damaged state useless. The word *kaputt*, the pragmatic presupposition of the play, is snatched back from the marketplace:

CLOV: [*He gets up on ladder, turns the telescope on the without.*] Let's see. [*He looks, moving the telescope.*] Zero . . . [*he looks*] . . . zero . . . [*he looks*] . . . and zero.

HAMM: Nothing stirs. All is –

CLOV: Zer –

HAMM: [*Violently.*] Wait till you're spoken to. [*Normal voice.*] All is . . . all is . . . all is what? [*Violently.*] All is what?

CLOV: What all is? In a word? Is that what you want to know? Just a moment. [*He turns the telescope on the without, looks, lowers the telescope, turns towards* HAMM.] Corpsed. [In the German translation quoted by Adorno, 'Kaputt!'.] (*CDW* 106)

The fact that all human beings are dead is smuggled in on the sly. An earlier passage gives the reason why the catastrophe may not be mentioned. Hamm himself is vaguely responsible for it:

HAMM: That old doctor, he's dead naturally?

CLOV: He wasn't old.

HAMM: But he's dead?

CLOV: Naturally. [*Pause.*] *You* ask *me* that? (*CDW* 104)

The situation in the play, however, is none other than that in which 'There's no more nature' (*CDW* 97). The phase of complete reification of the world, where there is nothing left that has not been made by human beings, is indistinguishable from an additional catastrophic event caused by human beings, in which nature has been wiped out and after which nothing grows any more:

HAMM: Did your seeds come up?

CLOV: No.

HAMM: Did you scratch round them to see if they had sprouted?

CLOV: They haven't sprouted.

HAMM: Perhaps it's still too early.

CLOV: If they were going to sprout they would have sprouted. [*Violently.*] They'll never sprout. (*CDW* 98)

The *dramatis personae* resemble those who dream their own death, in a 'shelter' in which 'it's time it ended' (*CDW* 93). The end of the world is discounted, as though it could be taken for granted. Any alleged drama of the atomic age would be a mockery of itself, solely because its plot would comfortingly falsify the historical horror of anonymity by displacing it onto human characters and actions and by gaping at the 'important people' who are in charge of whether or not the button gets pushed. The violence of the unspeakable is mirrored in the fear of mentioning it. Beckett keeps it nebulous. About what is incommensurable with experience as such one can speak only in euphemisms, the way one speaks in Germany of the murder of the Jews. It has become a total a priori, so that bombed out consciousness no longer has a place from which to reflect on it. With gruesome irony, the desperate state of things provides a stylistic technique that protects the pragmatic presupposition from contamination by childish science fiction. If Clov had really exaggerated, as his companion, nagging him with common sense, accuses him of doing, that would not change much. The partial end of the world which the catastrophe would then amount to would be a bad joke. Nature, from which the prisoners are cut off, would be as good as no longer there at all; what is left of it would merely prolong the agony.

But at the same time, this historical nota bene, a parody of Kierkegaard's point of contact between time and eternity, places a taboo on history. What existentialist jargon considers the *condition humaine* is the image of the last human being, which devours that of the earlier ones, humanity. Existentialist ontology asserts that there is something universally valid in this process of abstraction that is not aware of itself. It follows the old phenomenological thesis of the *Wesensschau*, eidetic intuition, and acts as though it were aware of its compelling specifications in the particular – and as though it thereby combined apriority and concreteness in a single, magical stroke. But it distils out the element it considers supratemporal by negating precisely the particularity, individuation in time and space, that makes existence existence and not the mere concept of existence. It courts those who are sick of philosophical formalism and yet cling to something accessible only in formal terms. To this kind of unacknowledged process of abstraction, Beckett poses the decisive antithesis: an avowed process of subtraction. Instead of omitting what is temporal in existence – which can be existence only in time – he subtracts from existence what time, the historical tendency, is in reality preparing to get rid of. He extends the line taken by the liquidation of the subject to the point where it contracts into a 'here and now', a 'whatchamacallit', whose abstractness, the loss of all qualities, literally reduces ontological abstractness *ad absurdum*, the absurdity into which mere existence is transformed when it is absorbed into naked self-identity. Childish silliness emerges as the content of philosophy, which degenerates into tautology, into conceptual duplication of the existence it had set out to comprehend. Modern ontology lives off the unfulfilled promise of the concreteness of its abstractions, whereas in Beckett the concreteness of an existence that is shut up inside itself like a mollusk, no longer capable of universality, an existence that exhausts itself in pure self-positing, is revealed to be identical to the abstractness that is no longer capable of experience. Ontology comes into its own as the pathogenesis of the false life. It is presented as a state of negative eternity. Dostoevski's messianic Prince Mishkin once forgot his watch because no earthly time was valid for him; for Beckett's characters, Mishkin's antithesis, time can be lost because time would contain hope. Bored, the characters affirm that the weather is 'as usual' (*CDW* 105); this affirmation opens the jaws of Hell:

HAMM: But that's always the way at the end of the day, isn't it, Clov?

CLOV: Always.

HAMM: It's the end of the day like any other day, isn't it, Clov?

CLOV: Looks like it. (*CDW* 98)

Like time, the temporal has been incapacitated; even to say that it didn't exist any more would be too comforting. It is and it isn't, the way the world is for the solipsist, who doubts the world's existence but has to concede it with every sentence. A passage of dialogue equivocates in this way:

HAMM: And the horizon? Nothing on the horizon?

CLOV: [*Lowering the telescope, turning towards* HAMM, *exasperated.*] What in God's name could there be on the horizon? [*Pause.*]

HAMM: The waves, how are the waves?

CLOV: The waves? [*He turns the telescope on the waves.*] Lead.

HAMM: And the sun?

CLOV: [*Looking.*] Zero.

HAMM: But it should be sinking. Look again.

CLOV: [*Looking.*] Damn the sun.

HAMM: Is it night already then?

CLOV: [*Looking.*] No.

HAMM: Then what is it?

CLOV: [*Looking.*] Grey. [*Lowering the telescope, turning towards* HAMM, *louder.*] Grey! [*Pause. Still louder.*] GRREY! (*CDW* 107)

History is kept outside because it has dried up consciousness' power to conceive it, the power to remember. Drama becomes mute gesture, freezes in the middle of dialogue. The only part of history that is still apparent is its outcome – decline. What in the existentialists was inflated into the be-all and end-all of existence here contracts to the tip of the historical and breaks off. True to official optimism, Lukács complains that in Beckett human beings are reduced to their animal qualities.[58] His complaint tries to ignore the fact that the philosophies of the remainder, that is, those which subtract the temporal and the contingent element of life in order to retain only what is true and eternal, have turned into the remains of life, the sum total of the damages. Just as it is ridiculous to impute an abstract subjectivist ontology to Beckett and then put that ontology on some index of degenerate art, as Lukács does, on the basis of its worldlessness and its infantilism, so it would be ridiculous to put Beckett on the stand as a star political witness. A work which sees the potential for nuclear catastrophe even in the oldest struggle of all will scarcely arouse us to do battle against nuclear catastrophe. Unlike Brecht, this simplifier of horror resists simplification. Beckett, however, is not so dissimilar to Brecht. His differentiatedness becomes an allergy to subjective differences that have degenerated into the conspicuous consumption of those who can afford individuation. There is a social truth in that. Differentiatedness cannot absolutely and without reflection be entered onto the positive side of the ledger. The simplification of the social process which is underway relegates it to the *faux frais*, the 'extras', in much the same way that the social formalities by means of which the capacity for differentiation was developed are disappearing. Differentiatedness, once the precondition of humanness [*Humanität*], is gradually becoming ideology. But an unsentimental awareness of this is not regressive. In the act of omission, what is left out survives as something that is avoided, the way consonance survives in atonal harmony. An unprotesting depiction of ubiquitous regression is a protest against the state of a world that so accommodates the law of regression that it no longer has anything to hold up against it. There is constant monitoring to see that things are one way and not another; an alarm system with a sensitive bell indicates what fits in with the play's topography and what does not. Out of delicacy, Beckett keeps quiet about the delicate things as well as the brutal. The vanity of the individual who accuses society while his 'rights' add to the accumulation of injustices is manifested in embarrassing declamations like Karl Wolfskehl's *Deutschlandsgedicht* [*Poem on Germany*]. There is nothing like this in Beckett. Even the notion that he depicts the negativity of the age in negative form would fit in with the idea the people in the Eastern satellite states, where the revolution was carried out in the form of an administrative act, must now devote themselves cheerfully to reflecting a cheerful era. Playing with elements of reality, taking no stand and finding pleasure in this freedom from prescribed activity, exposes more than would taking a stand with the intent to expose. The name of the catastrophe is to be spoken only in silence. The catastrophe that has befallen the whole is illuminated in the horrors of the last catastrophe; but only in those horrors, not when one looks at its origins. For Beckett, the human being – the name of the species would not fit well in Beckett's linguistic landscape – is only what he has become. As in utopia, it is its last day that decides on the species. But mourning over this must reflect – in the spirit – the fact that mourning itself is no longer possible. No weeping melts the armour; the only face left is the one whose tears have dried up. This lies at the basis of an artistic method that is denounced as inhuman by those whose humanness has already become an advertisement for the inhuman, even if they are not aware of it. Of the motives for Beckett's reductions of his characters to bestialised human beings, that is probably the most essential. Part of what is absurd in his writing is that it hides its face.

The catastrophes that inspire *Endgame* have shattered the individual whose substantiality and absoluteness was the common thread in Kierkegaard, Jaspers, and Sartre's version of existentialism. Sartre even affirmed the freedom of the victims of the concentration camps to inwardly accept or reject the tortures inflicted upon them. *Endgame* destroys such illusions. The individual himself is revealed to be a historical category, both the outcome of the capitalist process of alienation and a defiant protest against it, something transient himself. The individualistic position constitutes the opposite pole to the ontological approach of every kind of existentialism, including that of *Being and Time*, and as such belongs with it. Beckett's drama abandons that position like an outmoded bunker. If individual experience in its narrowness and contingency has interpreted itself as a figure of Being, it has received the authority to do so only by asserting itself to be the fundamental characteristic of Being. But this is precisely what is false. The immediacy of individuation was deceptive; the carrier of individual experience is mediated, conditioned. *Endgame* assumes that the individual's claim to autonomy and being has lost its credibility. But although the prison of individuation is seen to be both prison and illusion – the stage set is the imago of this kind of insight – art cannot break the spell of a detached subjectivity; it can only give concrete form to solipsism. Here Beckett runs up against the antinomy of contemporary art. Once the position of the absolute subject has been exposed as the manifestation of an overarching whole that produces it, it cannot hold up; expressionism becomes obsolete. Art is denied the transition to a binding universality of material reality which would call a halt to the illusion of individuation. For unlike discursive knowledge of reality, something from which art is not distinguished by degrees but categorically distinct, in art only what has been rendered subjective, what is commensurable with subjectivity, is valid. Art can conceive reconciliation, which is its idea, only as the reconciliation of what has been estranged. Were it to simulate the state of reconciliation by joining the world of mere objects, it would negate itself. What is presented as socialist realism is not, as is claimed, something beyond subjectivism, but rather something that lags behind it, and at the same time the pre-artistic complement of subjectivism. The expressionist invocation 'O Mensch' ['Oh Man'] is the perfect complement to a social reportage seasoned with ideology. An unreconciled reality tolerates no reconciliation with the object in art. Realism, which does not grasp subjective experience, to say nothing of going beyond it, only mimics reconciliation. Today the dignity of art is measured not according to whether or not it evades this antinomy through luck or skill, but in terms of how it bears it. In this, *Endgame* is exemplary. It yields both to the impossibility of continuing to represent

things in works of art, continuing to work with materials in the manner of the nineteenth century, and to the insight that the subjective
modes of response that have replaced representation as mediators of
form are not original and absolute but rather a resultant, something
objective. The whole content of subjectivity, which is inevitably self-
hypostasising, is a trace and a shadow of the world from which
subjectivity withdraws in order to avoid serving the illusion and the
adaptation that the world demands. Beckett responds to this not with
a stock of eternal truths, but with what the antagonistic tendencies
will still – precariously, and subject to revocation – permit.[59] □

The challenge of understanding what forms of protest do survive in
Beckett's universe, and how they are articulated, is one of the dominant
imperatives in Beckett criticism. As can be seen from this chapter, this
critical approach to Beckett, which seeks to understand how his radicalism subverts and deconstructs dominant ideological institutions, runs
alongside an opposite mode of criticism, which aims to interpret his formal dramatic gestures as closely as possible, whilst assuming that his art
is apolitical and benign. From these early days of Beckett criticism, two
contrasting Becketts emerge: a Beckett who represents universal truths
about human reality in concrete dramatic form, who rejects cultural and
political concerns as trivial and illusory, and whose artistic merit stems
from an unflinching, penetrating depiction of the world as it is, seasoned
with ineffable poetry and grace; and another Beckett, whose drama is a
dangerous challenge to the very notion of a universal humanity, whose
negativity is a residual and mournful form of protest, and whose poetry
is generated by a restless, formless antagonism. The history of Beckett
studies is the story of these two traditions, as they have interwoven and
contrasted through the decades of development of criticism and theory.
One of the values of *Godot* and *Endgame* is that, in their difficult and
sometimes abrasive relationship with the critical discourses that have
sought to account for them, they have exposed some of the mechanics of
the ongoing struggle for power, knowledge and authority that has driven
literary criticism in the second half of the twentieth century.

The following chapters will trace these two approaches to Beckett's
drama as they unfold, and as their fates are determined by the epistemological and theoretical battles fought in Anglo-American and European
critical institutions.

CHAPTER TWO

Humanising the Void

1. New Criticism and Esslin's Three Categories

THE DOMINANT mode of reception of Beckett's drama in the English-speaking critical community, from the sixties to the early nineties, has been an Anglo-American brand of liberal humanism that has affinities with the New Criticism and the Practical Criticism fashioned by the Leavises and I. A. Richards from the twenties to the forties.[1] The work of critics from Martin Esslin, Ruby Cohn and Hugh Kenner in the sixties and seventies, through John Fletcher, John Spurling, Michael Robinson and Bell Gale Chevigny in the seventies and eighties, to the exemplary work of James Knowlson and John Pilling, which has been dominant in Beckett studies from the seventies through to the nineties, has been largely contained within the boundaries of a liberal humanist critique. This critical approach, in achieving virtual hegemony in English-language Beckett criticism from the early sixties onwards, effectively marginalised the Marxist strand of criticism exemplified by Adorno's essay quoted in the last chapter, and confined it to the smaller field of German-language criticism. Adorno's emphasis on dramatic negativity as a radical challenge to modes of interpretation and theorisation was all but lost in a critical discourse that was geared to humanising Beckett's representation of 'the void', and making it accessible to a wide but discriminating audience. The years from Martin Esslin's 1965 collection of essays entitled *Samuel Beckett: A Collection of Essays*, to John Pilling and James Knowlson's influential *Frescoes of the Skull*, were years of consolidation, in which the basic approach to Beckett's drama laid out by Esslin in *The Theatre of the Absurd* was deepened and broadened to accommodate more fully not only the fifties drama, but also the whole emerging Beckett oeuvre. By the early eighties, it appeared that *Waiting for Godot* and *Endgame* had been fully incorporated, as flagships of the Beckett oeuvre, into T. S. Eliot's great literary tradition.[2] Far from being regarded as strange and threatening plays, they had been absorbed and understood so completely it seemed that there was little left to say about them. Indeed David Hesla comments, as early as 1971, that he doubts that there is anything worthwhile to say about Beckett's writing that has not already been said by Hugh Kenner.[3]

Of course, the writers that I am grouping together here under the loose heading of 'humanist' critics adopt a wide range of varying approaches, styles and priorities. Ruby Cohn's patient elaboration of the history of Beckett's comic devices,[4] for example, has little in common with Hugh Kenner's brilliantly quirky analysis of Beckett's preoccupation with the bicycle,[5] or G. C. Barnard's interest in schizophrenia.[6] But given this diversity, there is a level of consensus between these critics about the nature of art, the function of criticism, and Beckett's place and importance within the literary canon, as there is general agreement about the broad methodology that should be brought to his writing. This consensus is part of a much broader Anglo-American formalist critical movement that was flourishing as the Beckett institution headed by Esslin, Kenner and Cohn began to gather momentum in the early to mid-sixties. The study of literature in the English-speaking academy at this time was still influenced by the critical ideology of the Leavisites and the New Critics, who had won their battles to have literary studies recognised as a serious subject.[7] In the decade from 1920 to 1930, the work of F. R. Leavis, Q. D. Leavis, I. A. Richards and, to a certain extent, T. S. Eliot had taken English from an irrelevant and amateurish pastime to a central and vital discipline, which dealt with the most pressing intellectual problems facing post-war Europe. The periodical *Scrutiny*, in which much of the Cambridge New Critics' work was published, proved so influential that it forged a critical discourse that became almost invisible, such was its dominance.[8] The assumptions that lay behind New Critical judgements, which had been fought for so hard only a few years before, had become by the forties so firmly entrenched that some critics no longer even recognised them as assumptions. New Criticism had become natural law, and to write criticism was to partake of its wisdom.

The new critical discourse, however, was very much a product of a cultural moment that defined and delimited its approach. Leavis and Richards bequeathed to succeeding generations of scholars a revitalised and powerful discipline, which opened up possibilities for the reading and understanding of literary texts that had never before been apprehended. But the initial fragility of their position in the academy, and the specificity of their own agenda, led them to make pronouncements about the scope and nature of literature that exerted a deeply conservative influence on literary criticism that can still be felt today. The naturalisation of their critical approach, aided by its dominance in the creation of the new O- and A-level English syllabuses, made this conservatism more insidious, by causing it to appear as a bearer of incontrovertible cultural truth.

Leavis's redefinition of English studies was democratic in that it broke
down the aristocratic dominance of the subject at the traditional universities and made it accessible to the middle classes. It was also liberating
because it challenged the deferential attitude to literary texts that was
prevalent in pre-Leavis conventional criticism. New Criticism replaced a
respectful appreciation of literature as a sacred and untouchable object
with an aggressive critical approach, which was not afraid to break the
text down to its constituent parts in order to examine how it worked. It
introduced a much harder and more gritty, pseudo-scientific language
that brought the literary text to account, rather than simply congratulat-
ing it on being beautiful. But this new language of exacting
discrimination and cool-headed judgement, whilst being refreshing and
enabling, was also a feature of New Criticism that was to become restric-
tive and disabling. The 'discrimination' that the *Scrutiny* contributors
brought to bear on texts, which became such a naturalised form of
judgement in the English-speaking academy, was loaded with a great
deal of cultural baggage. The New Critics may have challenged the dominance of the Oxbridge aristocracy, but they were more interested in
consolidating the position of the emergent bourgeois intelligentsia within
an existing cultural framework than in posing too radical a threat to the
status quo, and their criticism reflected this conservatism. Critics such as
F. R. Leavis and T. S. Eliot were able, from very different standpoints, to
prioritise and energise the practice of literary criticism because they saw
it as an urgent antidote to the cultural disintegration caused by such
upheavals as rapid industrialisation, the rise of the bourgeoisie and the
First World War. As the certainties of the old world rapidly collapsed into
the disorder of the new, as rampant capitalism, mass consumerism and
the popular novel caused twentieth-century culture to drift from its
moral and ethical roots, it is in the authentic literary text that critics
found world order maintained. I. A. Richards exemplifies this reading of
literature as a kind of cultural guardian when he comments, in *Science
and Poetry*, that poetry is 'capable of saving us; it is a perfectly possible
means of overcoming the chaos'.[9] Literary criticism becomes radically
more exciting and dynamic at this period, precisely because it is seen as
the last form of protection against the forces that were threatening to
undermine the *status quo*.

In charging literature with such a monumental responsibility, these
critics fashioned a politics of reading that judged the literary text in terms
of its effectiveness in articulating the sacred truths that were preserved in
the literary canon. The emphasis on close reading, on scrupulous attention to the linguistic structure of the text, turned around this concern to
elaborate the means by which literature staved off the chaos. As Francis
Mulhern comments, Richards' pioneering work *Principles of Literary
Criticism* was, for all its technicality, 'less an academic disquisition on

aesthetics than a "loom on which . . . to reweave some ravelled parts of our civilisation"'.[10] The suggestion was that, in 'true', 'authentic' works, writers were able to develop a form of expression that could reveal the reality of experience in a way that other modes of expression could not. The job of the critic is, through a fine process of accurate and educated reading, to separate these special works from other, inauthentic works, and to inculcate sensitive, discriminatory faculties in the main body of readers. Criticism was seen as a kind of quality assurance, an advance guard of readers who check out the viability of new works with a magnifying glass, and keep up the standard of those that have already been admitted into the club of chaos-busting texts. Such an understanding of the critic's function, however, ended up reproducing some of the critical habits that the *Scrutiny* movement was most anxious to eradicate. This criticism was driven above all by an anxious concern to draw a non-negotiable barrier between legitimate, high art and the grubby popular entertainment that was accused of infecting the 'mind of Europe', but in policing such a boundary critics were led to refer to the very sacred, mystical qualities of literary texts that they objected to so strongly in their predecessors. The acid test for legitimacy, in this objective and scientific discourse, often turned out to be a question of whether or not the text was 'living', or other such obfuscatory and imponderable terms. The problem was that literature and criticism came to be justified as a form of defence of a liberal humanist ideology that was viewed as natural rather than cultural, and in deciding whether texts bore out the truths of a humanist ideology, critics were forced into using natural, organic terms rather than discriminatory, scientific ones to express their approval. It was still the case that literature was a 'special language' that you were either 'sensitive' enough to appreciate, or you weren't. Critics could distinguish good works from bad works through educated and finical examination, but they could not actually say *why* good literature was good, because the very mark of its quality lay in its mystical articulation of an ineffable truth in a living, vivid language that was not susceptible of translation or paraphrase. Despite its avowed rejection of the sanctity of art, the new critical discourse was an uneasy combination of empirical, objective observation and untheorised, quasi-theological mystification.

It is this somewhat unstable discourse that was inherited by Beckett's sixties critics. Whilst English-speaking Beckett criticism, as it emerged at this time, was influenced to some extent by the contemporary development of semiotics and structuralist theory, it drew from such theory very selectively, like a great deal of British criticism. The formalist approach that these critics adopted took some of its terminology from structuralists such as the early Barthes and Lévi-Strauss, but the ideological basis of this criticism remained deeply embedded in a Leavisite cultural conservatism. By the time Beckett's works became widely recognised as 'contemporary classics', after *Waiting for Godot* had amply demonstrated its ability to weather well, it became necessary for the guardians of the literary canon to construct an interpretative paradigm that could accommodate his growing oeuvre, without loosening the ties that held the delicate ideological–critical compound together. This proved to be a fairly awkward task, however, as the practice of interpreting Beckett's work tended to draw attention to the contradictions that lay beneath the surface of the critical discourse itself. It seems immediately clear that Richards' view of the function of art as a process of reweaving a ravelled civilisation sits somewhat awkwardly alongside a dramatic vision that represents civilisation as a bad joke. Kenneth Tynan's forthright rejection of *Endgame* as a legitimate artwork, because it could not 'help us' to face and overcome the difficulties that it dramatised, is symptomatic of the tensions that arise when a critical discourse that is structured around the power of art to maintain moral and ethical order is faced with an object that seems rather to collaborate in civic collapse than bravely and strenuously to resist it. Beckett's drama appeared not to fulfil many of the protective cultural functions that Eliot ascribed to traditional works of art, and yet it seemed beyond doubt that this was 'art' of the highest order. Indeed, it was taken by many to be one of the defining examples of the avant-garde high art that it was the function of the erudite and sensitive critic to defend against the ignorance and incomprehension of the general public. Despite its daring flirtation with forms of 'low' entertainment such as the music hall, which most certainly would not be admitted into the canon, Beckett's difficult, allusive drama became a bench mark for work of the 'high[est] level of artistic intensity and creativeness'.[11] The question arises – if good art is good because it keeps us in organic contact with the metaphysical truths enshrined in the canon, and if Beckett's drama is to be seen as a rejection of the values of civilisation, then in what sense can Beckett's work be regarded as good?

Those critics who, through the sixties and seventies, developed the liberal humanist paradigm for reading Beckett's drama, were forced to face this problem at the outset. Martin Esslin, who emerged in the fifties as an extremely influential reader of Beckett's work,[12] was at the forefront of the movement to construct a means of reading Beckett that did not offend New Critical sensibilities. In 1965, Esslin edited a collection of essays on Beckett's work, including one of Beckett's own critical essays, which formed one of the first concerted attempts to forge a coherent and inclusive response to the oeuvre. In the introduction to this collection, which P. J. Murphy has called the 'most influential fifteen pages in the history of Beckett criticism in English',[13] Esslin seeks to negotiate the apparent contradiction between Beckett's rejection of 'universal truths' and the universal human value of his literary achievement. Far from seeking to avoid or underplay the sense that Beckett's work does not constitute a defence of Western metaphysics, Esslin emphasises Beckett's absolute denial of the legitimacy of the truths upon which Western civilisation has been based. Relying heavily on a reading of Beckett's critical work 'Three Dialogues with Georges Duthuit', which he reprints in the collection, Esslin suggests that Beckett's writing constitutes an aesthetic of failure.[14] The oeuvre springs from the writer's recognition that art can no longer express abstract truths in a world in which civilisation has already died and can only be mourned. All that is left to us starved post-holocaust people is the recognition of the fruitlessness and the senselessness of our world, in which every individual subject is cut off and isolated from every other subject. In a move that will be familiar from the previous chapter, however, Esslin insists that this negativity, this radical meaninglessness, can be represented in an artistic form that itself is luminously meaningful and poignantly life-affirming. In fact, it is the very mysterious force with which Beckett is able to represent the bankruptcy of the human condition that lends his writing its undeniable vitality. The failure that forms the subject matter of Beckett's writing – the failure of language to express any meaningful truths – is held within a work of art that nevertheless represents the pinnacle of artistic achievement. Thus Esslin is quite happy to accept that 'no universal lessons, no meanings, no philosophical truths could possibly be derived from the work of a writer like Beckett'.[15] This does not put the validity of his work in question, because his 'categorical refusal to allow any philosophical meaning or thesis to be attributed to his work, is precisely the aspect of his activity that lifts his precarious and perilous enterprise into a sphere of significance beyond the scope of most other artists'.[16]

The category that mediates between Beckett's recognition of the failure of expression, and his adoption of an extremely successful art form, is that of 'authenticity'. In a language that shares the New Critical emphasis on the mystical, ineffable quality of the genuine work of art, Esslin suggests that it is Beckett's ability concretely and organically to reconstruct the *experience* of a life devoid of meaning that gives his work its power and weight. Beckett's work has such a 'living', direct quality that it manages to transcend the very collapse of meaning to which it bears witness. It does not speak in the quotidian language that has been cheapened by the marketplace and butchered by Auschwitz; rather it forges a special artistic language that, in its perfect balance, rhythm and weight, speaks to us about our hopelessness directly. In an emphasis on the formal quality of artistic discourse, which again has its roots in Leavis, Esslin repeatedly asserts (paraphrasing Beckett himself) that 'it is the shape of the thought, the symmetry that matters'. It is in Beckett's perfect symmetry and formal brilliance, reminiscent of music in its rhythmical poise, that his art gives expression to the void. Thus, while Beckett's writing does not 'lay claim to *meaning* anything beyond itself', it still has the function of staving off the chaos that so alarmed Eliot, Leavis and Richards, by pitting the earthy vitality of its language against what Beckett has called 'the mess'. Beckett's works 'may not express reality in terms of something outside itself, but they *are* reality, they *are* the world'. Paradoxically, therefore, Esslin suggests that Beckett, the arch-deconstructer of social values who confronts head on the meaninglessness of life, can after all be seen, in a certain Leavisite light, to be one of the great defenders of humanity against the void that threatens to engulf us.

The sleight of hand with which Esslin manages to incorporate Beckett into a liberal humanist critical framework whilst emphasising his resistance to such a framework, however, still leaves him with an embarrassing problem. If Beckett's value is to be found in his direct and untranslatable representation of reality, if his work is a concrete form of expression to which no abstract meanings can be attached, then how can the critic elucidate the oeuvre without falling into the trap of assigning to it such dreaded 'meanings'? How can a 'living', 'organic' art form, whose quality is to be found in its mystical, untranslatable and inexplicable rendering of the reality of life, possibly benefit from a critical gloss? Surely, if Beckett's work is a pure, concrete experience uncontaminated by any meanings that lie outside it, then it should be experienced first hand without any explanation. Esslin is uncomfortably aware of this difficulty, and he dedicates the second half of his introduction to solving it. In the passage quoted below, Esslin suggests that there are three areas in which the critic is able to make a legitimate contribution to our understanding of Beckett's work, and this prescription for the scope and the function of the Beckett critic forms a virtual manifesto for the humanist criticism that has been produced from the sixties to the present day.

■ But in that case – if there are no secure meanings to be established, no keys to be provided, guaranteed to unlock allegorical treasure-houses; if the only chance of approaching the writer's meaning is to experience his experience – what justification can there be for any critical analysis and interpretation of such a writer's work?

There is certainly no justification for criticism that will try to deliver cut-and-dried results, such as furnishing the discovery of the identity of Godot, or establishing that Hamm is James Joyce and Clov Beckett himself; nor is there point in importing Christian theology or Zen Buddhism into the work of a man whose basic attitude can be defined as a total rejection of ideology. Yet a wide area still remains that is legitimately open for critical analysis from a variety of different motivations and standpoints.

First of all, there is the entirely justifiable approach which seeks to elucidate the numerous allusions – literary, philosophical, geographical

– in the text. If a reader is to be capable of sharing in the existential experience embodied in these texts, he must have a full understanding of the references that are buried, at various levels, in the complex associative pattern of these intricate verbal structures. In Beckett's case the tracking down of these numerous cross-references and allusions, puns and assonances, demands such a high degree of skill and leads into such fascinating byways of recondite erudition that it can provide all the excitement and all the culminating pleasure in having found the solution that we get from the best detective thriller. There is, however, an important caution to be kept in mind: in retracing the intricate warp and woof of verbal and conceptual allusions, hidden clues and concealed correspondences, the critic may unwittingly suggest to the reader that the author has himself intentionally constructed his work as an intellectual puzzle. Such an 'intentional fallacy' would inevitably induce dangerous misconceptions about the motivation of a writer like Beckett as well as about the nature of the creative process that produces literature of this type; the writer will then appear to the reader as, above all, an intellect of almost superhuman ingenuity and calculation bent on devising superhumanly difficult conundrums for similarly ingenious and erudite intellects. Nothing could, in Beckett's case, be further from the truth. He is the least consciously intellectual of writers. His method of work is spontaneous and always has as its starting point the deeply concentrated evocation of the voice within his own depths. In this there are links between Beckett and the French surrealists of the '20's and '30's, some of whom he met during his first stay in Paris. He differs from the surrealists in that he does not, having summoned up the voices from his subconscious, merely record them in 'automatic writing'. He shapes them with all the skill and sense of style of a highly conscious craftsman, using the full discriminatory faculty of a skilled literary critic. Nevertheless, it is the spontaneously emerging voice that is the raw material on which he works. Inevitably, in the case of a man of such vast and varied learning as Beckett, the voices that emerge from the depths of his subconscious speak a language that reflects his past experience and the store of associations he has acquired, and will therefore be studded with allusions and a wealth of cross-references. But these are the outcome of a process that is largely subconscious, and certainly free of any premeditation or display of euphistic cleverness. The intricate texture the critic has to unravel is therefore nearer, in its structural principle, to the organic associative organisation of images in a dream than to the calculated pattern of a cross-word puzzle. The puzzle is there, but it is an organic growth, not a deliberate artefact of mystification. And the critic can help to solve it by elucidating the strands that have contributed to its growth. But the reader, once he has grasped the full import of the allusions, must accept the text as a spontaneous flow of images and allow himself to be carried along by it with equal spontaneity.

There is also, secondly (beyond the mere elucidation of associations and allusions, the provision of an annotated glossary, as it were, of verbal meanings), a wider and even more challenging task for the critic: namely, the uncovering of the structural principles, the outline of the main design, which must be present in an oeuvre in which the concept of the games that the consciousness must play to fill the void is of such importance.[17] Games have rules that can be deduced from observing the players. And only when the rules are known to the spectators can they fully enter into and share the excitement of the players. The elucidation of the structural principles governing each of Beckett's works is therefore another legitimate auxiliary function for the critic which should help the reader to achieve some degree of communication with the writer and to enter into the experience he is seeking to convey. In the same sense an art critic's explanation of the underlying pattern of design in a great painting will enhance the onlooker's ability to see it with the painter's own eyes. Moreover, in an oeuvre as single-minded and ruthlessly consistent with itself as Beckett's, the structural patterns thus uncovered will by no means be confined to each work by itself; it will also be possible to trace a larger pattern of design of a higher order of complexity that will emerge if all the single works are seen together as the constituent parts of the writer's total output. Here again the critic can help by allowing the reader to see the parts in their relation to the whole and in their true perspective. The gradual process of eliminating external events in Beckett's narrative prose from *More Pricks than Kicks* to *How It Is* and the progressive concentration of the action to a static pattern in his plays from *Waiting for Godot* to *Happy Days* and *Play* are cases in point.

Then, thirdly, and above all: if it is indeed true that *esse est percipi* [to be is to be perceived][18] (and for a writer's being *as a writer* it certainly is true; for his work exists only in the minds of those who read it; and the writer's activity itself has, from Horace to Proust, been frequently regarded by the writers themselves as an attempt to achieve permanent being beyond physical death, the only effective way to reach genuine immunity from the obliterating action of time), then it must also be true that a writer's very existence as a writer will depend on the manner in which his work is perceived and experienced by his readers. And this in turn will be largely shaped by the critics, who, if they fulfil their proper function, will determine the quality and depth of this experience by their account of the impact the works in question have made on themselves. It is the critics' experience that serves as an exemplar for the reactions of a wider public; they are the sense organs of the main body of readers: the first to receive the impact of a new writer and trained to experience it; their modes of perception will be followed by the mass of readers, just as in every theatre audience it is the few individuals with a keener than average sense of humour who determine whether the jokes in a play will be laughed at at all, and to what extent, by triggering off the chain-reaction of the mass of the audience.

If this is so, then the function of criticism is of particular importance for a writer like Beckett, who is not trying to communicate anything beyond the quality of his own experience of being; the quality of such a body of work, its very existence, will be determined by the quality of its reception, or by the sum total of the individual experiences it provokes in its individual readers. That is why a great writer's oeuvre can acquire a life of its own, that may well go beyond the author's conscious intentions, and expand by gaining layer after layer of new meaning through the experience it evokes in the minds and the emotions of succeeding generations. The richer a literary creation, the more directly derived from the depths of genuine human experience, the more varied and differentiated will be the reaction it evokes in its readers. Or to put it differently: it is the existential experience in a literary work, as distinct from its purely descriptive, ideological and polemical content, that, in evoking a direct, existential human response in the readers, will ensure its continued impact on succeeding generations. Always, however, it will be the critics who lead the way in discovering those aspects of such a literary creation that are of particular relevance to a given epoch. And it is the critics' work which remains as the permanent record of the quality of the experience provoked by the great writer's oeuvre in each epoch. The critics of one generation, by provoking the dissent of the next, provide the dialectical impetus for the expanding life of a great writer's creative achievement. Such a writer's work can thus be seen as the pebble thrown into a pool; from the point of impact of which an endless growing ring of circular waves spreads across the surface of the water. If, in Kierkegaard's sense, the subjective thinker's experience can never, finally and once and for all, be reduced to an abstract, dead *result* – its meaning being coterminous with itself and with the existential experience it evokes in its audience – and if the audience's reaction must necessarily be different in quality in each individual as well as from generation to generation, it follows that the mode of existence of such an individual thinker's work will eventually be seen as the movement of a living, constantly changing organic *tradition*; and at the centre of such a tradition there must necessarily be found the critics who reflect and shape the movement and the quality of the individual attitudes and experiences that constitute it.

The recognition of the fact that the very existence of such a writer's work is made up from the sum total of the reactions it evokes, does not, however, imply that each and every critical response is of equal value. While the impact of a text, emotional as well as intellectual, must and will be different on different individuals at different times and in different contexts and while many of these differing and seemingly even contradictory reactions may well have equivalent validity in highlighting different aspects of a richly structured literary creation existing on a multitude of levels, there are nevertheless definite and effective criteria that will, if only in due time, eliminate the irrelevant, insensitive, or factually mistaken critical evaluations from the body of the organic tradition that is continually forming and renewing itself around the work of a major creative writer.

In Beckett's case, the astonishing fact is the volume, the diversity, and the quality of the body of critical work he has evoked in so short a time. This is surely a measure of his relevance, richness, and depth. It might be objected that, being a difficult and puzzling writer, the volume of critical reaction merely reflects the fact that he presents a challenge to the ingenuity of critics eager to display their own discernment or erudition. There is, no doubt, a grain of truth in this argument; but any deeper examination of the great mass of critical work on Beckett must show that the argument is superficial. For it is precisely the emotional intensity of the response, even in the work of those critics who revel in the discovery of recondite allusions, that is the most striking common feature of all Beckett criticism; there can be no doubt that these critics are, above all, responding to an overwhelming emotional, almost a mystical, experience; and that this experience has sparked their zeal to elucidate and explain their author's meaning, to make him accessible to a larger number of readers. Whether they analyse the language and the structure of the texts, or track down the philosophical allusions and implications, or even use them as a starting point for sociological analysis (like Günther Anders) or psychological interpretation (like Eva Metman)[19] they are all clearly impelled by a profound experience of insight which has obviously had an exhilarating effect on them. In the terms of Kierkegaard's example of the thinker who faced the dilemma of proclaiming his discovery about the nature of truth by direct advertisement in the local paper or by its indirect expression through an account of his living experience, it is this emotional impact on the critics, as the representatives and advance guard of the public, that supplies the true measure of Samuel Beckett's achievement.

It is, moreover, highly significant that this emotional impact, in apparent contradiction to the recondite intellectual content of Beckett's work, is indeed an exhilarating one. How is it that this vision of the ultimate void in all its grotesque derision and despair should be capable of producing an effect akin to the catharsis of great tragedy?

Here we find the ultimate confirmation of our initial contention that it is not the content of the work, not *what* is said, that matters in a writer of Beckett's stamp, but the *quality of the experience* that is communicated. To be in communication with a mind of such merciless integrity, of such uncompromising determination to face the stark reality of the human situation and to confront the worst without even being in danger of yielding to any of the superficial consolations that have clouded man's self-awareness in the past; to be in contact with a human being so utterly free from self-pity, utterly oblivious to the pitfalls of vanity or self-glorification, even that most venial complacency of all, the illusion of being able to lighten one's anguish by sharing it with others; to see a lone figure, without hope of comfort, facing the great emptiness of space and time without the possibility of miraculous rescue or salvation, in dignity, resolved to fulfil its obligation to express its own predicament – to partake of such courage and noble stoicism, however remotely, cannot but evoke a feeling of emotional excitement, exhilaration.

And if it is the living, existential experience of the individual that matters and has precedence over any abstract concepts it may elicit, then the very act of confronting the void, or continuing to confront it, is an act of affirmation. The blacker the situation, the deeper the background of despair against which this act of affirmation is made, the more complete, the more triumphant must be the victory that it constitutes. The uglier the reality that is confronted, the more exhilarating will be its sublimation into symmetry, rhythm, movement and laughter. To attempt the impossible and to emerge having failed, but not completely, may be a greater triumph than total success in easier tasks. As Beckett himself says, in a fragment of verse hidden away among the addenda to *Watt*:[20]

who may tell the tale
of the old man?
weigh absence in a scale?
mete want with a span?
the sum assess
of the world's woes?
Nothingness in words enclose?[21] □

The contradictions that are to be found in this critical agenda are clear enough. Esslin's rather convoluted text seeks to reconcile implacably opposed positions, often without acknowledging that it is doing so. His main emphasis is on the freedom of interpretation of Beckett's texts – they can mean anything you want them to mean – and yet this emphasis is placed alongside an equal emphasis on the importance of accurate critical judgement – each and every response is not of equal value. Similarly, Beckett's texts should be regarded as a 'total rejection of ideology', and yet one has to be steeped in the lore of a specific ideology in order to be able to appreciate them fully. Or again, Beckett's work is the epitome of bravery, honesty and stoicism in that it does away with all forms of protection against the void and directly challenges the illusory consolation of communication, yet it is simultaneously an exhilarating act of affirmation whose primary quality is its ability to communicate directly to the audience or reader. These contradictions are the direct result of Esslin's application of a formulaic critical method to a body of texts that he claims are resistant, in their universal mystical significance, to any form of methodology. He wants to claim that these texts do not respect such petty distinctions as class difference or epistemological hierarchies, whilst at the same time rather hysterically insisting that you have to be a special person, with special sensitivity and knowledge, to understand them correctly. Time and time again in Esslin's work we find Beckett heralded as a supreme artist whose greatness resides in his rejection of ideology, while at the same time he is charged with the onerous burden of supporting the sometimes objectionable ideological assumptions that Esslin refuses explicitly to acknowledge that he is making.

Whilst Esslin makes these contradictions particularly blatant in this somewhat ungainly introduction, however, they are not simply the result of incompetent or disingenuous criticism. Rather, they arose because there was not a mainstream critical discourse available that was able to reconcile 'legitimate art' with a textual practice that does not say something affirmative about the human condition. This problem was not confined to Beckett studies. When D. H. Lawrence, whose work displayed a 'raging contempt for liberal and democratic values', was absorbed into the New Critical canon, he was 'effectively reconstructed as a liberal humanist, and slotted into place as the triumphant culmination of the "great tradition" of English fiction'.[22] Similarly, Brecht's work was available for admission into the league of Western literature only when 'Brecht the artist' was distinguished from 'Brecht the politician'.[23] The cultural agenda that saturated the critical approach adopted by the academy was such that it was extremely difficult for any form of expression that resisted or subverted liberal humanist ideology to escape the conversion to humanist affirmation. The manoeuvre by which Esslin recasts Beckett's negativity as affirmative is reproduced repeatedly by scholars who have produced some of the best Beckett criticism, because the critical field within which they worked demanded that they should. The three categories of legitimate critical analysis of Beckett's work that Esslin sketched out in his introduction survived intact for so long in Beckett studies because they were based on the limits of a humanist approach that was hegemonic in the English-speaking academy.

Beckett's humanist critics produced a great deal of extremely valuable scholarship, without which it would be impossible to read Beckett as accurately as we do today, but this scholarship was largely confined to Esslin's categories. There is a wealth of material that tracks down Beckett's references to the literary canon; that traces the development of Beckett's critical and literary oeuvre, and lends it coherence; that analyses the linguistic texture of the oeuvre and divines its structural principles; that points out rhythms and echoes and repetitions; and that provides the kind of intuitive response to the oeuvre as 'great art' that Esslin identifies as the final, most important function of the critic. But across the range of this criticism, a gap opens up between Beckett's art and its interpretation, that no amount of scholarly detail and intuitive response can close. This gap is caused by the insistence that Beckett's art, in its very organic structure, provides a kind of unmediated and absolute affirmation of a universal truth that is not reducible to its component parts. As much as this kind of criticism can provide a guide for the reader, and exercise its erudition to elaborate and clarify the texts' tangled contexts, it is forced to fall back repeatedly on the assertion that it is impossible to say what the works mean. Beckett's art remains finally impervious to criticism because it is the unspeakable mystery of the texts, their strange insusceptibility to the weaknesses and impurities of other forms of signifying practice, that allows them to adopt this unique position on the boundary between meaninglessness and supreme meaning. It is in stressing Beckett's mystical ability to give concrete expression to a natural human truth that critics were able to claim that they supported the tenets of a naturalised humanist ideology.

2. Kenner, Cohn and the Liberal Humanist Beckett

Two of the critics who were foremost in elaborating the humanist reading of *Waiting for Godot* and *Endgame*, which flourished through the sixties and seventies and has remained influential to the present day, were Hugh Kenner and Ruby Cohn. Their work on the plays, particularly in Kenner's *Samuel Beckett: A Critical Study* (1961, 1968) and *A Reader's Guide to Samuel Beckett* (1973), and in Cohn's *Samuel Beckett: The Comic Gamut* (1962), *Just Play: Beckett's Theatre* (1980), and *Casebook on Waiting for Godot* (1987), developed an approach to *Godot* and *Endgame* that became the standard for understanding Beckett's drama.

Hugh Kenner's work on Beckett is characterised above all by its deft elegance, its ability to demonstrate the plays' workings without appearing unduly to intrude upon them or to defile them. He produces a gentle, self-effacing criticism that works almost as an accompaniment to the drama. In a familiar reluctance to suggest that the critic has anything particularly valuable to say about *Godot* and *Endgame*, Kenner stresses that it is 'simpler', while watching the plays, to 'dismiss interpretations'.[24] The critic is there, as Esslin suggested, to demonstrate the oeuvre in its full range and to 'emphasise its coherence and unity';[25] to introduce to the reader Beckett's own thoughts and writings upon his and others' art; and to help the reader by fleshing out allusions and by drawing attention to discrepancies between French and English versions of the plays that may be illuminating. But, in what is again a familiar move, these critical props must be 'treated with caution',[26] as the analogies and similarities that the critic draws between one Beckett text and another, between one moment and another, are 'not meant for rigorous application'.[27] The striking thing about Beckett's work is its self-sufficiency, its ability to create within its own static world all the conditions of its existence. It is this formal repletion, this creation of an artistic shape on stage that brings forth its meaning unmediated, that has to be preserved. The meaning of *Godot* resides in its structural felicity: the 'molecule of the play, its unit of effect, is symmetry, a symmetrical structure'.[28] Beckett's dramatic language is 'shaped into phrases, orchestrated, cunningly repeated'.[29] The critic, by using an array of elucidatory procedures, can help the reader to see this structure clearly, but he or she must by no means mistake the crude detail for the artistic event proper, which is unapproachable. *Godot* and *Endgame* contain many references and details, but these external elements turn like a vortex around the purely Beckettian centre of the drama – the 'irreducible element which no style, no clarity, no ceremony will dissolve or explain: the thing which makes itself felt, in Beckett's cosmos, as a prevailing and penetrating mystery, seeping through the walls of stage or book'.[30]

Whilst Kenner is anxious to protect this purely artistic central element from the intrusion of explication, however, he does bring to the plays a critical agenda that is subtly present in all of his writings on the oeuvre. Beckett emerges in Kenner's work as a reluctant post-Cartesian, mourning the wholeness of a pre-enlightenment simplicity before Descartes separated mind from body, when it was easier to love and be loved. The trajectory of Beckett's work, from *Murphy* to *Play*, is a steady movement away from the possibility of harmony between mind, body and world, towards an increasingly desperate isolation of the thinking mind from any of the structures that could have redeemed it from its isolation. For Kenner, Beckett's work:

■ takes stock of the enlightenment, and reduces to essential terms the three centuries during which those ambitious processes of which Descartes is the symbol and progenitor (or was he too, like The Unnamable, spoken through by a committee of the *Zeitgeist*?) accomplished the dehumanisation of man. It is plain why Godot does not come. The Cartesian Centaur[31] was a seventeenth century dream, the fatal dream of being, knowing and moving, like a god. In the twentieth century he and his machine are gone, and only a desperate élan remains.[32] □

The shape that is formed on Beckett's stage, in all its perfect symmetry, rhythm and coherence, is the last bastion of coherence, erected against the chaos of the faithless, godless, post-Enlightenment universe like a shelter. Godot will not come from without to redeem those who wait for him; it is the beauty of the shapes that Gogo and Didi make whilst they wait that offers the only possibility of salvation in the name of art.

In the following extracts, Kenner's reading of *Godot* and *Endgame* as lamentations for a pre-Cartesian wholeness can be discerned beneath the elegant surface of his prose. In this first extract, Kenner draws attention to the self-reflexivity of *Godot*. Whilst emphasising the artificial elements of the play, which insistently reflects upon itself as a play, however, Kenner suggests (quoting Robbe-Grillet, who will be familiar from the last chapter) that this self-reflexivity turns around the ineluctable presence of the actors on the stage.

■ The drama is a ritual enacted in an enclosed space into which fifty or more people are staring. They are all more or less patiently waiting for something: the Reversal, the Discovery, the *Deus ex Machina*, or even the final curtain. Settled numbly for the evening, they accept whatever interim diversions the stage can provide: tramps in bowler hats for instance.

The space into which they are staring is characterised in some way: for instance, *A country road. A tree. Evening.* 'Evening' means that the illumination on stage is not much brighter than in the auditorium. 'A country road' means that there is no set to look at. As for the tree, an apologetic thing tentatively identified as a leafless weeping willow, it serves chiefly to denote the spot, like the intersection (co-ordinates 0,0) of the Cartesian axes. 'You're sure it was here?' 'What?' 'That we were to wait.' 'He said by the tree.' If it accretes meaning of an anomalous sort in the course of the evening, reminding us, when the two tramps stand beneath it with a rope, of ampler beams which once suspended the saviour and two thieves, or again of the fatal tree in Eden (and the garden has, sure enough, vanished), or even of the flowering staff in *Tannhäuser*,[33] it does this not by being explicated but simply by its insistent continual presence, during which, as adjacent events refract the bleak light, we begin to entertain mild hallucinations about it. Only in a theatre can we be made to look at a mock tree for that length of time. Drama is distinguished from all other forms of art by its control over the *time* spent by the spectator in the presence of its significant elements.

These events, these elements, assert only their own nagging existence. 'The theatrical character,' remarked Alain Robbe-Grillet in this connection, '*is on stage*, this is his primary quality – he is there.' Hence, 'the essential function of the theatrical performance: to show what this fact of *being there* consists of.' Or as Beckett was later to write of a later play, 'Hamm as stated, and Clov as stated, together as stated, *nec tecum nec sine te*, in such a place, and in such a world, that's all I can manage, more than I could.'[34]

In *Waiting for Godot*, the place with its tree is stated, together with a single actor engaged in a mime with his boot. His inability to get it off is the referent of his first words, 'Nothing to be done,' a sentence generally reserved for more portentous matters. To him enter the second actor, as in the medial phase of Greek theatre, and their talk commences. What they talk about first is the fact that they are both there, the one fact that is demonstrably true not only in the art's agreed world but before our eyes. It is even the one certainty that survives an evening's waiting:

BOY: What am I to tell Mr Godot, sir?

VLADIMIR: Tell him . . . [*He hesitates*] . . . tell him you saw us. [*Pause.*] You did see us, didn't you?

BOY: Yes, sir. (*CDW* 50)

The realities stated with such insistence are disquietingly provisional. The tree is plainly a sham, and the two tramps are simply filling up time until a proper dramatic entertainment can get under way. They are helping the management fulfil, in a minimal way, its contract with the ticket holders. The resources of vaudeville are at their somewhat incompetent disposal: bashed hats, dropped pants, tight boots, the kick, the pratfall, the improper story. It will suffice if they can stave off a mass exodus until Godot comes, in whom we are all so interested. Beckett, it is clear, has cunningly doubled his play with that absence of a play which every confirmed theatregoer has at some time or other experienced, the advertised cynosure having missed a train or overslept or indulged in temperament. The tramps have plainly not learned parts; they repeatedly discuss what to do next ('What about hanging ourselves?') and observe from time to time that tedium is accumulating:

Charming evening we're having.

Unforgettable.

And it's not over.

Apparently not.

It's only beginning.

It's awful.

Worse than the pantomime.

The circus.

The music-hall.

The circus. (*CDW* 34)

Thus a non-play comments on itself. Or the audience of the non-play is reminded that others the previous night sat in these seats witnessing the identical futility ('What did we do yesterday?' 'In my opinion we were here.') and that others in turn will sit there watching on successive nights for an indeterminate period.

We'll come back tomorrow (says tramp No. 1).

And then the day after tomorrow.

Possibly.

And so on. (*CDW* 16)

And so on, until the run of the production ends. It will end, presumably, when there are no longer spectators interested, though it is difficult to explain on Shakespearean premises what it is that they can be expected to be interested in. Or perhaps not so difficult. What brings the groundlings to *Macbeth*? Why, they are waiting for the severed head. And to *Hamlet*? They are waiting for Garrick (or Irving, or Olivier). And here?

Let's go.

We can't.

Why not?

We're waiting for Godot.

[*Despairingly.*] Ah! (*CDW* 46–47)

The French text manages an inclusiveness denied to English idiom: 'Pourquoi?' 'On attend Godot.' Not '*nous*' but '*on*': Didi, Gogo, and audience alike.

If the seeming improvisation of the tramps denies theatricality, it affirms at the same time quintessential theatre, postulating nothing but what we can see on stage: a place, and men present in it, doing what they are doing. And into this quintessential theatre there irrupts before long the strident unreality we crave:

> POZZO: [*Terrifying voice.*]. I am Pozzo! [*Silence.*] Pozzo! [*Silence.*] Does that name mean nothing to you? [*Silence.*] I say does that name mean nothing to you? (*CDW* 23)

This is at least the veritable stuff, that for which we paid our admissions: an actor, patently, with gestures and grimaces, who has furthermore memorised and rehearsed his part and knows how they talk in plays. He make his entrance like Tamburlaine driving the pampered jades of Asia[35] (represented, in this low-budget production, by one extra); he takes pains with his elocution, assisted by a vaporiser, like an effete *Heldentenor*; he recites a well-conned set speech on the twilight, with 'vibrant', 'lyrical' and 'prosaic' phases, and contrapuntal assistance from well-schooled hands (two hands lapsing; two hands flung amply apart; one hand raised in admonition; fingers snapped at the climax, to reinforce the word 'pop!'). This is theatre; the evening is saved. Surely he is Godot?

But he says not; and we are disconcerted to find him fishing for applause, and from the tramps. They are his audience as we are his and theirs. The play, in familiar Beckett fashion, has gotten inside the play. So too when Lucky (who has also memorised his part) recites his set speech on the descent of human certainty into 'the great cold the great dark' ('for reasons unknown but time will tell'), it is for the amusement of his master, and of the tramps, and incidentally of ourselves. The same is true of his symbolic dance, a thing of constrained gestures, as in Noh drama.[36] So the perspective continues to diminish, box within box. In this theatre, the tramps. Within their futile world, the finished theatricality of Pozzo. At Pozzo's command, Lucky's speech; within this speech, scholarship, man *in posse* and *in esse*, all that which, officially endorsed, we think we know, notably the labours of the Acacacacademy of Anthropopopometry; within these in turn, caca (Fr. Colloq., excrement) and popo, a chamberpot: a diminution, a delirium.

Such metaphysics as the Beckett theatre will permit is entailed in this hierarchy of watchers and watched. Throughout, and notably during Lucky's holocaust of phrases, we clutch at straws of meaning, persuaded at bottom only of one thing, that all four men exist, embodied, gravid, speaking; moving before us, their shadows cast on the wall, their voices echoing in the auditorium, their feet heavy on the boards.

The second act opens with the song about the dog's epitaph, another infinitely converging series of acts and agents. *The Unnamable* also meditates on this jingle, and discovers its principle: 'third verse, as the first, fourth, as the second, fifth, as the third, give us time, give us time and we'll be a multitude'; for it generates an infinite series of unreal beings, epitaph within epitaph within epitaph. Correspondingly, near the end of the act Didi muses over the sleeping Gogo:

> At me too someone is looking, of me too someone is saying, he is sleeping, he knows nothing, let him sleep on. (*CDW* 84–85)

So we watch Didi move through his part, as he watches Gogo, and meanwhile Lucky's God with the white beard, outside time, without extension, is loving us dearly 'with some exceptions for reasons unknown but time will tell.'

It remains to recall that the Beckett universe, wherever we encounter it, consists of a shambles of phenomena within which certain symmetries and recurrences are observable, like the physical world as observed by early man. So this stage world has its structure and landmarks. We observe, for example, that bowler hats are apparently *de rigeur*, and that they are removed for thinking but replaced for speaking. We observe that moonrise and sunset occur in conjunction two nights running, for this is an ideal cosmology, unless we are to suppose the two acts to be separated by an interval of twenty-nine days. The tree by the same token has budded overnight, like an early miracle. All this is arbitrary because theatrical. Our play draws on Greek theatre with its limited number of actors, its crises always offstage, and its absent divinity; on Noh theatre with its symbolic tree, its nuances and its ritual dance; on *commedia dell'arte*, improvised before our eyes; on twentieth century experimental theatre; and on vaudeville with its cast-off clowns, stumblings, shamblings, delicate bawdry, acrobatics and astringent pointlessness. The final action partakes of the circus repertoire

> [*They each take an end of the cord and pull. It breaks. They almost fall.*]
> (*CDW* 87)

synchronised with a burlesque house misadventure with trousers

> *... which, much too big for him, fall about his ankles.* (*CDW* 87)

The student of *Finnegans Wake* will identify this mishap as the play's epiphany,[37] the least learned will note that something hitherto invisible has at last been disclosed, and everyone can agree that the final gesture is to a static propriety:

VLADIMIR: Pull ON your trousers.

ESTRAGON: [*Realizing his trousers are down.*] True. [*He pulls up his trousers. Silence.*]

VLADIMIR: Well? Shall we go?

ESTRAGON: Yes, let's go.

[*They do not move.*] (*CDW* 88)[38] □

Kenner suggests that the naked presence of the actors on *Godot*'s stage should be understood in the context of Beckett's oeuvre, and in particular in relation to his prose work, which *Godot* interrupted at its height, during the intensely creative period in the late forties to early fifties that produced *Molloy, Malone Dies*, and *The Unnamable*. He points out that *Godot* displays many affinities with a novel written in French just before *Godot*, entitled *Mercier et Camier*. This novel also treats of an aimless couple who are laconically waiting for a revelation that never appears, and the similarities are such that some stretches of dialogue are transplanted straight from the novel into the play. The major difference between the two works, however, is the characters' and objects' physical presence on the stage. Following Robbe-Grillet, and anticipating John Peter's influential work *Vladimir's Carrot*,[39] Kenner suggests that the stage is the place to which Beckett turned in order to allow him to represent more effectively a world of objects that have become entirely divorced from their social, collective meaning. By placing Vladimir, Estragon, and their sorry collection of paraphernalia on the stage, he is able to show them stripped of their history, stranded in the eerily beautiful space of an interminable wait. Pointing to a structural distinction between journeying and waiting that runs throughout the oeuvre, Kenner suggests that those who journey (Pozzo and Lucky, Mercier and Camier) are still caught up in the big world of objects and objectives, whereas those who wait (Vladimir and Estragon) have gained admission to a pocket of calm if bleak retirement from the world, which is the best that can be hoped for in Beckett's universe.

■ [W]hy, in transforming the ambiguously aimless journey of the novel into the ambiguously empty waiting of the play, [does] Beckett empt[y] the protagonists' world of objects[?] Objects, in his universe, go with a journey: bicycles, for instance, crutches, a hat secured by a string; in *Comment c'est*, a jute sack, tins of fish, a can opener, used in the journeying, absent in the waiting.[40] The objects Malone inventories in his immobility – a needle stuck in two corks, the bowl of a pipe, equipped with a little tin lid, a scrap of newspaper, a photograph of an ass wearing a boater – these constitute no exception, for Malone's immobility is not a waiting but by definition a terminal phase in a journey, toward nothingness.[41] Thus Malone's objects have histories. Since they joined his entourage they have made a journey through time in his company, undergoing modifications not always at random (he knows under what circumstances the brim came off his hat; he removed it himself, so that he might keep the hat on while he slept). It is even possible to speculate concerning their pre-Malone history; the pipe bowl which he found in the grass must have been thrown away by a man who said, when the stem broke, 'Bah, I'll buy myself another.' ('But all that is mere supposition.') Thus the static object, like Malone's own immobility, is a momentary cross-section of a duration, the present index of a movement in time which may parallel or continue movement in space, as the Beckett journey is apt to become identical with the process of being alive.

But the scanty tale of objects that concern the bums in *Waiting for Godot* contains no item owning a past, a future, or a duration with which our vital sentiments may feel empathy. Like the elements at the beginning of a mathematical problem, the bowler hats, the boots, the pants, the rope, the tree are simply *given*, and the operations that are performed on them do not modify them (as, at the end of the most prolonged computation, x is still x).

There are, it is true, in the play a few things that undergo changes of a different order. These are irreversible changes, the sort prescribed by the Second Law of Thermodynamics, the law with whose gross effects Lucky's great speech is concerned. Reversible events are trivial, like rearrangements of the furniture, or of the terms in an equation. By this criterion the status of most of the events in the play is slight, or at most ambiguous. Irreversible things are the ones that *happen*, that declare something more than a system of tautologies, or an economy of displacements. It is the sum of those happenings, however small, whose terms and agents can never again be put back the way they were – the carrot uneaten, the leaves unbudded – that advances by today's quantum the system's articulation, or perhaps its entropy. Of these *Waiting for Godot* contains a real but insignificant number.

Though this is a play in which, as Vivian Mercier wittily observed, 'nothing happens, twice,' things at the fall of the curtain are not precisely the same as they were. Before our eyes a carrot has come into visibility out of Didi's pocket and vanished again into Gogo's mouth; its subsequent decomposition may be conjectured. Before our eyes, also, the rope has been broken, into two pieces whose combined length will equal the original length, but which can never again be combined. These are both irreversible actions; the world is now poorer by one carrot and one rope. In the interval between the acts there have been three organic changes: the tree has acquired leaves, and Pozzo his sight and Lucky his speech. (We have only Pozzo's word for the latter two.) It is not clear whether these count as irreversible events, though certainly the leaves cannot be expected to go back into the tree. In the same interval Gogo's boots have been taken, and a pair of a different colour substituted. Didi ventures an explanation of this, inaccurate because based on inadequate data. With the benefit of our later knowledge that the new boots are larger than the old, we can readily amend his hypothesis. The play's other substitution occurs before our eyes: as a result of a series of permutations too long to reconstruct, Didi midway through Act II has Lucky's hat on his head, and Didi's hat has replaced Lucky's on the ground. And one further item comes from outside the visible economy of the play, viz. Lucky's second hat, the hat he is wearing on his reappearance in Act II, after having left his first hat on the ground before his exit in Act I. These substitutions are presumably reversible, though it is not clear how Lucky's second hat would have to be disposed of.

Nor can the tedium of the two evenings be said to redeem its own nullity by enhancing the experience of Didi and Gogo, as one may learn by watching bees move about. They exist in an eternity of stagnation, Gogo's memory defective ('Either I forget immediately or I never forget'), Didi's an eventless assimilation of the same to the remembered same. They are, unlike Murphy, Mercier, Molloy, Moran and Malone, utterly incapable of the kind of experience you can later tell a story about, and utterly detached from the least affection for objects. They have only their bodies and their clothes: hence the mathematical speed with which their situation can be exhibited. Not having chosen suicide ('sans le courage de finir ni la force de continuer'),[42] they have grown committed, in a kind of fierce negative sanctity, to waiting for the figure with sheep, goats, many affairs and a white beard (we need not credit any of these details). Their lives correspond exactly to St. John of the Cross's famous minimal prescription, divested of the love of created things, and the divine union is awaited beside the tree, one evening, another evening, every evening, since two terms, in the absence of indications to the contrary, imply a series, perhaps infinite. They are blessed, says Didi, in knowing the answer to the question, what it is they are doing there. They are waiting for Godot to come, or for night to fall. They have kept their appointment, that too they can claim, and it is not by accident that he refers to the saints. 'We are not saints, but we have kept our appointment. How many people can boast as much?'

Lest we be tempted to take this rhetorical question for the ridge pole of the play, Gogo replies, 'Billions,' and Didi concedes that he may be right. The question, climaxing the longest speech either of them is to deliver, retains its torque.

Having reduced the whole of two men's lives to a waiting which epitomises a moral issue, Beckett causes this situation to be intersected by his other key situation, a journey. Pozzo and Lucky are a little like Moran and his son, seen from the outside instead of through Moran's narrative.[43] They are loaded, as if to emphasise the distinction between waiters and travellers, with every kind of portable property, notably a heavy bag (of sand), a folding stool, a picnic basket (with chicken and wine), a greatcoat, a whip, a watch (genuine half-hunter, with deadbeat escapement,[44] gift of Pozzo's grandfather), a handkerchief, a pocket vaporiser, a rope, glasses, matches, and a briar pipe (by Kapp and Peterson). The watch is often consulted; there is a schedule to observe. If these two, master and servant, steadily on the move, epitomise the busy world from which Didi and Gogo have seceded, there is no record of the act of secession. Rather, the contrasting pairs appear to epitomise not ways of life so much as ways of being. Amid the great void which they contrive to fill up with exercises and conversation, Didi and Gogo circulate about one another with numb but delectable affection, Didi perpetually responsible for Gogo, enraged when Gogo is kicked, and offering to carry him (*Pause*) 'if necessary.' Gogo for his part rejects a proposed system for hanging themselves on the sole ground, he says, that if it fails his friend will be left alone. Both strike noble if temporary rages on behalf of Lucky, and even, when Lucky is put in the wrong, on behalf of Pozzo; and with infinite delay and ratiocination they do eventually help the blind Pozzo of the second act to his feet. Pozzo, on the other hand, absurd, theatrical, glib, patronising ('so that I ask myself is there anything I can do in my turn for these honest fellows who are having such a dull, dull time') is capable of nothing but stage turns: the judicious stranger, the picnicker at his ease, the eulogist of twilight, the man whose heart goes pit-a-pat – very much, in each of his roles, someone we have seen before. This kaleidoscope of impostors learned all that he knows from Lucky, and we are given at some length a specimen of Lucky's capacity for imparting the things he has in his head. They live with their heads, these two, moving hither and thither, Pozzo talking of buying and selling, and imposing with his campstool and ceremonial a prissy elegance on their halts; Lucky treacherous, miserable, obeying with a precision that does not quite approximate to ritual, and dancing or thinking on command. There is no love here, and the play's waiting seems incontestably preferable to its journeying.[45] □

It is with Beckett's turn to *Endgame*, Kenner claims, that the stage as a perfectly symmetrical space of waiting, whose finely balanced contours offer the only legitimate form of defence against the void, is given its definitive shape. In the following extract, Kenner draws an extended parallel between the world of *Endgame* and the world of chess (whilst insisting on the familiar caveat that such an interpretative analogy should not be taken too seriously). The force of this parallel lies in its emphasis on the self-reliance of *Endgame* as a complete, enclosed system. In a critical approach that treats Beckett's texts as mathematical equations whose symmetry is calculated with infinite precision,[46] Kenner suggests that the structure of *Endgame*, like that of chess, is based on a number of inflexible but arbitrary rules that have relevance only to the game in hand. None of the character's moves may make sense with relation to the big world that the audience share, but in terms of the play's internal economy, each move is finely tuned to have its desired effect. The play may not 'mean' anything – its objects and its characters are divorced from any social or cultural context that would give their actions objective meaning – but in the 'self-sufficient world' of *Endgame*, which contains its own 'order of reality',[47] these abstract rules impose a rigorous and self-consistent law that provides the play with its meaning and with its epiphany. It is this structural control that makes *Endgame* the great artwork that it is, as 'nothing satisfies the mind like balance'.[48]

■ For the stage is a place to wait. The place itself waits, when no one is in it. When the curtain rises on *Endgame*, sheets drape all visible objects as in a furniture warehouse. Clov's first act is to uncurtain the two high windows and inspect the universe; his second is to remove the sheets and fold them carefully over his arm, disclosing two ash cans and a figure in an armchair. This is so plainly a metaphor for waking up that we fancy the stage, with its high peepholes, to be the inside of an immense skull. It is also a ritual for starting the play; Yeats arranged such a ritual for *At the Hawk's Well*, and specified a black cloth and a symbolic song. It is finally a removal from symbolic storage of the objects that will be needed during the course of the performance. When the theatre is empty it is sensible to keep them covered against dust. So we are reminded at the outset that what we are to witness is a dusty dramatic exhibition, repeated and repeatable. The necessary objects include three additional players (two of them in ash cans). Since none of them will move from his station we can think of them after the performance as being kept permanently on stage, and covered with their dust cloths again until tomorrow night.

The rising of the curtain disclosed these sheeted forms; the removal of the sheets disclosed the protagonist and his ash cans; the next stage is for the protagonist to uncover his own face, which he does with a yawn, culminating this three-phase strip tease with the revelation of a very red face and black glasses. His name, we gather from the program, is Hamm, a name for an actor. He is also Hamlet, bounded in a nutshell, fancying himself king of infinite space, but troubled by bad dreams; he is also 'a toppled Prospero,'[49] remarking part way through the play, with judicious pedantry, 'our revels now are ended';[50] he is also the hammer to which Clov, Nagg and Nell (Fr. *clou*, Ger. *nagel*, Eng. *nail*) stand in passive relationship; by extension, a chess player ('Me – [*he yawns*] – to play'); but also, (since Clov must wheel him about) himself a chessman, probably the imperilled King.

Nag and Nell in their dustbins appear to be pawns; Clov, with his arbitrarily restricted movements ('I can't sit.') and his equestrian background ('And your rounds? Always on foot?' 'Sometimes on horse.') resembles the Knight, and his perfectly cubical kitchen ('ten feet by ten feet by ten feet, nice dimensions, nice proportions') resembles a square on the chessboard translated into three dimensions. He moves back and forth, into it and out of it, coming to the succour of Hamm and then retreating. At the endgame's end the pawns are forever immobile and Clov is poised for a last departure from the board, the status quo forever menaced by an expected piece glimpsed through the window, and King Hamm abandoned in check:

> Old endgame lost of old, play and lose and have done with losing.
> . . . Since that's the way we're playing it . . . let's play it that way . . .
> and speak no more about it . . . speak no more. (*CDW* 133)

Even if we had not the information that the author of this work has been known to spend hours playing chess with himself (a game at which you always lose),[51] we should have been alerted to his long-standing interest in its strategy by the eleventh chapter of *Murphy*, where Murphy's first move against Mr. Endow, the standard P-K$_4$, is described as 'the primary cause of all [his] subsequent difficulties.'[52] (The same might be said of getting born, an equally conventional opening.) Chess has several peculiarities which lend themselves to the metaphors of this jagged play. It is a game of leverage, in which the significance of a move might be out of all proportion to the local disturbance of its effects ('A flea! This is awful! What a day!'). It is a game of silences, in which new situations are appraised: hence Beckett's most frequent stage direction, '*Pause.*' It is a game of steady attrition; by the time we reach the endgame the board is nearly bare, as bare as Hamm's world where there are no more bicycle wheels, sugarplums, pain killers, or coffins, let alone people. And it is a game which by the successive removal of screening pieces constantly extends the range of lethal forces, until at the endgame peril from a key piece sweeps down whole ranks and files. The king is hobbled by the rule which allows him to move in one direction but only one square at a time; Hamm's circuit of the stage and return to centre perhaps exhibits him patrolling the inner boundaries of the little nine-square territory he commands.

To venture further will evidently expose him to check. ('Outside of here it's death.') His knight shuttles to and fro, his pawns are pinned. No threat is anticipated from the auditorium, which is presumably off the board; and a periodic reconnaissance downfield through the windows discloses nothing but desolation until near the end. But on his last inspection of the field Clov is dismayed. Here the English text is inexplicably sketchy; in the French one we have,

> CLOV: Aïeaïeaïe!
>
> HAMM: C'est une feuille? Une fleur? Une toma – [*il bâille*] – te?
>
> CLOV: [*regardent*] Je t'en foutrai des tomates! Quelqu'un! C'est quelqu'un!
>
> HAMM: Eh bien, va l'exterminer. [*Clov descend de l'escabeau.*] Quelqu'un! [*Vibrant.*] Fais ton devoir![53]
>
> It's a leaf? A flower? A toma [*he yawns*] to.
>
> To hell with your tomatoes! It is someone! It's someone!
>
> Ah well, go and kill him. [*Clov descends the stepladder.*] Someone! [*vibrantly*] Do your duty.

In the subsequent interrogatory we learn the distance of this threat (fifteen metres or so), its state of rest or motion (motionless), its sex (presumably a boy), its occupation (sitting on the ground as if leaning on something). Hamm, perhaps thinking of Jesus, murmurs 'La pierre levée,' then on reflection changes the image to constitute himself proprietor of the Promised Land: 'Il regarde la maison avec les yeux de Moïse mourant.' It is doing, however, nothing of the kind; it is gazing at its navel. There is no use, Hamm decides, in running out to exterminate it: 'If he exists he'll die there or he'll come here. And if he doesn't . . .' And a few seconds later he has conceded the game:

> It's the end, Clov, we've come to the end. I don't need you any more. (*CDW* 131)

He sacrifices his last mobile piece, discards his staff and whistle, summons for the last time a resourceless Knight and an unanswering Pawn, and covers his face once more with the handkerchief: somehow in check.

Not that all this is likely to be yielded up with clarity by any conceivable performance. It represents, however, a structure which, however we glimpse it, serves to refrigerate the incidental passions of a play about, it would seem, the end of humanity. It is not for nothing that the place within which the frigid events are transacted is more than once called 'the shelter,' outside of which it is death; nor that the human race is at present reduced to two disabled parents, a macabre blind son, and an acathisiac servant. Around this shelter the universe crumbles like an immense dry biscuit: no more rugs, no more tide, no more coffins. We hear of particular deaths:

> CLOV: [*Harshly*.] When old Mother Pegg asked you for oil for her lamp and you told her to get out to hell, you knew what was happening then, no? [*Pause.*] You know what she died of, Mother Pegg? Of darkness.
>
> HAMM: [*Feebly*.] I hadn't any.
>
> CLOV: [*As before.*] Yes, you had. (*CDW* 129)

We observe particular brutalities: Hamm, of his parents: 'Have you bottled her?' 'Yes.' 'Are they both bottled?' 'Yes.' 'Screw down the lids.' What has shrunken the formerly ample world is perhaps Hamm's withdrawal of love; the great skull-like setting suggests a solipsist's universe. 'I was never there,' he says. 'Absent, always. It all happened without me. I don't know what's happened.' He has been in 'the shelter'; he has also been closed within himself. It is barely possible that the desolation is not universal:

> HAMM: Did you ever think of one thing?
>
> CLOV: Never.
>
> HAMM: That here we're down in a hole. [*Pause.*] But beyond the hills? Eh? Perhaps it's still green. Eh? [*Pause.*] Flora! Pomona! [*Ecstatically.*] Ceres! [*Pause.*] Perhaps you won't need to go very far.
>
> CLOV: I can't go very far. [*Pause.*] I'll leave you. (*CDW* 111)

As Hamm is both chess man and chess player, so it is conceivable that destruction is not screened off by the shelter but radiates from it for a certain distance. Zero, zero, words we hear so often in the dialogue, these are the Cartesian co-ordinates of the origin.[54] □

With an elegant balance that mirrors that of the plays themselves, Kenner's reading of *Waiting for Godot* and *Endgame* finally comes full circle to re-emphasise the importance of self-reflexivity in *Endgame*. The self-enclosure of the play has to be understood, for Kenner, within the terms of its own self-conscious theatricality. It never seeks to represent anything outside itself ('The set does not *represent*, the set is itself'[55]), or to disguise the fact of its own artificiality – rather the play's structure is dedicated to exposing the scriptedness of all the characters' actions. Again, though, Kenner is very careful to stress that this self-reflexivity does not undermine the effect of the play's unmediated and absolutely self-contained presence. Although the play draws attention to the fact that Hamm the actor and Hamm the stage character are not identical, it does not suggest that the play therefore fails to dramatise a universal truth in its entirety. Self-reflexivity does not signal for Kenner, as it does for some other theorists,[56] an uncertainty about the possibility of a perfect match between the text and the world, or an anxiety about the power of any form of representation to represent fully. If *Endgame* may lead us to think that 'all the world's a stage', in which our actions are always determined by an invisible script-writer, and in which we are never fully present to ourselves, then it also suggests that 'this stage is all the world'.[57] The world of *Endgame* becomes, by virtue of the universal power of the performance, a world entire, and rather than doubt about the relation between being and presence, the play presents us with an organic certainty that the characters on stage exist 'embodied, gravid, speaking; moving before us, their shadows cast on the wall, their voices echoing in the auditorium, their feet heavy on the boards'.[58]

■ Bounded in a nutshell yet king of infinite space, Hamm articulates the racking ambiguity of the play by means of his dominance over its most persuasive metaphor, the play itself. If he is Prospero with staff and revels, if he is Richard III bloodsmeared and crying 'My kingdom for a nightman!', if he is also perhaps Richard II, within whose hollow crown

> Keeps death his court, and there the Antic sits,
> Scoffing his state and grinning at his pomp,
> Allowing him a breath, a little scene
> To monarchize, be feared, and kill with looks – [59]

these roles do not exhaust his repertoire. He is (his name tells us) the generic Actor, a creature all circumference and no centre. As master of his revels, he himself attends to the last unveiling of the opening ritual:

[*Pause.* HAMM *stirs. He yawns under the handkerchief. He removes the handkerchief from his face. Very red face. Black glasses.*]

HAMM: Me – [*he yawns*] – to play. [*He holds the handkerchief spread out before him.*] Old stancher! [. . . *He clears his throat, joins the tips of his fingers.*] Can there be misery – [*he yawns*] – loftier than mine? (*CDW* 93)

The play ended, he ceremoniously unfolds the handkerchief once more (five separate stage directions governing his tempo) and covers his face as it was in the beginning. 'Old stancher! [*Pause.*] You . . . remain.' What remains, in the final brief tableau specified by the author, is the immobile figure with a bloodied Veronica's veil in place of a face: the actor having superintended his own Passion and translated himself into an ultimate abstraction of masked agony.

Between these termini he animates everything, ordering the coming and going of Clov and the capping and the uncapping of the cans. When Clov asks, 'What is there to keep me here?' he answers sharply, 'The dialogue.' A particularly futile bit of business with the spyglass and the steps elicits from him an aesthetic judgement, 'This is deadly.' When it is time for the introduction of the stuffed dog, he notes, 'We're getting on,' and a few minutes later, 'Do you not think this has gone on long enough?' These, like comparable details in *Godot*, are sardonic authorizations for a disquiet that is certainly stirring in the auditorium. No one understands better than Beckett, nor exploits more boldly, the kind of fatalistic attention an audience trained on films is accustomed to place at the dramatist's disposal. The cinema has taught us to suppose that a dramatic presentation moves inexorably as the reels unwind or the studio clock creeps, until it has consumed precisely its allotted time which nothing, no restlessness in the pit, no sirens, no mass exodus can hurry. 'Something is taking its course,' that suffices us. Hence the vast leisure in which the minimal business of *Godot* and *Endgame* is transacted; hence (transposing into dramatic terms the author's characteristic pedantry of means) the occasional lingering over points of technique, secure in the knowledge that the clock-bound patience of a twentieth-century audience will expect no inner urgency, nothing in fact but the actual time events consume, to determine the pace of the exhibition. Clov asks, 'Why this farce, day after day?' and it is sufficent for Hamm to reply, 'Routine. One never knows.' It is an answer of an actor in an age of film and long runs. In *Endgame* (which here differs radically from *Godot*) no one is supposed to be improvising; the script has been well committed to memory and well rehearsed. By this means doom is caused to penetrate the most intimate crevices of the play. 'I'm tired of going on,' says Clov late in the play, 'very tired,' and then, 'Let's stop playing!' (if there is one thing that modern acting is not it is playing). In the final moments theatrical technique, under Hamm's sponsorship, rises into savage prominence.

HAMM: . . . And me? Did anyone ever have pity on me?

CLOV: [*Lowering the telescope, turning towards* HAMM.] What? [*Pause.*] Is it me you're referring to?

HAMM: [*Angrily.*] An aside, ape! Did you never hear an aside before? [*Pause.*] I'm warming up for my last soliloquy. (*CDW* 130)

Ten seconds later he glosses 'More complications!' as a technical term: 'Not an underplot I trust.' It is Clov who has the last word in this vein:

HAMM: Clov! [CLOV *halts, without turning.*] Nothing. [CLOV *moves on.*] Clov! [CLOV *halts, without turning.*]

CLOV: This is what we call making an exit. (*CDW* 132)

By this reiterated stress on the actors as professional men, and so on the play as an occasion within which they operate, Beckett transforms Hamm's last soliloquy into a performance, his desolation into something prepared by the dramatic machine, his abandoning of gaff, dog, and whistle into a necessary discarding of props, and the terminal business with the handkerchief into, quite literally, a curtain speech. *Endgame* ends with an unexpected lightness, a death rather mimed than experienced; if it is 'Hamm as stated, and Clov as stated, together as stated,' the mode of statement has more salience than a paraphrase of the play's situation would lead one to expect.

The professionalism also saves the play from an essentially serious sentimental commitment to *simpliste* 'destiny.' Much of its gloomy power it derives from contact with such notions as T. H. Huxley's view of man as an irrelevance whom day by day an indifferent universe engages in chess. We do not belong here, runs a strain of western thought which became especially articulate in France after the war; we belong nowhere; we are all surds, ab-surd. There is nothing on which to ground our right to exist, and we need not be especially surprised one day to find ourselves nearly extinct. (On such a despair Cartesian logic converges, as surely as the arithmetic of Pythagoras wedged itself fast in the irrationality of $\sqrt{2}$.) Whatever we do, then, since it can obtain no grip on our radically pointless situation, is *behaviour* pure and simple; it is play acting, and may yield us the satisfaction, if satisfaction there be, of playing well, of uttering our *cris de coeur* with style and some sense of timing. We do not trouble deaf heaven, for there is only the sky. ('Rien,' reports Clov, gazing through his telescope; and again, 'Zéro.') We stir and thrill, at best, ourselves. From such a climate, miscalled existentialist, Beckett wrings every available *frisson* without quite delivering the play into its keeping; for its credibility is not a principle the play postulates but an idea the play contains, an idea of which it works out the moral and spiritual consequences. The despair in which he traffics is a conviction, not a philosophy. He will even set it spinning like a catharine wheel about a wild point of logic, as when he has Hamm require that God be prayed to in silence ('Where are your manners?') and then berate him ('The bastard!') for not existing.⁶⁰

The play contains whatever ideas we discern inside it; no ideas contain the play. The play contains, moreover, two narrative intervals, performances within the performance. The first, Nagg's story about the trousers, is explicitly a recitation; Nell has heard it often, and so, probably, has the audience; it is a vaudeville standby. Nagg's performance, like a production of *King Lear*, whose story we know, must therefore be judged solely as a performance. Its quality, alas, discourages even him ('I tell this story worse and worse'), and Nell too is not amused, being occupied with thoughts of her own, about the sand at the bottom of Lake Como. The other is Hamm's huffe-snuffe narrative, also a recitation, since we are to gather that he has been composing it beforehand, in his head. This time we do not know the substance of the tale, but contemplate in diminishing perspective an actor who has memorised a script which enjoins him to imitate a man who has devised and memorised a script:

> The man came crawling towards me, on his belly. Pale, wonderfully pale and thin, he seemed on the point of – [*Pause. Normal tone.*] No, I've done that bit. (*CDW* 116)

Later on he incorporates a few critical reflections: 'Nicely put, that,' or 'There's English for you.' This technician's narcissism somewhat disinfects the dreadful tale. All Hamm's satisfactions come from dramatic self-contemplation, and as he towers before us, devoid of mercy, it is to some ludicrous stage villain that he assimilates himself, there on the stage, striking a stage-Barabbas pose ('Sometimes I go about and poison wells.') It is to this that life as play-acting comes.

> In the end he asked me would I consent to take in the child as well – if he were still alive. [*Pause.*] It was the moment I was waiting for. [*Pause.*] Would I consent to take in the child . . . [*Pause.*] I can see him still, down on his knees, his hands flat on the ground, glaring at me with his mad eyes, in defiance of my wishes. (*CDW* 118)

'It was the moment I was waiting for': the satisfaction this exudes is considerably less sadistic than dramatic, and the anticlimax into which the long performance immediately topples would try a creator's soul, not a maniac's:

> I'll soon have finished with this story. [*Pause.*] Unless I bring in other characters. [*Pause.*] But where would I find them? [*Pause.*] Where

would I look for them? [*Pause. He whistles. Enter* CLOV.] Let us pray to
God. (*CDW* 118)

So the hooks go in. There is no denying what Beckett called in a letter
to Alan Schneider 'the power of the text to claw.' It strikes, however,
its unique precarious balance between rage and art, immobilising all
characters but one, rotating before us for ninety unbroken minutes the
surfaces of Nothing, always designedly faltering on the brink of utter
insignificances: theatre reduces to its elements in order that theatrical-
ism may explore without mediation its own boundaries: a bleak
unforgettable tour de force and probably its author's single most
remarkable work.[61] □

Kenner's understanding of the drama as a powerful formal statement of
a universal truth about the human condition in a time of cultural crisis,
and his reading of self-reflexive presence on the stage as a dramatic
assertion of the human certainty of 'being there' when all other metaphysical 'props' fail, is shared by Ruby Cohn, the other founding parent
of liberal humanist Beckett studies. There are differences between Cohn
and Kenner – Cohn adopts a much grittier, less elegant style than
Kenner, and is more emphatic that cultural contextualisation is necessary for a full understanding of Beckett's work – but the basis of her
reading is that Beckett's drama is a last-ditch theatrical stand against the
collapse of the values of Western civilisation. In one of her most influential works on Beckett, *Samuel Beckett: The Comic Gamut*, Cohn conducts an
illuminating and rigorously detailed analysis of the modes of comic
device employed by Beckett across the range of the oeuvre. The dominant theme of this reading is that Beckett's humour reflects critically
upon the death of a civilisation that nevertheless continues to inform the
contemporary creative imagination. Beckett's drama represents above all
a world that has been deserted by the ethical, moral and cultural values
that used to sustain it – 'the dramatic action presents the death of the
stock props of western civilisation – family cohesion, filial devotion,
parental and connubial love, faith in God, empirical knowledge and
artistic creation'[62] – but the works derive their energy and their drive,
their ironic gradient, from the fact that they are saturated with the very
civilisation that they mourn. The mass of detail that Cohn provides in
her readings is geared to demonstrating the extent to which Beckett's
drama is absolutely full of references to a now degraded, impoverished
Western classical tradition. The comedy of Beckett's work derives from
the inappropriateness of this once rich and noble tradition to the bleak
and grim post-holocaust landscape in which it fitfully and scabbily lives
on. In Beckett's drama, this ironic comment on the collapse of our sheet
anchors even extends to the artwork itself, as Beckett's comedy 'shoves

the artist off a pedestal, down into our lowly human midst'.[63] The plays 'hit below the belt of logic and literature. Evocative of both compassion and derision, Beckett's bums present us with an image of ourselves. Shivering in the rags of our classico-Christian heritage, they sing frantically for an uncertain supper'.[64]

Cohn suggests, however, that our denuded civilisation is finally redeemable in the name of Beckett's own art. Even whilst the subject matter of his work is the cultural poverty of contemporary life, it remains, in the hands of a supreme artist such as Beckett, a 'rich poverty'.[65] Through the mysterious operation of the great artwork, the drama both mourns a civilisation that is lost, and produces the most civilised art that we have available to us. The classical heritage that is present in Beckett's work is not simply ironised, it is also and at the same time preserved in the rich texture of the plays themselves. In the following extracts, Cohn traces some of the biblical and classical allusions that are to be found in *Godot* and *Endgame*, whilst exploring the comic effect of these allusions in the bleakly Beckettian universe of the plays. We join her critique as she turns to *Waiting for Godot*:

■ Beckett deliberately emphasised the duration of the waiting, in contrast to and at the expense of the action. But there *is* action, and, like much of the dialogue, it depends for its comic effect upon incongruity and absurdity. Thus, it is not Lucky's job to carry, but we see him doing little else. Estragon, less verbal than Vladimir, was once a poet, whose medium is words. Vladimir cannot laugh, and urinates torrentially. Estragon helps Vladimir only when the latter stops requesting it, and both aid Pozzo for lack of anything else to do. In Act II the friends help Pozzo to his feet, as they did Lucky in Act I. Master and slave, hat and shoe, carrot and turnip, rope and tree, goat and sheep, and above all pagan and Christian reference seem to be absurdly irrelevant to one another in the cosmos created on stage.

On the basis of Vladimir's pondering upon the thief who was saved (according to the Gospel of St. Luke), and Estragon's comparison of himself to Christ, several critics have read Christian hope into *Waiting for Godot*.[66] But Christ and thief have long been treated ironically by Beckett. In *Murphy* the puppet Neary ironically urges the other puppets to take heart, since one thief was saved; Mercier and Camier in Beckett's unpublished French novel compare themselves to the two thieves without Christ; in the French text of *Molloy* A and C are referred to as 'mes deux larrons'; in *Malone Dies* Moll's crucifix earrings stand for the two thieves, and her single, cruciform yellow tooth, for Christ. Even the rationalist Watt articulates proper names 'such as Knott, Christ, Gomorrah, Cork with great deliberation'; Molloy describes his misery as a mock Calvary; an Easter Chorus suggests to

Malone the one 'who saved me twenty centuries in advance'; the narrative of *The Unnamable* is punctuated with blasphemy.

In *Waiting for Godot*, as in other works, the biblical echoes are mocking echoes, probably because Christianity (like love, another major Beckett target) seemed to promise so much to man. Vladimir thinks of the thief who was saved, only after he declares man's foot is at fault (in French, 'coupable'). Of the Gospels, Estragon remembers only the map of the Holy Land, where the blue of the Dead Sea awakens his thirst. Frightened by noises he assigns to Godot, Estragon dimly echoes a verse from St. Matthew: 'The wind in the reeds.' Vladimir quotes with comic incompleteness from Proverbs: 'Hope deferred maketh the something sick.' Vladimir calls Lucky an 'old and faithful servant,' then accuses him of crucifying Pozzo, who, in turn, calls Lucky his 'good angel'; Pozzo laughs to see that Estragon and Vladimir are of the same species as himself, 'Made in God's image!' If the friends repent, it is not of sin, but of being born. Estragon's comparison of himself to Christ culminates in a bitter contrast, 'And they crucified quick'. Vladimir's 'Christ have mercy on us' punctuates the information that Godot's beard is neither fair nor black, but white. The final promise of salvation *if* Godot comes is comically undercut by the dialogue about Estragon's fallen trousers.

Greek deities also find their way into *Godot*, since Pozzo refers to Atlas and Pan. Estragon, tired of supporting Pozzo, informs the blind tyrant that he and his friend are not caryatids. Thus, true to Beckett's habit, he mocks the whole classico-Christian tradition in *Godot*.

Again true to his habit, Beckett evokes explosive as well as subtle laughter. Copious urination, possible lice, and obscenities provide a comic shock effect. As in the fiction, details of cruelty, comically conveyed, delineate man's metaphysical situation. Early in the play, man's position is succinctly summarised. While waiting for Godot, Estragon asks, 'Where do we come in?' 'Come in?' Vladimir snorts, 'On our hands and knees.' In each act, Estragon enters after 'they' have beaten him; occasionally, he speaks of his unhappiness. The two friends sporadically entertain the idea of suicide. Estragon mentions that Vladimir has killed 'the other' and 'billions of others.' Pozzo treats Lucky brutally; he finds it a 'good sign' when Estragon's leg bleeds after he has been assaulted by Lucky. Estragon does not hesitate to seize an opportunity for revenge. The two friends impersonally discuss the possibility of Lucky's being dead. Lucky's heavy burden is revealed to be sand. In Act II when Estragon pleads for God to pity him, Pozzo arrives, seeking help and pity for himself. At the end, the two friends wistfully renounce their hope of hanging themselves, for the only cord they have, Estragon's belt – similar in length to the cord that binds a dumb Lucky to a blind Pozzo – binds Vladimir and

Estragon to this life and the absurd, compulsive wait for Godot.

It is not surprising that most people who came to know Beckett by way of *Waiting for Godot* compared him to Kafka, since both are impassive creators of a cruel cosmological comedy, revealing man's awkward situation in an absurd universe. For those who examine the play in the context of Beckett's other works, there are also hints of the more epistemological comedy of the fiction. The hat remains a symbol of knowledge, and the identical bowlers worn by the four characters suggest that they all belong in the same play, in the same comic context. It is significant, too, that Vladimir, the mental bum, harps on his hat, and that Lucky cannot think without his hat on his head. On the other hand, Lucky's hat on Estragon's head, or even Vladimir's, does not produce the same flow of discourse.

In the process of self-discovery through narration (of dreams, parables, jokes, or parodies) each monologist needs an audience. In the stichomythic dialogue of the two friends, there is a subtle transfer from their inexhaustible 'we' to 'dead voices' who talk about 'their' lives, because merely to have lived is not enough, and to be dead is not enough. 'They' are compelled to speech, to pass the endless wait for Godot in discourse, in words of indeterminate origin, shifting significance, and dubious communicability.

If language is the primary level of doubt, close upon it follows doubt of events, and of their co-ordinates in time and space. Implicitly mocking Descartes, the friends exist because they wait, whereas their pervasive doubt includes a doubt of their very existence. Whistling in the dark, Estragon asks pathetically, 'We always find something, eh Didi, to give us the impression we exist?' But the impression is fleeting, as doubt insinuates itself again.

Specific doubt begins with conversation about the scheduled rendezvous with Godot: 'He said by the tree. Do you see any others?' Vladimir worries, 'What are you insinuating? That we've come to the wrong place?' But Estragon bridles, 'I didn't say that.' Places are not meant to be recognised; the friends are 'not from these parts.' References to Ireland and France (sometimes to non-existent places that merely sound as though they are in these countries) give a veneer of locality, but the references to the Board and the physical confines of the theatre cast doubt on larger spaces.

Even more pointedly, time is called into question. Vladimir attempts to schedule their appointment with Godot: 'He said Saturday. [*Pause.*] I think.' But Estragon gnaws at the date, 'But what Saturday? And is it Saturday? Is it not rather Sunday? [*Pause.*] Or Monday? [*Pause.*] Or Friday?' Vladimir looks *'wildly about him as though the date was inscribed in the landscape.'* By Act II Vladimir can scarcely tell the morning from the evening. In the play, time is mentioned in conventional units (hours, days, seasons, years), and the very plethora of units serves to belittle and abstract it, as does the hysterical insistence on past, present and future in *Comment c'est*. Like Pozzo's watch, time is almost perceptible, then lost from perceptibility, and even mistaken for Pozzo's heart. In Lucky's speech, God is 'outside time, without extension.'

Doubt of time and space leads to doubt of human memory. At the beginning of Act I, the fallibility of witness is implied, since only one of the four Evangelists reports that a thief was saved. A little later, it is Vladimir who cannot remember that the friends have already waited for Godot by this tree; it is Estragon who comments, 'Off we go *again*' [Cohn's italics], when Godot's boy arrives. In Act II, it is first Estragon's memory that is deficient, but this is followed by a similar defection on Pozzo's part. By the end of Act II it is Vladimir who comments, 'Off we go again,' when Godot's boy arrives again, Estragon, asleep, does not even see him. Vladimir supposes that someone watches him as he watches Estragon, equally sure he is asleep and oblivious to what is happening.

The comedy of failing memories sets up an expectation that the boy will not recollect appearing before, seeing Pozzo and Lucky before, meeting Vladimir and Estragon before. More certainly now, Godot will not come, and yet the tragi-comedy lacks absolute certainty; for doubt exists to the degree that word, thing, and event have been undermined. In *Waiting for Godot*, Beckett contrives to approach the classical unities, only to leave us more aware of the monotonous infinitude of time, the repetitive indeterminacy of place, and the absurd discontinuity of action.

Waiting for Godot, written while Beckett was at work on the trilogy of novels, was called by him (in translation) a 'tragicomedy.' One cannot be sure what Beckett means by the word, but it seems likely that the *New English Dictionary* definition of 'a play mainly of tragic character but with a happy ending' was less his intention that Sir Philip Sidney's 'mungrell Tragy-comedie' as described in his *Defense of Poesie*. Sidney decried the Elizabethan plays which were, in his classical view, 'neither right Tragedies, nor right Comedies mingling Kings and Clownes, not because the matter so carrieth it, but thrust in Clownes by head and shoulders to play a part in majesticall matters with neither decencie nor discretion.'

'Majesticall matters' are dim and undependable memories to Beckett's bums. In Godot's continued absence, man becomes a king of shreds and patches, of blindness and dumbness, fit only to play the clown and feed the worms, 'with neither decencie nor discretion.' Fallen too low to be a subject for 'right Tragedy,' feeling too much anguish to be capable of 'right Comedy,' Beckett's man, whilst waiting for Godot, plays a part in a tragicomedy – a slapstick part of victim in a world that he did not make, and that resists his efforts to make sense of it.[67] □

From this contextualisation of *Godot* in terms of an ironically failing Christian classical tradition, Cohn then turns to *Endgame*. Here, too, we are presented with a theatrical world that is replete with allusions to a Christian heritage that can no longer support or sustain it.

■ With characteristic irony, Beckett accents the cruel inhumanity of *Endgame* by frequent evocation of the Bible in the light of its delineation of man's role, particularly with respect to the superhuman. Thus, Hamm, son of Nagg, instantly recalls Ham, son of Noah. Nagg, like Noah, has fathered the remnant of humanity, but rather than make a covenant with God, he tells a joke at God's expense. Biblical Noah faithfully follows God's command to perpetuate all species by thriftily introducing couples into the ark; but Beckett's Nagg is indifferent to, or unaware of, the universal death outside the shelter.

Although Noah's animals are absent from *Endgame*, the play abounds in animal associations: Hamm is an edible part of pig, and Clov either its spice or accompaniment, or perhaps a reference to the cloven-hoofed animals which, pigs excepted, were the only permissible meat for Biblical Jews. A nag is a small horse, and Nell a common name for a horse; Nagg-nag and Nell-knell are puns as well. Hamm refers to Clov as his dog, and Clov makes a toy dog for Hamm. Clov feeds Nagg Spratt's medium animal biscuits. An off-stage rat and an on-stage flea are objects of Clov's murderous intent, for rather than propagate all species, Nagg's progeny, Hamm and (perhaps) Clov, seek to extinguish them. The flea in Clov's trousers is fiercely and farcically destroyed lest a new evolutionary line lead to humanity again. Even a punning sex joke is made to serve the theme of universal destruction. After applying insecticide freely, with exaggerated, slapstick gestures, Clov adjusts his trousers. He has killed the flea 'unless he's laying doggo.'

HAMM: Laying! Lying you mean, unless he's *lying* doggo.

CLOV: Ah? One says lying? One doesn't say laying?

HAMM: Use your head, can't you. If he was laying we'd be bitched. (*CDW* 108)

In Genesis, 'Hamm, the father of Canaan, saw the nakedness of his father, and told his two brethren without' (9:22). Beckett's Hamm, by ironic contrast, has no brethren and cannot see; his Canaan is circumscribed to the 'bare interior' of the room on the stage, and his father is relegated to an ash bin in that room. Biblical Noah curses his son for seeing him naked, and Beckett's Hamm curses his father for conceiving him. The biblical curse of Noah to Ham is: 'a servant of servants shall he be unto his brethren' (9:25). Nagg also curses his son, but not with a prophecy of servitude, for Hamm is master of his domain, which is reduced to the stage room.

Hamm refers to his kingdom – an ironic name for the room before our eyes. In production, his armchair looks like a mock-throne, his toque like a mock-crown. He utters high-handed orders to Clov, a servant who is intermittently good and faithful. Both Hamm and Clov suggest that the world off stage perished by Hamm's will. Even more cruel than Hamm's own lust for destruction is that of the 'I' of Hamm's story, which, like the play proper, is full of biblical reminders.

Hamm sets his chronicle on Christmas Eve, that time of birth rather than death, of peace on earth, and good will towards men. But Hamm, ironically, fills the narrator-protagonist of his tale with ill will in a desolate world, which Hamm describes in terms of numbers on thermometer, heliometer, anemometer, and hygrometer. Just as Hamm is lord of a lifeless earth, and sole custodian of its dwindling supplies, so Hamm's narrator-hero rules a similar domain. The father of a starving child crawls before him, begging for food. With charity towards none, but cruelly recalling a divine charity towards a people in exile, Hamm's 'I' screams at the grovelling father, 'But what in God's name do you imagine? . . . That there's manna in heaven still for imbeciles like you?'

Similarly, the blindness, darkness, suffering, and above all death that fill *Endgame* comment ironically on a biblical context. The most frequently repeated line of the play is Hamm's 'Is it not time for my pain-killer?' Although Hamm is literally asking Clov for a pill, it becomes increasingly evident that the only true pain-killer is death. When Clov asks Hamm whether he believes in the life to come, the sardonic answer is, 'Mine was always that.' The ring of the alarm clock is 'fit to wake the dead!'

On two separate occasions, Hamm cries out in anguish, 'Father, Father!' and, as Jean-Jacques Mayoux has suggested, 'How can we not think of the "Eli Eli" of that other supreme moment?' Towards the end of the play, Hamm utters several phrases which derisively twist Scripture: 'Get out of here and love one another! Lick your neighbour as yourself! . . . The end is in the beginning . . . Good . . . Good . . . Peace to our – arses.' In the French text Hamm compares the small boy outside the shelter to a dying Moses gazing at the promised land.

Since *Endgame* is unmistakably a play about an end of a world, there are many recollections of the Book of Revelations. In the vision of St. John the Divine, Christ says he has the 'keys of hell and death,' in ironic contrast to Hamm, who knows the combination of a cupboard that presumably contains the wherewithal to keep them *alive* in their hell in the shelter.

Revelations is full of phrases about light and darkness, sea and earth, beginning and end, life and death. After the destruction of Babylon, a great voice from heaven utters the words, 'It is done.' In the New Jerusalem, 'The length and the breadth and the height of it are equal,' even as the length, breadth, and height of Clov's kitchen, whose thousand cubic feet might be a caricature reminder of the millennium of Revelations.

Within the tight text of *Endgame*, the frequency and mockery of the biblical echoes cannot be ignored in any interpretation of the play, and the fourth gospel is crucial for such interpretation. Not only does the English *Endgame* contain the fugal variations upon Christ's last words, 'It is finished,' but in this gospel particularly, Christ affirms that He is the light; He speaks of 'my Father' and 'my Father's house.' Beckett's Hamm has dispensed and extinguished light; he calls upon his father and insists that his house is the only asylum.

St. John tells the story of Lazarus, resurrected by Christ, and we learn both from that account and the Passion that in biblical times corpses were wrapped in linen clothes, a napkin around the head, and anointed with oil and spices. In *Endgame*, Clov may be a spice among corpses; it is he who lifts the sheet from near-corpses, but it is Hamm who focuses attention on the napkin that covers his head when the play opens and closes – even as a napkin covered the head of Lazarus and of Christ.[68] □

Within the dramatic economy of *Endgame*, in which these classical details have been drained of their meaning to become merely ironically critical reflections on a society in its death throes, the only hope of salvation, redemption, or resurrection, is through the form of the play itself, its shape, its tautness, the bleak beauty of its structure. As Cohn brings her reading to a close, it is to the redemptive powers of the artwork itself that she turns, in a critical manoeuvre that has become very familiar in this chapter. *Endgame* offers an ambivalent promise of a double resurrection from the lifelessness of its own *mise en scene*, and this resurrection stems directly from the play's formal brilliance.

■ Perhaps *Endgame*, with characteristic Beckett ambivalence, implies two resurrections – one occurring just after the curtain rises, and one just after it finally falls. As has been mentioned, the opening action, silent except for five brief laughs (possibly recalling Christ's five wounds?), is performed like a mock-ritual. Sheets are removed from inert objects, and three people come to life – slowly and feebly – stage. The opening word is Clov's paradoxical 'Finished,' but his phrases trail off in some doubt. Hamm, the word-man made flesh, is 'getting on' in years. He is blind and can therefore not rely on knowledge through perception. He has relegated his parents – both their teachings and tenderness – to ash bins and night-caps.

Far, far in the past are those days when his parents rode through France and Italy on a tandem, when Hamm himself manipulated a bicycle, when Clov pleaded for a bicycle and rode a horse, when body was in efficient union with mind, and man and his carrier could complement each other.[69] By the time of *Endgame*, the delights of the body are grotesque anachronisms. Nagg and Nell laugh uproariously at the accident in which they lost their legs. Keats's line, 'Bold lover, never, never canst thou kiss,' is hideously if hilariously caricatured when Nagg and Nell strain towards each other from their respective ash bins, their 'very white' faces like death masks. Beauty is dead, truth is dead, happiness a subject for farce. 'Nothing is funnier than unhappiness,' Nell sets the tone of *Endgame*. Once born, or resurrected, or merely set in motion, Hamm reluctantly yet compulsively forces the show to go on.

Paralysed himself, he directs the action, even as a director does a play, even as God perhaps directs the world. The infinitesimal movements of his armchair, human life and death – all are subject to Hamm's commands, as long as he is in command. And yet, his activities are ridiculously restricted to composing a chronicle, to praying halfheartedly when he runs out of characters, and above all to giving orders to Clov, variously designated as his dog, menial, creature, and son.

Early in the play, Hamm makes a prophecy about Clov, and we recall other blind prophets – Tiresias, Oedipus, Samson. Hamm's prophecy ends, 'Infinite emptiness will be all around you, all the resurrected dead of all the ages wouldn't fill it, and there you'll be like a little bit of grit in the middle of the steppe. [*Pause.*] Yes, one day you'll know what it is, *you'll be like me*, except you won't have anyone with you, because you won't have had pity on anyone and because there won't be anyone to have pity on' [Cohn's italics] (*CDW* 109–110).

Ironic as the word 'pity' sounds in Hamm's mouth, there *is* someone for Clov to pity, once the small boy is sighted. This little child – real or imagined – is the cue for Hamm to dismiss Clov: 'I don't need you any more.' Perhaps the small boy will take Clov's place as Hamm's servant, while Clov goes out to die in the desert. If, after the final curtain, Hamm is resurrected, the small boy would remove the sheets in the opening ritual, and Hamm, uncovering his face, would replay his part as hero-victim-director-actor-author. The pattern of such a resurrection would be circular.

[. . .]

The verbal spareness of *Endgame* is a startling contrast to the unparagraphed rush of the trilogy, but in both works the heroes are word-men, and in both works one word-man is replaceable and (perhaps) replaced by another. In *Endgame*, Clov, Hamm, and Nagg – three generations – are also three stages of physical decomposition. Like Malone in the trilogy, it is Hamm, the middle member, who is at the height (such as it is) of his creative powers. But as the focus of *Endgame* narrows to the Hamm–Clov relationship, the tension is tautened between creator and creature until, finally, after the end of the play as played, one is (perhaps) replaced by the other, and the whole absurd, heartbreaking cycle begins again. Resurrection into another and reduced life, into another and slower death, may take place – if at all – only through the play of creation.[70] □

The critical approach sketched out here by Cohn and Kenner became increasingly influential throughout the following decades, and continues today to be one of the most dominant means of understanding the plays. The story of critical development throughout the seventies, and well into the eighties, was the story of consolidation of this approach, and a growing wealth of information and detail that fuelled a number of scholarly monographs. With the appearance of Deirdre Bair's pioneering but extremely controversial biography in 1978, and the foundation, by James Knowlson, of the Beckett archive at Reading University in the seventies, the stage was set for a massive increase in the amount of knowledge available that made it possible to contextualise and elucidate Beckett's texts. John Fletcher and John Spurling published the influential *Beckett: A Study of his Plays,* which set the tone for humanist criticism in the seventies, and the high-water mark of this contextualising criticism came with John Pilling's penetrating and detailed study of the oeuvre, entitled *Samuel Beckett,* published in 1976. Since then, scholarly humanist criticism has continued to emerge with the appearance of the *Journal of Beckett Studies* and work by critics such as Stanley Gontarski, Rosemary Pountney, Katharine Worth, Bert O. States and Edith Kern. Perhaps one of the most recent detailed examples of work in this tradition is the biography published by James Knowlson, entitled *Damned to Fame: The Life of Samuel Beckett,* which seeks more thoroughly than ever before to place Beckett's work in its historical, geographical and biographical contexts.

Whilst the Beckettian critical industry has been so shaped by this mode of criticism, however, during the eighties Beckett criticism began to be influenced by the growing range of theoretical approaches that made a growing impact on British literary criticism throughout the decade. The assumptions upon which the liberal humanist approach was based – that the literary text preserves universal truths about the human condition in a mystical language and a living, organic form that cannot be translated or even fully understood – were being challenged by the development of this new theoretical discourse. With the emergence of critics such as Michel Foucault, Roland Barthes and Jacques Derrida, the notion that any discourse, artistic or otherwise, was capable of articulating a natural, extra-ideological truth was being brought very much into question, and the understanding of the nature and the function both of art and of literary criticism was transformed as a result. As the seismic upheaval in the intellectual world caused by the development of post-structuralism and deconstruction began to be powerfully felt within Beckett studies in the late eighties, the grip that Esslin's three categories had exerted over the critical community began to loosen. It appeared that maybe Beckett's work had not been so effectively incorporated and defused, and that perhaps Beckett's plays still had disturbing, challenging and exciting things to tell us about the world that had not yet been glimpsed by his critics. It is to the impact of post-structuralist criticism on Beckett studies that I turn in the next chapter.

CHAPTER THREE

Beckett and the Emergence of Theory

1. Beckett, Derrida and the Resistance to Theory

POST-STRUCTURALIST theory comes late to Beckett. One of the characteristics of Beckett's oeuvre is its relative resistance to ongoing developments in contemporary thought. Whilst critical discourses are mutating and evolving, finding ever new ways to think about the relation between text and world, Beckett criticism has sometimes seemed to draw a protective ring around his work, to create a safe haven from the theoretical uncertainties and insights that have characterised the last few decades. Whilst, from the sixties to the nineties, the sometimes heady critical climate has been influenced by the uneven development from phenomenology to structuralism and semiotics, to post-structuralism and psychoanalysis, Beckett has been in a sense preserved in the formaldehyde of the formalist, liberal humanist criticism considered in the last chapter. This is not to suggest that Beckett criticism has been ineffective over these decades, or to imply that theoretical developments during this time would necessarily have been any more effective as a means of analysis. Rather it is to point out the curious phenomenon that Beckett's writing, which has produced such a wealth of critical analysis and which is widely regarded as central to the twentieth-century literary canon, has been virtually cut off from its literary, critical and theoretical contexts. In this sense, Beckett appears to be both central and marginal – his work seems in important ways to speak for a generation and to articulate the concerns of post-war Europe, but in equally important ways his writing has seemed unapproachable, untouched by contemporary concerns, verging on the timeless, the ahistorical, the untheorisable.

This combination of centrality and marginality is reflected in the way that Beckett was received by those critics who were prominent in setting new structuralist, post-structuralist and deconstructive theoretical agendas.[1]

There was a strong sense that Beckett was a central figure in the modernist and post-modernist literary landscape, and it was clear to many that his writing offered an opportunity to think through some of the new reading and writing practices that were being experimented with throughout Beckett's writing career. Despite this prominence, however, theorists seemed reluctant to approach his work, preferring to concentrate on other major modernists such as Joyce, Eliot, Woolf or Pound.[2] Michel Foucault describes Beckett's 'indifference' as 'one of the fundamental ethical principles of contemporary writing' at the opening of his important essay 'What is an Author', but nowhere in his work does he attempt a direct analysis of Beckettian indifference as an ethical principle.[3] Julia Kristeva writes a short and somewhat hesitant essay on Beckett in *Desire in Language*, but it is clear that she is much more comfortable writing about Joyce, Kafka or Proust.[4] Roland Barthes avoids Beckett, and he is a noticeably absent figure in the work of Jacques Derrida. It is true that Maurice Blanchot writes on Beckett periodically, and indeed has produced some of the best reviews of his work,[5] but this has proved the exception, as theorists have been more or less explicitly unwilling to deal with this major but somehow displaced author. A critic like Colin MacCabe, who exploits Joyce's work as the raw material on which to carry out the theoretical work that was to have a marked influence on the direction of literary theory in the British academy,[6] is strangely silent about the Irish modernist whom it is customary to describe as Joyce's natural heir or successor.[7]

This peculiar doubleness in the response of major critics to Beckett's writing is partly due to the sense that it is simply easier to route the massive proliferation of theoretical ideas that emerged from the sixties to the eighties through a writer like Joyce, whose expansiveness and verbal profusion provides footholds for so many varied new approaches. If you want to develop a psychoanalytic approach, or a deconstructive approach, or a new historical approach, then Joyce's texts are there to welcome you. Their sheer openness and inclusiveness provides so much to work on, that Joyce became a kind of testing ground for new ways of thinking. In the work of pioneering post-structuralists such as MacCabe, Joyce offers the best example of the revolutionary potential of the word. For MacCabe, Joyce turns from the grubby political landscape of post-war Europe to the vast expanses of a poetic language that, freed from tyrannical relationship between signifier, signified and referent, can create a new world in the image of an internationalist modernism.[8] The post-structuralist appetite for texts that, liberated from the job of actually referring to the world, are able to create an infinite surplus of meaning in the play of the signifier, is amply appeased by a work such as *Finnegans Wake*. Beckett's writing, on the other hand, clearly offers no such linguistic plenitude. His work, rather than tending towards the maximum of expressiveness, appears to tend towards the minimum. Language is not set free in his writing, but is brought to the point of collapse. If the ultimate goal of a work such as *Finnegans Wake* is a language that can give expression to all cultures simultaneously, then the goal of Beckett's writing is often taken to be silence. Beckett uses words to whittle away words until words, exhausted, plead to stop. Beckett himself refers to this distinction between himself and Joyce. For Joyce, he claims, words were enabling, whereas for himself, words led to depletion, to 'ignorance, inability and intuitive despair'. In an interview with Israel Schenker, which loses none of its significance as a comment on the critical understanding of the relationship between Beckett and Joyce for being purportedly invented by Schenker himself, 'Beckett' expands on this contrast.

■ [T]he difference is that Joyce was a superb manipulator of material, perhaps the greatest. He was making words do the absolute maximum of work. There isn't a syllable that's superfluous. The kind of work I do is one in which I am not master of my material. The more Joyce knew the more he could. His tendency is towards omniscience and omnipotence as an artist. I'm working with impotence, ignorance. I don't think that impotence has been exploited in the past. There seems to be a kind of aesthetic axiom that expression is an achievement – must be an achievement. My little exploration is that whole zone of being that has always been set aside by artists as something unusable – as something by definition incompatible with art.[9] □

Whilst Beckett's putative intention to expose the limit where language borders on silence rather than on absolute expression is a long way from MacCabe's revolution of the word, however, it does not run contrary to the spirit of much of the post-structuralist and deconstructive theory that was emerging in the seventies and eighties. Indeed, it has been suggested that Beckett's works are the closest we have to texts that deconstruct themselves. Whilst in the work of modernists such as Joyce, Woolf and Eliot the signifier tends to float free of the signified in order to develop alternative meanings, and to open up signifying practices to the 'difference' that 'ordinary' language excludes, the signifier in Beckett's work threatens to rid itself of significance altogether, as language seems to absorb the nothingness that it has to ward off in order to achieve expression. When Molloy claims, in Beckett's novel *Molloy*, that 'you would do better, at least no worse, to obliterate texts than to blacken margins, to fill in the holes of words till all is blank and flat and the whole ghastly business looks like what it is, senseless, speechless, issueless misery',[10] he could be speaking for Beckett himself, whose language is always trembling on the verge of collapse into the nothingness or the silence that it only just withstands.[11] This tendency for Beckett's language to self-destruct, or to self-deconstruct, would suggest that his writing, far from scaring off deconstructive criticism, should offer itself up to the Derridean critic as exemplary. Indeed, Derrida himself, in another version of the simultaneously central and marginal status of Beckett's writing that we have already discussed, comments both on the suitability of Beckett's writing to deconstructive analysis, and on his own (partly consequent) reluctance to embark on a reading of the oeuvre. In an interview with Derek Attridge in 1989, Derrida suggests that Beckett's writing is so close to his own deconstructive philosophy, itself carries out the activity of deconstruction so well, that it undermines his ability to construct an 'academic metalanguage' that could adequately respond to it. Beckett's work strikes at the very heart of what Derrida is doing, but as a result it is alarmingly difficult to find a stable theoretical language with which to reflect upon or critique the writing. Explicitly comparing this reluctance to approach Beckett with his relative willingness to write on Joyce, Kafka or Celan, Derrida focuses on Beckett's use of the French language as a strategy that makes him both more distant and more familiar.

■ This is an author to whom I feel very close, or to whom I would like to feel myself close; but also too close. Precisely because of this proximity, it is too hard for me, too easy and too hard. I have perhaps avoided him a bit because of this identification. Too hard also because he writes – in my language, in a language which is his up to a point, mine up to a point (for both of us it is a 'differently' foreign language) – texts which are both too close to me and too distant for me even to be able to 'respond' to them. How could I write in French in the wake of or 'with' someone who does operations on this language which seem to me so strong and so necessary, but which must remain idiomatic? How could I write, sign, countersign performatively texts which 'respond' to Beckett? How could I avoid the platitude of a supposed academic metalanguage? It is very hard. You will perhaps say to me that for other foreign authors like Kafka, Celan or Joyce, I attempted it. Yes, at least attempted. Let's not speak of the result. I had a kind of excuse or alibi: I write in French, from time to time I quote the German or the English, and the two writings, the 'performative signatures,' are not only incommensurable in general, that goes without saying, but above all without a 'common language,' at least in the ordinary sense of the term. Given that Beckett writes in a particular French, it would be necessary, in order to 'respond' to his oeuvre, to attempt writing performances that are impossible for me (apart from a few stammering [and thus oral] tries in some seminars devoted to Beckett in the last few years). I was able to risk linguistic compromises with Artaud, who has his own way of loving and violating, of loving and violating a certain French language of its language. But in Artaud (who is paradoxically more distant, more foreign for me than Beckett) there are texts which have permitted me writing transactions. Whatever one thinks of their success or failure, I have given myself up to them and published them. That wasn't possible for me with Beckett, whom I will thus have 'avoided' as though I had always read him and understood him too well.[12] □

As the interview continues, Attridge suggests to Derrida that Beckett's work is not only unapproachable because it occupies an uncomfortable, hybrid position in terms of the French that, for both Derrida and Beckett remains to some extent a 'foreign' language,[13] but also because the literature itself robs the critic of the moment of deconstruction. In a slightly wry question, Attridge asks whether there is a sense in which Beckett's writing is already so 'deconstructive', or 'self-deconstructive', that there is 'not much left to do?'.[14] Derrida's response, again contrasting the relative accessibility to critique of Joyce with the uncooperative distance of Beckett, focuses on the difficulty of extracting a Beckettian 'signature' (which he claims is nevertheless there) from texts that so resolutely fold in on themselves, and refuse to offer up isolated moments of significance.

■ No doubt that's true. A certain nihilism is both interior to metaphysics (the final fulfilment of metaphysics, Heidegger would say) and then, already, beyond. With Beckett in particular, the two possibilities are in the greatest possible proximity and competition. He is nihilist and he is not nihilist. Above all, this question should not be treated as a philosophical problem outside or above the texts. When I found myself, with students, reading some Beckett texts, I would take three lines, I would spend two hours on them, then I would give up because it would not have been possible, or honest, or even interesting, to extract a few 'significant' lines from a Beckett text. The composition, the rhetoric, the construction and the rhythm of his works, even the ones that seemed the most 'decomposed', that's what 'remains' finally the most 'interesting', that's the work, that's the signature, this remainder that remains when the thematics is exhausted (and also exhausted, by others, for a long time now, in other modes).

With Joyce, I was able to pretend to isolate two words (He *war* or *yes, yes*); with Celan, one foreign word (*Shibboleth*); with Blanchot, one word and two homonyms (*pas*). But I will never claim to have 'read' or proposed a general reading of these works. I wrote a text, which in the face of the event of another's text, as it comes to me at a particular, quite singular, moment, tries to 'respond' or to 'countersign,' in an idiom which turns out to be mine. But an idiom is never pure, its iterability opens up to others. If my own 'economy' could provoke other singular readings, I would be delighted. That it should produce 'effects of generality' here or there, of relative generality by exceeding singularity, is inscribed in the iterable structure of any language, but in order to talk about that seriously, it would be necessary to re-elaborate a whole 'logic' of singularity, of the example, the counter-example, iterability, etc. That is what I try to do in another mode elsewhere, and often in the course of the readings I have just mentioned. They are all offered, simultaneously, as reflections on the signature, the proper name, singularity. All this to explain that I have given up writing in the direction of Beckett – for the moment.[15] □

This sense that Beckett awkwardly, and sometimes alarmingly, undermines theoretical language by picking apart the very processes that allow critics to respond to him, and by presenting deconstruction with a disabling image of itself, has been shared by many theorists. Beckett is 'important', but somehow unspeakable, unapproachable, unnamable. The effect of this has been to limit Beckett criticism largely to Beckett specialists. A humanist formalist critical discourse that has proved effective in articulating Beckett's nihilist tendencies *without* unravelling the discourse itself has grown up around the oeuvre, and the critical method of dealing with Beckett adopted by 'Beckett studies' has had very little truck with the main (French, German, Anglo-American) currents of theoretical thought developing from the sixties onwards. There is of course some crossover – it is possible to read the influence of structuralist thinkers such as Lévi-Strauss and the early Barthes in the work of Ruby Cohn, and Martin Esslin draws on populist readings of continental existentialism – but the gap between Beckett criticism and the larger theoretical community is a marked feature of Beckett studies. The stress on Beckett's humanism, and the related critical insistence upon converting his threatening negativity into an affirming positivity, has allowed Beckett studies to prosper by avoiding the self-destruction anticipated by Derrida, but it has caused the scholarship to become isolated from those fields of thought for which humanist criticism was no longer a valid response. A writer whose work is so central to some of the main concerns of post-structuralist theory has thus repeatedly been reconstructed as a universal humanist, and deflected from the mainstream of literary theoretical life, partly as a consequence of such unnerving centrality.

2. Beckett, Iser and Reader Response

Whilst the gap between Beckett criticism and mainstream theory was largely maintained from the beginning of Beckett's writing career to the mid to late eighties, however, there were a small number of (largely non-English-speaking) theorists who gave Beckett a more central place in their thinking. Amongst the most notable of these is Wolfgang Iser, the German critic who was prominent in the development of what became known as 'reader response theory'. In his major works, such as *The Implied Reader* (1974) and *The Act of Reading* (1978), Iser sought to adapt the hermeneutic methods elaborated by his predecessors such as E.D. Hirsch and Hans-Georg Gadamer, to incorporate the process of reading into the critical moment. For Iser, the most crucial thing to grasp about literature is that it only 'happens' when it is read or experienced by its audience. To imagine any literary artefact as a stable, self-sufficient object, independent of historical and cultural change, is to overlook the fundamental fact that it is born at its point of reception. In order to know what happens when a literary work comes into being, therefore, it is not only necessary to understand the cultural conditions under which it was originally produced, and the intentions of the author who was producing it, but also the conditions in which it is received, as these latter provide at least as many ingredients for the literary experience as the former. What Iser suggests, in effect, is that the critic should concentrate on the moment of interpretation as the point at which the literary work arrives, rather than the distant moment of inception. The focus is thus shifted from the transcendent mind of the author (as in traditional criticism), or the self-regulating and legitimising text (as in New Criticism), to the dynamic, shifting interface between text and reader.

The impact of this shift from author and text to reader was to have important theoretical consequences, as it marked the movement away from the notion that the text was a complete artefact that needed only to be correctly analysed in order to yield up its store of precious truths, towards a critical method that regarded the text as always incomplete and in process. The insights of later theorists owe a great deal to the insistence of reception theorists that the text should be read as much for what it doesn't say as for what it does. The literary moment takes place not in a space that is prescribed by the text, and under the jurisdiction of the author, but in a social space that is beyond the text's control, and that is being constantly made and remade in the ceaseless dialogue between text and reader. Unusually for a theoretical innovation of such importance, Iser draws heavily on Beckett's work in the elaboration of his ideas. From his 1961 essay entitled 'Samuel Beckett's Dramatic Language', through his substantial work on Beckett in *The Implied Reader* (1974) and *Prospecting: From Reader Response to Literary Anthropology* (1989), to *The Fictive and the Imaginary* published in English translation in 1993, Iser returns again and again to Beckett. This choice of Beckett's work as exemplary is related to Iser's recognition of its negativity. Where the failure of his writing to fend off the 'nothingness' that threatens it is reconstituted by his humanist critics as a positive triumph over the void, and regarded by critics such as Derrida as a deconstructive tendency that makes it difficult to find a critical foothold, Iser sees in such failure an openness to interpretation that emphasises the role of the reader in creating the work. The 'negativeness' of Beckett's texts, their refusal to 'satisfy our needs' as readers/audience, causes us constantly to provide possible explanations or interpretations that would complete them. But the texts' equally constant refusal to allow such interpretations causes us to realise that the interpretations we have provided are inadequate fictions. The final consequence of this rhythmical movement between the goading and denial of interpretative faculties, Iser suggests, is to raise the interpretative process to consciousness. Beckett's works show us

■ that we are constantly fabricating fictions in order to create reliable guidelines or even realities for ourselves, though in the end they turn out to be no such thing. These texts also show clearly that in spite of the knowledge revealed to us concerning our needs, we still cannot do without our fictions, so that these needs become the basis of our own entanglement with ourselves.[16] □

When Iser came, in 1979, to write a concentrated analysis of *Waiting for Godot*, an approach to the play began to emerge that differed widely from that which had become orthodox in Beckett studies. The critique of *Waiting for Godot* was important for Iser, partly because the application of reader response analysis to the stage, as opposed to the more obviously text-based medium of fiction, posed central questions of the theory. To suggest that a novel has no existence independent of its readers was an important and innovative step, but as the novel is not conventionally reduced to its material existence as a bound commodity, the work of imagination that this required was not too demanding. The novel has commonly been regarded as an idea – it is just that Iser was asking readers to consider that the idea belonged partly to them, as well as to the author, or to the text. But the suggestion that a *play* exists only in the process of its being interpreted has to deal with the element of material presence that looms much larger in drama criticism than in other fields. In some ways, of course, reader response theory is suited to drama, as it relies to an extent on the notion that every work of art is a performance, but in others it seemed radically unsuited. When faced with the self-evident physicality of actors on the stage, it is difficult to suggest that the artwork has no reality apart from its interpretation. In suggesting a reader response analysis of *Waiting for Godot*, Iser had to rethink the relation between the space of the stage, the text and the audience. In the process, the concrete reality of the players in the geography of the theatre lost some of that direct 'presence' that has been held up by so many critics as a guarantor of identity and fullness of being, or as a proof of the Heidegerrian certainty of 'being there'. As we have already seen, it is an insistence on the fundamental affirmation of Vladimir and Estragon's presence on the stage that allowed Beckett's critics such as Robbe-Grillet and Esslin to cast *Waiting for Godot* as a positive and essentially redemptive vision of the human condition, and Iser's reading radically challenged the certainty of this stage presence.[17] The stage for Iser was not a timeless space with trans-cultural, trans-historical humanity standing nakedly upon it, but a space that comes fitfully and problematically into being in a dialectical relationship between audience, stage and text.

Iser's essay, entitled 'Counter-sensical Comedy and Audience Response in Beckett's *Waiting for Godot*', focuses, in its analysis of the relation between play and audience, on the role of comedy. In the introduction to the essay, Iser draws on terms borrowed from structuralism and semiotics, such as paradigm and syntagm, to suggest ways in which the comic devices in *Godot* control and manipulate the audience's interpretative faculties.[18] Drawing a distinction between 'comic paradigm' and 'overall plot', Iser discovers what he calls a 'toppling effect' in the play's comic structure. The comedy deriving from Vladimir and Estragon's clown like stupidity does not harmonise with the general tendency of the play (for example, the possibility of salvation), but rather clashes with it, and it is as a result of this clash in the basic structure of the play that the toppling effect that Iser identifies takes place. *Godot* does not lead to a satisfying catastrophe, in which comic paradigm and overall plot discover an overarching unity, but is built around a 'minus function', a gap into which the play topples. It is into this gap that the audience's interpretative urge is led and, for Iser, the resultant confrontation between the drama and its interpretation is what constitutes the play's artistry.

■ A basic feature of the technique in *Godot* is the unmistakable miscarriage of comedy . . . The failed action, as one comic paradigm, . . . shows through action what is actually meant by 'nothing to be done'. Similarly, the repetition does not signify the futility of failed actions, but the fact that nothing can be learnt from failed actions. Consequently, the link between comic paradigms and overall plot is dislocated, so that the latter completely loses its syntagmatic function and the only relation left between the two different levels is one of mutual toppling. This instability results in a breakdown of the basic structure of comprehension, as syntagmatic and paradigmatic levels are flattened to equality and the interchangability of their contents serves to emphasise the apparent futility of these contents. This levelling out, however, produces a carnival effect, manifested in enjoyment of the nonsense, even though the tendency has disappeared upon which the inversions of the carnival or the relieving devices of comic pleasures are based.

It goes without saying that such dislocated comedy is bound to mobilise the interpretative faculties; indeed, if one might anticipate the effects produced by these structures, one might say that, in the manner in which the failure is presented, the artistry lies in the manipulation of these mobilised faculties. The comic paradigms, the mutually upsetting levels of action, the carnival effect, the enjoyment of nonsense, and finally the basic theme-and-background structure of perception and comprehension – all constitute 'minus functions', and this means that because of what they are, they always evoke that which they have excluded. Such a process continually compels the spectator to provide his own background, but at the same time it tells him nothing about why his expectations have been thwarted, or what sort of relationship exists between these thwarted expectations and what has actually been presented. He is therefore left with an array of empty spaces into which his mobilised interpretative faculties are relentlessly drawn and which are manipulated by them in a specific manner. For the purposes of laying bare the mechanics of this process, we will now try to give a schematised description of the interpretative activities triggered off by the play; we may thereby understand the text-guided processes occurring in the spectator's mind, and these in turn will serve as an indication of the kind of aesthetic experience which is to be imparted.[19] □

The section of the essay that follows is an attempt, which again draws on structuralist as well as phenomenological criticism, to provide as accurate as possible a 'schema' of the interpretative 'processes occurring in the spectator's mind'.

■ Vladimir and Estragon, the main characters, both seem to be tramps; we learn right at the beginning that Estragon spent the night in a ditch. But they also seem like clowns, as many critics have pointed out, although in fact neither 'tramp' nor 'clown' is ever mentioned in the text.[20] This clowning effect comes about through their constant failures and through their inability to learn through their failures, as evidenced by their endless repetitions. In Joachim Ritter's words: 'The clown is simply the outcast, the dropout, yet he proclaims this non-conformity not by antithesis of meaning, but by an extreme distortion of it. His clothes are very different from normal clothes, but the long gloves, the countless jackets, the giant trousers represent a distortion, a perversion of ordinary dress. He carries around with him a meaning-ful piece of equipment, a garden gate, but it is totally detached from its usual context, and so he uses it to keep entering the realm of nonsense, which becomes nonsense when set against sense, and thereby raises the liberating laughter that breaks down the barriers of seriousness and moderation.'[21] The laughter with which we greet the clown's actions is liberating because we perceive the naïveté in which he is trapped. Everything he does goes wrong, but he persists, as if the repetition denoted constant success. Such distortions are generally so absolute that the naïveté of the failure is immediately apparent, and so is greeted by immediate and spontaneous laughter. No mental activity is really required to put the distortion right, and the momentary perplexity can be relieved at once. The clown's naïveté places the spectator in a position of superiority which, as Freud observed, arises out of a comparison between the mental and spiritual qualities perceived in the comic character, and the qualities that determine one's own situation. The comparison of intellectual qualities is funny 'if the other person had made a greater expenditure than I thought I should need. In the case of mental function, on the contrary, it becomes comic if the other person has spared himself expenditure which I regard as indispensable (for nonsense and stupidity are inefficiencies of function). In the former case I laugh because he has taken too much trouble, in the latter because he has taken too little.'[22] The clown's 'inefficiencies of function' signalise his being trapped in his naïveté, and it is precisely this impression that makes Vladimir and Estragon seem like clowns. People appear naïve if they do not know the restraints imposed by civilisation – restraints of which we ourselves are aware and which, in the given situation, we would also expect them to be aware of. We laugh at such people when, in their ignorance, they cross the borders of these restraints. In *Godot* these borders are set by the fact that the characters are waiting for Godot – a fact which seems to determine their whole lives, even though with their constant failures they behave as if the situation did not exist. Now if these characters seem to us like clowns, then we are already caught up in a process of interpretation; and in our efforts to find plausible reasons for the never ending repetition of failed actions, we ourselves become prisoners of the play.

Viewing the characters as clowns, or making them into clowns, is an interpretation arising out of a process of comparison which is comforting in so far as it enables one to reduce the unfamiliar to terms of the familiar, the abstract to the concrete, and so to master a strange and puzzling world. So long as Vladimir and Estragon represent comic paradigms through their repeated failures, we are misled into such a comparison. This is encouraged at first by the level of the overall comic plot-line. The characters are waiting for Godot; but they frequently behave as if they did not have any such purpose, and so we are constantly tempted to explain their conduct as naïveté; we begin to laugh because they constantly seem to transgress the limits set by their overall purpose. Our laughter is evidence of our position of superiority, but this position depends upon conditions that we have produced for ourselves. For this reason, our laughter does not make us happy; it has no cathartic effect because, at the very moment when we believe we can take the protagonists for clowns, this idea begins to fall apart owing to the increased indifference they show towards their avowed aim of waiting for Godot. Consequently our reaction is, in the last analysis, not to the clowning of the play, but to our own interpretation of it as clowning, which manifests itself in the flaring up and dying down of our laughter.

This cut off reaction is not due solely to the fact that we make the protagonists into clowns; it results in an even greater measure from a preconceived pattern of audience response that is built into the structure of the play. Whenever the diverse and apparently non-sensical actions seem to converge unequivocally into clowning, the characters suddenly relate once more, with detailed and often weighty allusions, to the overall plot-line of waiting for Godot. Biblical references to the crucified thieves (CDW 14), an intricate casuistic debate, reminiscent of St Augustine, as to which of the thieves was saved (CDW 14f), Estragon's comparison of himself to Jesus (CDW 50–51), all permeate the play with a density of allusions that have, logically enough, led many to conclude that the two men might in fact be waiting for God. But there is nothing in the text to confirm this, and Beckett himself, when asked who Godot was, merely replied that he would have said so if he had known it himself.[23] But whatever the heart of the matter may be, it is clear that our mobilised interpretative endeavours are guided in a certain direction. If these characters are waiting for God or some such all-powerful figure, if their identities are somehow connected with the thieves on the cross, then clearly we can no longer regard them as clowns. This means we have erected a concept of the characters – admittedly with the guidance of the text – and are then forced to dismantle this concept as soon as we are made to relate the comic paradigms to the overall action.

Now in conventional comedy, the overall plot-line provides the background for the humour of the comic paradigms. In *Godot*, however, the overall plot-line seems to be the background against which the comic paradigms *lose* their humour. Naïveté as a source of comedy is not denied; but only when we ourselves deny its humour, does it become possible for us to relate the two levels of action to one another. And even if we were to persist in viewing the characters as naïve, this naïveté would be very dangerous in the light of their purpose, so that the situation would still take on a seriousness that would stifle our laughter. But whose is this seriousness? At times, it is true, the characters themselves cry out in despair, but we can never be sure of its extent or even its reality; at times we may project seriousness onto them without their knowing it; at times this projection of seriousness constitutes a perfectly natural and instinctive reaction akin to that of children at a pantomime, when they cry out to warn the unsuspecting hero that the villain is behind him.

There is no need to go on illustrating these patterns of reaction, for one can already pinpoint the structure underlying and guiding the processing of such a text, as well as the function the structure is to perform. The play leads us into making a whole series of projections in order to provide some kind of overall background that will give coherence to the events that we are witnessing. But, remarkably, our projections do not function as a substitute for cancelled expectations at all; on the contrary, we find ourselves compelled to abandon them. We conceive of the protagonists as clowns, but this view is upset by the allusions that deepen and intensify the dialogue. However, the apparent depth provided by the overall plot-line itself begins to topple when the characters fall back into the characteristic futility of their normal dialogue. The most striking features of this normal dialogue are its simplicity of syntax and vocabulary, the ease with which it can be understood, and above all the fact that it only describes what they do.[24] What is said means nothing but what in any case we can see – in other words, the language is purely denotative, so that we even begin to project intentions onto the absence of connotations. We feel ourselves being pushed into processes of interpretation because the actions denoted by the language seem to have no representative value, whereas the overall plot-line leads us to believe that there must be a representative value hidden somewhere. But if we think we have found such a value, it is quickly invalidated by the characters themselves. Furthermore we are tempted to project references onto the purely denotative language, but these are then wiped out whenever the dialogue itself becomes allusive. If we sense a pattern through the reference to the crucified thieves, it is wiped out by the fact that no one can say which of the thieves was saved, since even the apostles disagree (*CDW* 14). What cannot be decided cannot be significant, and so the overall action ceases to impart any syntagmatic articulation to the comic paradigms; once the two levels come into contact, the overall plot-line is made trivial. The relation between the two levels is obviously such that whatever missing links the spectator may provide will at once begin to fall apart when they take on any degree of equivocalness. Thus the view of the protagonists as clowns begins to topple when set against the Godot level; and the latter as a concept of possible salvation begins to topple when viewed against the protagonist's indifference.

This mutual destruction of interpretive concepts stimulated by the text does, however, constitute a 'connection' between the two levels of action, even if this connection is far from that which one would expect from a comic plot. Thus, the process of overturning our concepts – whatever their substance may be – implies that we are incessantly forced to build up a concept in the one instance, and then are forced to dismantle it in the next. It follows that the aesthetic object of the drama, which the spectator is always bound to assemble for himself in realising the intentions laid down for him, here comprises this very alternation of building and dismantling imaginary concepts. If one thinks back to the carnival effect, which permeates the whole atmosphere and construction of the play, the aesthetic object consists in the switching between what, for the sake of brevity, one might classify as clowning and salvation – two concepts which so undermine one another that they both disintegrate. Now with the carnival effect, as with one's enjoyment of nonsense, these confusing switches normally stabilise themselves by way of one tendency or another, but in Beckett's plays there is no tendency to latch onto, because the two levels of theme and background, or comic paradigm and overall plot-line, have been levelled out. But it is this very absence of any tendency that acts as a goad to the spectator's interpretative faculties, for an aesthetic object that constitutes itself through dismantling constructed concepts can only consolidate itself by means of a tendency. Any tendency in *Godot*, however, can only be in the form of a projection, as is only too clear from the well documented range of audience responses and interpretations since the play was first performed. Whatever the nature and the substance of this projected tendency may be, it functions structurally as the syntagmatic articulation that balances out the 'minus function' of the overall plot-line of waiting for Godot, whose articulating force has become inoperative. It re-establishes the theme-and-background structure basic to comprehension, although it may remain completely open as to whether the comic paradigms are the background and waiting for Godot the theme, or vice-versa. Our interpretation will vary depending on which is which. When the prisoners of St Quentin recognised themselves in Vladimir and Estragon, the protagonists constituted the theme and the helpless waiting the background.[25] When the play is experienced as an existential apocalypse,[26] the helpless waiting is the theme, and the apathetic characters the background. In both interpretations one can see the compulsion to impose on the play a tendency which will allow a syntagmatic organisation of its paradigms.

Whatever the tendency projected onto the play, it is not an arbitrary act on the part of the spectator. It is the response to three central expectations relating to 1. the carnival effect and enjoyment of nonsense, 2. the theme-and-background structure of comprehension with its resultant organisation of the levels of action, and 3. the significance and precision necessary for each and every interpretation. Points 1 and 2 concern cancelled expectations pertaining to genre and cognition within the structure of the drama; point 3 denotes a basic requirement of comprehension in so far as meaning is only meaningful to the degree in which its significance is precise. As we have seen, the text of *Godot* undermines this basic requirement of meaning, and it is this process that gives rise to the peculiarity of the aesthetic experience offered by the play. For the continual building and dismantling of concepts that brings about the aesthetic object not only compels the projection of tendencies, but also challenges the significance essential to those tendencies. Thus the sense and the nonsense and the counter-sense of the play translate themselves into an experience for the spectator.

What *is* this counter-sense, and what are the reactions that such an experience can bring about? Counter-sense – as Plessner has emphasised[27] – is the basis of the comic situation. The counter-sense of *Godot* consists in the fact that on the one side we have the characters' incessant repetition of failed actions, and on the other the hopeless wait for an unforseeable change through an unknown being. The spectator will react to these divergent themes by seeking a point of intersection. He can only find one to the extent that the protagonists' behaviour seems reduced to the level of clowning without actually *being* so, and the wait for salvation sinks into apathy without ever actually being lost from view. Thus the mutual distortion of the two 'senses' brings out a common element which we become aware of when we recognise that the source of these distortions is our own interpretations. In trying to impose significance and preciseness on the counter-sense, we experience our own interpretations as that which has been excluded by the counter-sense. Now this is also a comic effect, albeit an insidious one. If comedy focuses on that which is excluded by prevailing norms, thereby subverting their claim to comprehensiveness,[28] the resultant sense will, in Beckett's case, keep drawing our interpretations into the play in order either to exclude them again on account of their incompleteness, or to unmask their distortive nature. In both cases, the projected norms of the spectator become part of the play, and there arises the effect which Beckett himself once described as his plays' 'clawing' into the spectator.[29] For the spectator is no longer confronted with a comic conflict; instead the comedy *happens* to him because he experiences his own interpretations as that which is to be excluded. If the basic effect of comedy is to illuminate the whole of life[30] by showing the excluded striking back at the excluder (i.e. the norm), in Beckett this effect is inverted, as the spectator experiences the shortcomings of his interpretative norms just when he thinks they will enable him to grasp the whole.

This experience is conditioned by various factors connected with our own dispositions and, above all, with the expectations which we bring to art and which are deliberately exploited by Beckett's plays. The counter-sense in these plays does not come about by means of contrastive positions, such as one finds in traditional comedies. Instead it is present to us as an experience because, to begin with, we must formulate the aesthetic object by continually building and dismantling concepts, and ultimately – through this very same inescapable process – we are forced to realise (in both senses of the term) the incompleteness of our interpretations. However, the counter-sense of comedy has always been accompanied by a pattern which, so to speak, holds in store an overall resolution. It is the constant availability of such a pattern that allows us to remain detached from the events depicted and, furthermore, to experience these events as fiction rather than fact. So long as we live through the play as a presentation and not a reality, the events – particularly when the situation threatens danger – will always allow for a degree of distance, thereby providing the relief necessary to enable us to disentangle ourselves. But if the counter-sense is our very own experience, from which we cannot detach ourselves (because the attempt to free ourselves and to understand the experience reveals that even such attempts are only partial and restricted), then the situation seems to us more real than fictional. Here we have a comic structure which denies us the relief normally inherent in such structures. Freud once wrote: 'It is a necessary condition for generating the comic that we should be obliged, *simultaneously or in rapid succession,* to apply to one and the same act of ideation two different ideational methods, between which the "comparison" is then made and the comic difference emerges.'[31] But if this difference does not emerge, because the counter-sense is so total that any comparative operations will only succeed in uncovering their own inadequacies, then the comedy of the structurally comic situation will remain open-ended if not actually threatened with destruction. In conventional comedy, the differences resulting from the process of comparison point in the direction of a whole, albeit a whole that is signalised by way of transgressing limits that are caused by repression and by substitutions for taboos violated; but in Beckett's play the differences are wiped out by the continual overturning of the counter-senses, so that the whole can never be produced even though it is present in the toppling effect. This whole, evidenced only by the toppling effect of the counter-senses, might be described as the 'human condition', which can only be perceived as such by warding off every individual interpretation in order that it should not become a mere token for something other than itself. It cannot be referentially subsumed, and it cannot be represented either; it can only be experienced as a reality. And in experiencing this reality, we gain some insight into the very reality of this experience.[32] □

In the final section of the essay, Iser expands out from his very precise and close reading of audience response to *Waiting for Godot*, to draw some broader conclusions concerning Beckett's writing, and its treatment of what he describes as the 'human condition'.

■ A presentation of the human condition through comedy seems in fact to be a logical continuation of the 'genre'; the play evokes specific expectations which it then proceeds to juggle with. The laughter which always greets the play might well be equated with the responses expected in any comedy. But this laughter is of a very special kind. Joachim Ritter writes in his classic analysis of laughter: 'Laughter as a sound has its moment: namely the precise moment at which comprehension has taken place, which is when the material has emerged with the ideas already present in the listener or observer. However, this excludes the possibility that laughter should be attributed to particular layers of the inner being, particular moods, particular feelings during a particular "pleasure"; but at the same time it includes another implication: that laughter is only possible when an excluded and opposing idea can be grasped as an inalienable part of human existence; i.e. when it can be integrated as a meaningful component into this very existence.'[33] Now the laughter of Beckett's audiences does not seem to fit in with this definition at all. It has been noted time and time again that the laughter that greets his plays is not contagious or communal. The latter category of mirth is confirmatory in its effect, for it communicates to others that 'an opposing idea' has been 'grasped as an inalienable part of human existence'. But laughter at Beckett's plays is always isolated, apparently robbed of its contagious qualities; indeed in *Endgame* and *Happy Days* it is often accompanied by a sort of shock effect, as if the reaction were somehow inappropriate and must therefore be stifled.

The stifled burst of laughter is an individual reaction indicative of the breakdown of the liberating function of laughter. We normally laugh when our emotive or cognitive faculties have been overtaxed by a situation that they can no longer cope with. 'The disorientated body takes over the responses from it (i.e. the mind), no longer as an instrument for action, speech, movement or gesture, but simply as a body. Having lost control of it, having renounced any relation to it, man still evinces a sovereign understanding of the incomprehensible, displaying his power in his impotency, his freedom and greatness in his constraint. He can even find an answer where an answer is no longer possible. He has, if not the last word, at least the last card in a game whose loss is his victory.'[34] But in Beckett's theatre, this victory out of defeat turns into defeat again.

We have seen how, in Beckett's play, the different levels upset one another – an effect which becomes increasingly potent and virulent. The result of this mutual overturning is the collapse of the theme-and-background structure essential to comprehension. In attempting to stabilise this structure, we are forced to dismantle the tendencies we have projected onto the play. This means that the comic action, the structure of comprehension and the structure of participation all collapse the moment we try to stabilise them. This collapse involves the continual neutralisation of contrastive differences, and as has been shown by de Saussure and his structural semantics, if not by others before him, contrastive opposition is the basic condition of meaning. The toppling effect consequently cancels out each meaning as soon as it seeks to establish itself. This is the reason for the isolation of laughers in Beckett's audiences. The timing of the toppling effect will largely depend on the disposition of the individual spectator, so that laughter as a reaction to and a relief from his entanglement is deprived of a collective confirmation at the very moment when it is most needed; the individual spectator then finds that he is laughing alone, and is thus made conscious of his own loss of control. This can be highly embarrassing. It should be borne in mind that inherent in the sound of laughter, in Plessner's words, 'is the power of self-affirmation: one hears oneself'.[35] But supposing one also sees oneself, because the others are silent?

This brings us to the very special nature of the laugh that is elicited by the toppling effect. Freud made an interesting observation in his practice: 'Many of my neurotic patients who are under psychoanalytic treatment are regularly in the habit of confirming the fact by a laugh when I have succeeded in giving a faithful picture of their hidden unconscious to their conscious perception; and they laugh even when the content of what is unveiled would by no means justify this. This is subject, of course, to their having arrived close enough to the unconscious material to grasp it after the doctor has detected it and presented it to them.'[36] Now surprisingly, this observation coincides with a remark of Beckett's about laughter, which also sheds light on a strange feature of his plays: in *Godot*, *Endgame*, and *Happy Days* there are brief, violent bursts of laughter from the characters, that end as abruptly as they began. In Beckett's *Watt*, there is a short catalogue of laughs: 'Of all the laughs that strictly speaking are not laughs, but modes of ululation, only three I think need detain us, I mean the bitter, the hollow and the mirthless. They correspond to successive, how shall I say successive . . . suc . . . successive excoriations of the understanding, and the passage from the one to the other is the passage from the lesser to the greater, from the lower to the higher, from the outer to the inner, from the gross to the fine, from the matter to the form. The laugh that now is mirthless once was hollow, the laugh that once was hollow, once was bitter. And the laugh that once was bitter? . . . The bitter laugh laughs at that which is not good, it is the ethical laugh. The hollow laugh laughs at that which is not true, it is the intellectual laugh. Not good! Not true! Well well. But the mirthless laugh is the dianoetic laugh . . . it is the laugh of laughs, the *risus purus*, the laugh laughing at the laugh, the beholding, the saluting of the highest joke, in a word the laugh that laughs – silence please – at that which is unhappy.'[37] For Beckett, then, the real gradation of laughter begins where the laughter of comedy normally ends: with derision of that which is bad or malicious. But it is the mirthless 'laugh of laughs', the dianoetic mockery of unhappiness, that brings about its transparency and, interestingly enough, draws Freud and Beckett together. The raising of what has been displaced to the threshold of its perception allows one to face up to unhappiness, which in being faced is no longer exclusively itself, but appears in the perspective of its being perceived.

Unhappiness raised to consciousness is the source of dianoetic laughter. This observation would seem to explain the frequent, apparently unmotivated laughter of Beckett's characters. They burst out laughing when they have interpreted their own situations. Now if hollow and mirthless laughs are a response to untruth and unhappiness respectively, this means that the application of the cognitive faculties can no longer cope with the untruth and the unhappiness. For such an intervention would inevitably lead to interpretations through which the unhappiness would not be raised but covered up and displaced even and so, in its ultimate effect, intensified because interpretations are commitments with a presumption of reality whereas when set against reality, their claims to authenticity fall apart. Laughter as a physical response to such a precarious situation is a last attempt at liberating oneself from a seemingly hopeless challenge; with our cognitive exertions stalled and our urge for interpretation (as a means of warding off unhappiness) frustrated, laughter remains as the one reaction that can cut itself off from unhappiness, thus banishing fear. It is true that Beckett's characters show, through their laughter, that they cannot avoid interpreting their situation; but at the same time they seem to know that clinging to such interpretations – even though these are doomed to eternal failure – embodies the source of untruth and unhappiness, the awareness of which announces itself through the physical reaction of laughter.

This laughter has no cathartic effect, but in its mirthlessness it is still a response to the human condition, which is lit up by the laughter and is accepted as itself and not an interpretation of itself. If unhappiness arises from our need to stabilise our situation, our ultimate liberation would be to escape from the norms we have chosen or adopted in our efforts at stabilisation. And this is precisely what Beckett's characters are forever doing, which is why they seem so alien to us. This impression communicates itself through the extraordinary feeling that the characters, although they appear to behave like clowns, reveal a striking superiority which tends to efface the clowning element without removing it altogether. This is because they go the whole way in liberating themselves from the normally inescapable need to stabilise situations by means of interpretation, and their laughter marks the shattering of all self-imposed censorship. It has no healing power, for here the human condition presents itself, not as something that can be contained within prevailing systems of norms, but as something that demands continual explanations only in order to appear as itself by dissociating itself from these explanations. Such laughter is physical, and so elemental; it has no definable content of its own, because it lies beyond the scope of the defining intellect. In this respect, it is an entirely appropriate expression of the human condition, which is equally beyond definition and reveals itself only through an irremediable insufficiency of interpretative frameworks that are moulded, not by reality, but by man's need to explain reality.

The laughter and embarrassment with which Beckett's audiences react to a manifestation of the human condition indicates the fact not only that they are facing this condition, but also that they cannot cope with it. Why not? The answer can only be hypothetical, for as we have seen the laughter defies ultimate definition. It produces a mixed reaction in so far as it registers the nonsensical conduct of the characters who constantly turn aside from their own opinions and intentions; at the same time, however, we are unable to fulfil our enjoyment of the nonsensical by laughter, as we realise that the abandonment of purposes has a liberating effect on the characters. We see the tendency of the nonsense, but we do not understand it. Clearly, the laughter of the characters themselves destroys their own interpretations of precarious situations, for they seem to know that their unhappiness will only increase if they continue to seek compensatory resolutions. We, however, are not able to free ourselves in the same way, for we cannot suddenly regard our interpretations and guiding norms as nonsense. Consequently we are left dangling, and our laughter dies. This position – being trapped halfway – is an almost insoluble paradox. Beckett's play compels us to construct the aesthetic object by continually building up and dismantling concepts, and through this process we are inescapably drawn into the experience that whatever objects we construct can only be a fashioning of objects – in other words, reality is never reality as such, but can only be a fashioning of reality. And yet we generally act as if our fashioning were identical to reality – i.e. as if our realities were more than mere fashioning. In fact they are simply pragmatic arrangements of reality, through which we gain security. Beckett's plays force us to develop a sense of discernment, so that we find ourselves playing off our need for security against our insight into the products of this need. Thus we come to the very borders of our own tolerance. But this is not the whole of the paradox. Beckett's play seems to dissatisfy us, because it makes us block our own paths to possible solutions. It is, however, not the play itself that denies us solutions; we are 'left darkling' so long as we continue to identify with the world of our own concepts. This is a problem revealing and relevant for modern consciousness: we always long to be free from constraints, repressions and prefabricated solutions imposed upon us – and yet we are bewildered and shocked when such solutions are withheld from us in the theatre. Could it be that the ultimate source of laughter at Beckett's play is the fact that it confronts us with this unpalatable contradiction within ourselves? And could it be that this very same fact is the source of irritation? If we were able to laugh in spite of it all, then laughter might – at least momentarily – indicate our readiness to accept our buried life, thus liberating it from the displacement caused by social and cultural repression. But are we really able to free ourselves from our unhappiness by facing up to it? Perhaps we might leave the final comment to Beckett himself, speaking through Nell in *Endgame*:

NELL: Nothing is funnier than unhappiness, I grant you that. But –

NAGG: [*Shocked.*] Oh!

NELL: Yes, yes, it's the most comic thing in the world. And we laugh, we laugh, with a will, in the beginning. But it's always the same thing. Yes, it's like the funny story we have heard too often, we still find it funny, but we don't laugh any more. (*CDW* 101)[38] □

This reading of *Godot*, and of Beckett's drama in general, was an exciting development in Beckett criticism, in that it provided an alternative to the more familiar humanist readings that were proliferating at the time that Iser wrote this essay. Iser's suggestion that *Godot* confronts us with the idea that all our realities are fashioned in the ongoing process of interpretation was a long way from Esslin's insistence that the play opens out onto the transcendent, permanent and essential reality of being. Similarly, his claim that freedom from 'constraints, repressions and prefabricated solutions' is 'withheld' in Beckett's theatre directly contradicted the then dominant view that it is on the Beckettian stage that precisely such freedom is given to Vladimir and Estragon, and consequently to the audience. Even the argument that humour in Beckett's theatre does not necessarily provide an antidote to the existential misery that it dramatises met with some resistance in the mainstream of Beckett criticism. In offering such counter arguments to the powerful orthodoxy that gripped the reception of Beckett's drama in the late seventies, Iser's contribution was extremely valuable. His reading of *Waiting for Godot* opened up Beckett's drama to interpretative possibilities which had been sidelined within the English-speaking critical community, and his prominence as a theorist in fields other than Beckett studies ensured that his challenging work on Beckett reached a wide and varied audience.

Whilst Iser's work offered such a welcome variation upon a dominant critical theme, however, his reader response approach to Beckett's drama is not as radical or as far-reaching as it promises to be. Indeed, he shares many assumptions with the humanist critics to which his work is, in some senses, so opposed. His focus on reception as the point at which the artwork comes into being would seem to offer Iser the opportunity to free writing to some extent from ideological prescription – if the content of the work is formed by its interaction with an infinite number of unknowable future readings, then texts can never be controlled or stabilised in advance, but are open to ever new and challenging manifestations. But it is just this uncontrollable proliferation of meaning in the text that Iser's reading tends to resist. His emphasis on 'experience' as a stable category that underlies interpretation, and his structuralist faith in his ability as a critic to 'lay bare the mechanics' of interpretation – to provide a 'schematised description of the interpretative activities' occurring in 'the spectator's mind' – seems curiously to contradict the spirit of a mode of enquiry that gives the reader free reign. By suggesting that the reader is the agent who supplies the text with its meaning, whilst also insisting that the critic can draw a diagram of exactly what kind of meaning 'the reader' will produce, Iser seems to be granting freedom, independence and the possibility of textual difference with one hand only to withdraw it with the other. The work is released from the tyrannical control of author or text, only to be placed under the jurisdiction of an ideal and idealised 'reader' or 'spectator', whose 'experience' of the play is just as readable as the most transparent of texts.

To this extent, Iser's work on Beckett could be regarded as marking a transitional moment, between the orthodox humanism with which it was contemporary, and a more adventurous theoretical approach for which it partly paved the way. As we have seen, the reception theory that he brought to Beckett served to loosen the critical consensus that had held the drama so tightly, and to question some of the fundamental assumptions upon which Beckett's reception was based, but Iser's own humanist tendencies prevented him from pushing the consequences of his reading to their conclusions. It was not until the late eighties that a new burst of theoretical activity gave Iser's earlier theoretical inquiries new momentum, and presented the humanist school of Beckett criticism with its first significant challenge.

3. Beckett, Post-structuralism and Feminism

At around the time that Derrida was telling Derek Attridge that Beckett was beyond his reach as a theorist, a group of critics were publishing new work that, for the first time, sought to develop a theoretical language capable of articulating the deconstructive tendency of Beckett's writing. Writers such as Steven Connor, Mary Bryden, Leslie Hill, Paul Lawley and Carla Locatelli began to produce criticism that amounted to a radically new way of thinking about Beckett.[39] Where Iser's critique maintained a belief in the capacity both of art and of criticism to reconstruct and communicate a common human experience, the theoretical approaches emerging in the late eighties suggested that Beckett's work posed a radical challenge to the very possibility that language could communicate any experience authentically. Rather than offering a stark, whittled down but honest representation of essential human truths, Beckett's experiments in fiction and drama were seen by these critics to be orchestrated around a dramatisation of the failure of words to communicate presence. His prose and stage geographies do not stave off or even persist within the existential void, but rather slide into the gaps left in language between presence and representation, original and copy. As such, the value of his writing lies not in what it reveals about the human condition, but in the operations it performs on language itself – its skill in uncovering and exploring the limits of representation, where words fold in on themselves.

Two of the major contributors to this new wave of criticism were Steven Connor and Mary Bryden. Connor's monograph, *Samuel Beckett: Repetition, Theory and Text*, which offers an analysis of the textual effects of repetition as they are played out throughout the oeuvre, and Bryden's *Women in Samuel Beckett's Prose and Drama*, which suggests that Beckett's writing, particularly his later drama, deconstructs gender positions in radical and progressive ways, proved extremely influential in setting a new agenda for Beckett criticism. The impact of this new criticism on the reception of *Waiting for Godot* and *Endgame* is suggested in the collection of essays, entitled '*Waiting for Godot*' and '*Endgame*', which was edited by Steven Connor in 1992. This collection of essays can be compared in its influence to that edited by Martin Esslin in 1965, in that it set the tone for a whole body of criticism that followed it. Whilst it republishes some work that is representative of 'traditional' Beckett criticism, the collection introduces a range of theoretical approaches to the plays, from deconstruction to feminism and psychoanalysis, which demonstrate just how elastic and open to interpretation they are. It is this collection, amongst other work that was appearing around the same time, that breathed a new life into Beckett criticism that can still be felt today.

Steven Connor's essay printed in the collection, taken from *Samuel Beckett: Repetition, Theory and Text*, analyses the effect of repetition on the space of Beckett's stage. In this essay, Connor skilfully reads the various repetitive devices that are set up in *Waiting for Godot* and *Endgame*, focusing on the ways in which repetition undermines the certainty of presence on the stage. In the introduction to the essay, Connor explicitly contrasts his deconstructive approach with the emphasis of earlier critics, such as Robbe-Grillet and Michael Robinson, on the physical tangibility of the stage space. He addresses two of the thematic concerns that have been prominent in Beckett criticism from its beginning – presence on the stage and self-reflexivity – in order to suggest new ways of thinking these concerns through. Reading Beckett against theorists such as Robbe-Grillet and Antonin Artaud, Connor claims that Beckett's stage is a place where presence is worn away, eroded by the repetition that is inherent in all acts of representation. The self-reflexivity that is characteristic of Beckett's drama does not function as a guarantor of self-present identity, as it does for critics such as Ruby Cohn and Sidney Homan, but is one of the repetitive devices that most effectively undermines the capacity of the stage to represent the human tendency to 'be there'.

■ Beckett's turn to the theatre has often been represented as the expression of a longing for an art of visibility and tangibility as a relief from the epistemological disintegrations of the Trilogy which Beckett described in his interview with Israel Schenker in 1956 – 'no "I", no "have", no "being", no nominative, no accusative, no verb. There's no way to go on.'[40] Michael Robinson, for example, sees the theatre as 'the only direction in which a development was possible', since the theatre 'promises a firmer reality than a subjective monologue written and read in isolation; perhaps on stage the reality behind the words may be revealed by the action which often contradicts that literal meaning'.[41] Beckett himself has testified to the sense of relief that he gets from working in drama: 'For me, theatre is first of all a relaxation from the labour of the novel. You are working with a certain space and with people in this space.'[42]

Perhaps the most emphatic statement of this view of Beckett's turn to the theatre is that offered by Alain Robbe-Grillet. Writing early in Beckett's dramatic career, he stressed the sense of sheer *presence* which is given by Vladimir and Estragon, deprived as they apparently are of all the conventional dramatic supports of script, plot or properties. We see them, he says, 'alone on stage, standing up, futile, with no future or past, irremediably present'.[43] For Robbe-Grillet, Beckett's theatre embodies the Heideggerrian apprehension of *Dasein*, of primordial being-there: 'The human condition, Heidegger says, is *to be there*. Probably it is the theatre, more than any other mode of representing reality, which reproduces this situation most naturally. The dramatic character is on stage, that is his primary quality: he is *there*' (*P* 119). As Bruce Morrissette observes, Robbe-Grillet also finds in *Waiting for Godot* an assertion of Sartrean freedom *en situation*. The very absence of programme or a priori principles is what guarantees this freedom. Vladimir and Estragon have nothing to repeat; everything is happening for the first and last time: 'They are *there*; they must explain themselves. But they do not seem to have a text prepared beforehand and scrupulously learned by heart, to support them. They must invent. They are free' (*P* 126).[44]

Other writers have elaborated or modified this theme by stressing the self-reflexiveness of the plays which, instead of undermining the audience's sense of presence, seems to intensify it, by focusing attention on the actual forms of the performance.[45] William Worthen argues that Beckett 'literalises' the plight of his characters in the visibly straitened conditions in which his actors are required to work, so that a piece like *Play* 'dramatises the essential dynamics of stage performance'.[46] Sidney Homan argues in a similar way for self-reflection as a guarantee of presence. The plays turn in on themselves, he argues, to join playwright, play and audience in a mutually mirroring autonomy. The plays therefore no longer require reference to a pre-existing world, or the addition of any commentary to elucidate meanings which are hidden or allegorically elsewhere; the plays are simply what they are, in an elementary performing present, without before or after, the action 'complete, pure, itself – and immediately experienced by the audience'.[47] Beckett's occasional remarks about his plays have encouraged this view of their 'extreme simplicity of dramatic situation',[48] and his intense jurisdiction over his plays embodies this sense of their almost physical simplicity of form. In his direction, Beckett is concerned not so much to control the meaning of interpretation of his plays as to control this physical form, in the details of light, sound, décor and pacing.

In many ways, this view of Beckett's turn to the theatre reproduces conventional views about the theatre itself and its relation to other arts. It is conventional, for instance, to oppose the living art of the theatre to the dead or abstract experience of private reading. If we merely imagine characters and events in written texts, it is often said, then in the theatre, and in other visual media, we 'actually see' those characters and events, 'actually hear' their voices. Of course, the dramatic text usually exists in a written as well as in a physical form, but this double existence often focuses claims about the drama's difference from other arts. Whilst it is usual to see the dramatic performance as subsidiary or secondary to the written text – in that it must be 'faithful' to it, must repeat it accurately and efficiently – it is also quite common to find the hierarchy reversed with the performance of the play claimed as its real or primary condition. Here, it is the written text which is considered to be empty or incomplete, while the essence of the play is embodied in that perfect production which fuses text and performance, idea and utterance. This need not be imagined as a single or particular performance: in one of the subtlest formulations of this principle, Hans-Georg Gadamer suggests that the essential nature of a play is developed in its slow organic evolution through different forms. In Gadamer's formulation, the model of the text as absolute origin and the performance as variable and imperfect repetition is abandoned, for now reproducibility guarantees the permanence of the being of the play through multiple embodiments.[49]

Another influential formulation of the belief in the priority of the performed play is that of Antonin Artaud. What makes Artaud's writings particularly useful for examining Beckett's work and the critical constitution of it is not only the widely diffused influence of Artaud's ideas, but his particular stress upon and opposition to repetition as a model for theatre. Throughout his essays of the 1930s, Artaud argues for a non-repetitive theatre, one no longer slavishly obedient to the written texts which precede and control it. The Theatre of Cruelty projected by Artaud escapes the tyranny of the verbal altogether, and speaks its own, intrinsically theatrical language of mime, gesture, dance, music, light, space and scene. Throughout the essays in *The Theatre and its Double*, Artaud insists on the physicality of the theatre, maintaining that 'the stage is a tangible, physical place that needs to be filled and ought to be allowed to speak its own concrete language'.[50] Once the drama rediscovers its own language, Artaud argues, 'we can repudiate theatre's superstition concerning the script and the author's autocracy. In this way also we will link up with popular, primal theatre sensed and experienced directly by the mind, without language's distortions and the pitfalls in speech and words' (*TD* 82–83). This escape from the script is an escape from the compulsion to repeat. The spectator of the drama will no longer be forced to try to read the performance back into its original script, since what he or she beholds will be both performance and text. Closing the gap between text and performance will also eradicate the hiatus between meaning and interpretation for the spectator: 'This involved gesticulation we see has a goal, an immediate goal, towards which it aims by effective means, and we are able to experience its direct effectiveness. The thought it aims at, the states of mind it attempts to create, the mystical discoveries it offers are motivated and reached without delay or periphrasis' (*TD* 42).

Of course, there is much in Artaud's formulation that is very unlike Beckett's theatre. Where the self-sufficiency of means in Beckett's work is a function of restriction and indigence, the self-proclaiming autonomy of Artaud's Theatre of Cruelty is an enactment of its 'blind zest for life'. Nevertheless, there are times when Artaud's arguments suggest very strongly the features of Beckett's theatre – or those features which criticism of Beckett has found most congenial: 'We might say the subjects presented begin on stage. They have reached such a point of objective materialisation we could not imagine them, however much one might try, outside this compact panorama, the enclosed, confined world of the stage' (*TD* 43).

If, in one sense, Beckett's theatre is aptly described as a theatre of presence, or, in Artaud's terms, a theatre freed from repetition, then there are also important ways in which his work seems to undermine not only the particular claims of individual critics, but the more general cultural claims upon which they often rest and from which they derive their authority. It is no accident that Beckett's international fame came first of all as a playwright and not as a novelist, for it has been the prevailing critical and cultural consensus about the theatre and its strengths and capacities that has allowed his work to be absorbed and rewritten as a humanist theatre of presence, a theatre which directly and powerfully embodies real and universal predicaments. In various ways, and particularly in the intricate play of its different repetitions, Beckett's theatre makes this critical representation seem inadequate, and asks questions of common conceptions about the theatre as a whole.[51] □

In the second and last section of the essay, entitled 'The Doubling of Presence', Connor goes on to a close reading of *Waiting for Godot* and *Endgame*, which elegantly traces the impact of this doubling on the plays themselves.

■ One can understand why Robbe-Grillet should have found his views about the theatre so amply demonstrated in *Waiting for Godot*. It is undeniable that the restriction of the play's plot, setting and dialogue focus attention on the sheer fact of being on stage in a way that had never before been experienced so unrelievedly in the theatre. But what Robbe-Grillet doesn't explore are the implications of the fact that, as Vivian Mercier puts it, this is a play in which nothing happens, *twice*, in which Vladimir and Estragon undergo the ordeal of their sheer presence on the stage, *twice*.[52] It is a repetition that makes all the difference, for it demonstrates to us that the sense of absolute presence is itself dependent upon memory and anticipation. We may see Vladimir and Estragon with our own eyes, and see them nowhere else but on the stage which is their only home, but this seeing has to contend with the knowledge that they have actually left the stage, have been or imagine themselves to have been elsewhere. At the beginning of Act II, we only recognise their being-back-again, or even their still-being-there, because of our awareness of the break that has taken place between the acts. Indeed the appearance and meeting is established for us at the beginning of both acts as a repetition: – 'Is that you again?', 'You again' (*CDW* 10, 53). This, combined with the fact that Vladimir and Estragon do not leave the stage at the end of each act, but seem mysteriously to have left it at some point between Acts I and II, makes their continuing 'presence' on the stage something other than simple or unbroken.

To reappear, to be on stage again, is in itself to allow the shadow of absence or non-being to fall across the fullness and simplicity of *Dasein*. It opens up the dual anxiety of living in time, an anxiety expressing itself in the two questions 'am I the same as I was yesterday' and 'will I be the same as I am today?' When Vladimir and Estragon meet, they have painfully to reconstruct the events of the previous day. As an audience we are in the same position as Vladimir and Estragon, certain or almost certain of what we can remember about the events of the previous act, though we cannot be certain that this is indeed the previous 'day' that Vladimir refers to. To reconstitute the day in memory and representation is to open up that gap between the original and its repetition which can never entirely be closed, either for the characters or for their audience; we can never be sure again of the simple factuality of the day and of its events. What is more, the present moment will come to seem more and more dependent on re-capitulation in the future. So, when Vladimir sees the boy for the second time, he is concerned to make sure that he will indeed tell Godot that he has seen them. Despite the uncertainties of memory and recapitulation, it is not enough simply for Vladimir to be there: he must confirm this simple present tense by reference to an anticipated retrospect.

Once repetition has been set up in the play, it proves to be congenital. Once the second act is revealed to be a repetition or near-repetition of the first, then the first itself loses its self-sufficient repletion. If the second act encounter with the boy sends us back to the similar encounter in the first act, then we may remember that this has already struck Vladimir as a repetition:

VLADIMIR: I've seen you before, haven't I?

BOY: I don't know, sir.

VLADIMIR: You don't know me?

BOY: No, sir.

VLADIMIR: It wasn't you came yesterday?

BOY: No, sir.

VLADIMIR: This is your first time?

BOY: Yes, sir.

[*Silence.*] (*CDW* 49)

In a similar way, every presence in *Waiting for Godot* seems likely to turn out to be a ghostly repetition, or even an anticipation. (In the curious *déjà vu* structure of *Waiting for Godot*, it might even be possible to read the boy in the first act as a repetition-in-advance of the boy who appears at the end.) Stranded as they are in their agonising space of waiting, Vladimir and Estragon seem to encounter the paradox of all time; that is, that the only tense we feel has real verifiable existence, the present, the here-and-now, is in fact never here-and-now. The present tense can never simply 'be', because the 'now' of the present tense can only be apprehended the split-second before it happens, or the split-second after. It is never itself, but always the representation of itself, anticipated or remembered, which is to say, non-present. Vladimir and Estragon, stranded in the not-yet or intermission of waiting, poised between the past they no longer inhabit and the future which cannot commence until the arrival of Godot, can never *be* fully in their present either. The longer they spend on the stage, the more, for them and for the audience, the simple immediacy of the present becomes drawn into the complex web of relationship and repetition that is all experience of time.

In fact, there seem to be two main versions of the repetitive enacted in *Waiting for Godot*. The first is circular, and suggests the impossibility of any stable present because past and future are ranged about it so ambiguously. The model for this kind of repetition is provided by the circular song which Vladimir sings at the beginning of Act II. In this, priority and progression seem to be disallowed, since every element in the song is both before and after every other element. The other model of repetition is linear. Some of the repetitions in *Waiting for Godot* seem to indicate not endless reduplication, but entropic decline. Chief among these is the reappearance of Pozzo in Act II, blind and without his watch, with a servant who is now unable to think because he is dumb. In later plays, Beckett insists more and more on this kind of repetition-with-decrease, to give us, for example, the gradual burying of Winnie in the earth, the slowing down of the speakers in *Play*, the weakening of the auditor's gestures in *Not I* and the enfeebling of the woman's voice in *Rockaby*.

All these suggest repetitive series rather than repetitive circles. It is hard to say whether this kind of repetition is more or less corrosive of the audience's sense of presence. It would seem to be true that the idea of a repetitive series at least retains the direction of time, and therefore stabilises the repetition, for in a repetitive series it is possible to distinguish and rank different stages of decline, and consequently possible to mark the passage of time by them. This kind of repetitive series also seems to promise an end point which circular repetition does not.

But even in repetitive series there is a decentring effect which makes the sense of immediate presence difficult to sustain. For how do we begin to consider the two 'halves' of a Beckett da capo play? As with all such repetitions the first time through will strike us as new, and primary, and the second is likely to seem a derivation from the first, its ghost, or shadow. But the ubiquity of repetition and the insistence of series in Beckett's work prevents us from seeing the first time through as necessarily primary, or the second time through as terminal. Both are equally repetitions, and we are therefore deprived of the sense of priority or finality; each is doubled on the inside, as it were, by what it repeats, and what will repeat it. This is surely the reason why Beckett's repetitive structures rarely go into a third phase (though the trilogy might seem to be an important exception). To pass into a third phase is to risk suggesting transcendence, or committing oneself at least to the triangular shape of transcendence as it has been conceived in many philosophical models; it is to rank the previous two possibilities as opposites and perhaps to suggest their dialectic subsuming or resolution in the third repetition. Here, repetition is the sign of redemption, the guarantee of memory and destiny. It might also be to remind one, in a less exalted way, of the superstitious values attached to the third repetition in myth and fairy tale, which always marks the moment of return, or the resolution into pattern of endless open process. The fixity conventionally established by the triad is most plainly stated by Lewis Carroll's Bellman, in *The Hunting of the Snark*, when he declares 'what I tell you three times is true'.[53] Beckett's theatre, on the other hand, leaves repetitive possibilities to extend arbitrarily and uncontrollably into the future beyond the play – and therefore in a sense to infiltrate the performance too.

One exception to this prevailing double-structure might seem to be *Endgame* – and this is also the most uncompromising representation in Beckett's work of repetition allied to entropic running down. Certainly, Hamm and Clov may be on the point of leaving at the end. But it might still be argued that withholding the repetition of the day from the audience has the effect of highlighting the self-sufficiency, the unique presence of this particular passage of time in a way that distinguishes it from other plays. We know that these players will return to the stage night after night – but, in the theatre, we see them once and for all.

Another way of putting this might be to say that *Endgame* impresses us with its unity. It is a unity that is foregrounded by repetitive devices. Beckett said of the play that it 'is full of echoes, everything answers itself',[54] and there does indeed seem to be a thickening of internal repetition in the play. The various parallels in the action, Clov watching Hamm at the beginning and the end of the play, Hamm taking off and putting on his old handkerchief, and the verbal echoes in Hamm's first and last soliloquies, as well as the repetition of words and phrases shared by Hamm and Clov, all seem to give a sense of closure, completeness and self-identity to *Endgame*.

But against all this are the various factors which resist this apprehension of unity. Near the beginning of the play, Hamm asks Clov 'What's happening, what's happening?', only to receive the reply 'Something is taking its course' (*CDW* 98). These words suggest the non-identity of experience and meaning. If all that is happening is precisely what we see, consists simply in the two characters being there, then, for Hamm and Clov, this being there is agonisingly insufficient. For Hamm especially, meaning or significance cannot inhere in experience, but must be imposed from the outside, as the supervention of an imagined outsider, a 'rational being' who, as he surmises, might happen to visit them and 'get ideas into his head' (*CDW* 108). Because of this dependence on meanings ascribed from the outside, the endless process of Hamm's and Clov's lives never comes of itself to any point of significance or understanding; the best that can be managed is the asymptomatic approach to meaning or identity which is imaged in the allusions to the millet heap of the philosopher Sextus Empiricus. Clov looks forward to the coming of being as one looks for the moment when a succession of millet grains added to one another can suddenly be recognised as a heap: 'Grain upon grain, one by one, and one day, suddenly, there's a heap, a little heap, the impossible heap' (*CDW* 93). When the metaphor recurs in Hamm's words, it seems clear that the moment when the grain becomes a heap will recede infinitely: 'Moment upon moment, pattering down, like the millet grains of . . . [*he hesitates*] . . . that old Greek, and all life long you wait for that to mount up to a life' (*CDW* 126). In this hell, as in Sartre's *Huis Clos*, it proves impossible to imagine a life brought to completeness. When death comes it will not confer a meaning, but will simply, arbitrarily, bring the process of living to a halt.

So we can see that *Endgame* refuses the consummation of an ending which its form and title suggest. Time and again in Beckett's work, we encounter the anxiety that it will not be possible to come to an end because there will have been no full existence prior to that ending; and for all its powerful theatrical presence, *Endgame* shows us characters who fear that they will never have been enough in the present to vanish. Hamm shares with the characters in the Trilogy, especially with the voice in *The Unnamable*, that repetitive structure of consciousness, in which it is impossible to be fully oneself, because fullness of being is always one step further on, always deferred to the future. Hamm's life, as he says, was always 'the life to come' (*CDW* 116). As Robbe-Grillet recognises, a present contaminated in this way by lack ceases to exist: 'under these conditions, the present becomes nothing, it disappears, it too has been conjured away, and lost in general bankruptcy' (*P* 129).

If Hamm's life is always deferred, then it is also true that it is a life lived in repetition and retrospect. It is as though every unfinished moment requires repetition to bring it to completeness, or significance. So, as we listen to his endless attempt to retrieve the past in his portentous narrative we sense what may happen to the present moment. As in *Waiting for Godot*, the present fades into its reconstitution in future repetition. Indeed, for all the locked closure of this play, there is an insistent self-doubling that takes place at every moment. This, surely, is the effect of all the moments of theatrical self-reflexiveness in the play, Hamm's posturing grandiloquence, mimicked by Nagg's story, Clov's sarcasm at the audience's expense and the references to 'playing' of all kinds, from Hamm's opening words to the explicit references to asides, exits and soliloquies. All these features induce consciousness not of the stage as simply itself, but of the stage as a space of representation – even if it is the minimal representation of itself. No matter what is stripped away of character, plot and setting on the stage, there always persists, within the most reduced performance, a residual self-doubling – the stage presenting itself *as* stage, *as* performance. If we see *Endgame* initially as a play which acts out the coming to an end of one kind of repetitive series, then in another clear sense it is a play which demonstrates the necessary and inescapable continuation of repetition. This necessity is described well by Jacques Derrida in his critique of Artaud's prescriptions for the Theatre of Cruelty:

There is no theatre in the world today which fulfils Artaud's desire. And there would be no exception to be made for the attempts made by Artaud himself. He knew this better than any other: the 'grammar' of the theatre of cruelty, of which he said that it is 'to be found', will always remain the inaccessible limit of a representation which is not repetition, of a *re*-presentation which is full of presence, which does not carry its double within itself as its death, of a present which does not repeat itself, that is, of a present outside time, a non-present. The present offers itself as such, appears, presents itself, opens the stage of time or the time of the stage only by harbouring its own intestine difference, and only in the interior fold of its original repetition, in representation.[55]

The moment of pure theatre which Beckett seems to show us, Hamm declaiming as an actor in the dying moments of the play, with no pretence that he is anything else, is in reality not the limit of full self-identity. The actor who plays the part of Hamm cannot – by definition – be the same actor whose part Hamm represents himself as playing. There is certainly close resemblance between the two, but if we recognise the collusion between the actor who speaks the words of the text and the character who repeats the words of his oft-rehearsed story, then that is because we also recognise the sustaining difference between them. In other words, we recognise the resemblance as one of repetition rather than identity. And the closer the performance comes to an identity with its text, the more Derrida's obstinate 'interior fold of its original repetition' reasserts itself.

There is another way of thinking about this. For the theatre to be theatre, it must be observed, must be staged in a particular place for a particular audience. Traditionally, the playwright and actor have depended upon, and sometimes regretted, this necessity. Billie Whitelaw has recently said that Beckett himself thinks of his plays as ideally a drama without an audience. But, though it is certainly possible to imagine a performance without an audience, it is doubtful whether such a thing could count for anyone as a performance unless the element of spectacle were retained. This residual doubling asserts itself at the moment of Hamm's withdrawal from the theatre at the end of the play. After he has discarded all his petty theatrical paraphernalia, he is left merely with words and, when they cease, with darkness and silence. His final words seem to show him embracing this final retreat. His story has concerned his rebuff to the man he has hired (Clov?), whose son he would not permit to live with them. But if Clov is a kind of son to Hamm, then the closure of possibility in Hamm's story is contradicted by Clov's continuing presence on the stage. Hamm's words may seem like an embracing of solitude, but they show in their hesitations and gaps the awareness of a potential audience – for example in the phrase 'there we are, there I am, that's enough', in which the second phrase sounds like a retraction or correction of the first. However, the first person plural recurs a little later when, having whistled and sniffed to see if Clov is still alive and then having cautiously called his name, he settles back, saying 'Good . . . Since that's the way we're playing it . . . let's play it that way . . . and speak no more about it' (*CDW* 133). The conventional 'we' here includes the possibility that Clov may still be there, as indeed he is, and may help to confirm the audience's suspicion that this little scene has been played out between them before. The last lines of the play have Hamm withdrawing into solitude, after he has pierced the barrier between audience and spectacle with the whistle that he throws into the auditorium. But Hamm's solitude remains an enacted solitude, enacted for us and the still-visible Clov. Hamm has discarded all but his 'old stancher', and closes his soliloquy with an affectionate address to it – 'You . . . remain' (*CDW* 134). The irresistible effect of his words is to suggest the presence of the audience who do indeed remain, for the time being anyway, watching him. Hamm's words seem to acknowledge the necessity of the Other, even as he repudiates it. Only as long as they 'remain' to watch can he 'remain' in enacted solitude.[56] □

Connor's influential reading of Beckett's drama as staging the ongoing dialogue between self and other, in which characters whose identities are under threat of erasure or duplication are compelled constantly to represent themselves in order to make themselves present, paved the way for several other related approaches to the plays. Amongst the most notable of these was the emergence of a number of feminist critiques which emerged in the late eighties and early nineties. Up to this point, Beckett's work had not encouraged a great deal of feminist criticism. His writing appeared either to express a violent loathing for women, or to dismiss women altogether, and this perceived misogyny, coupled with a critical insistence upon the 'universalism' of Beckett's vision, led to a sense that Beckett's putative representation of 'everyman' was a deeply phallocentric one which excluded or oppressed a female voice. With the increase in theoretical activity in the eighties, however, this reading of Beckett's work as representing a monological image of male-as-species began to be questioned. If Beckett, far from offering a static picture of an ahistorical mankind, was dramatising identity in process, then it seemed possible that his treatment of gender may be more critical than had previously been recognised. Work by post-structuralist feminists such as Mary Bryden and Linda Ben Zvi sought to theorise Beckett's writing in terms of its identity politics and its gender politics.[57] Bryden's essay, 'Gender in Transition: *Waiting for Godot* and *Endgame*' is an example of this emerging criticism. In it, she argues that *Waiting for Godot* and *Endgame* are transitional works in Beckett's oeuvre (in one of the two senses of 'transition' referred to in the title). In the early fiction, and the prose up to *First Love*, Beckett's women are objectified, vilified, 'grounded in alterity', but with the turn to the stage and the writing of *Godot*, Beckett's work undergoes an epiphanal transformation. Gender ceases to be a prescribed cultural norm in Beckett's writing and is placed (in the second sense of the title) in a state of transition. As Beckett's work progresses to the stage in which 'the very notion of a stable selfhood is destabilised',[58] both men and women are seen in the process of forging their own subject positions. As a result, women are freed from the 'essentialist straitjacket which might seek to preserve gender hierarchies'[59] into the free play between self and other in which all subjects come into being. In this environment, to regard Beckett's treatment of gender as a straightforward reflection of ideological prescriptions of gender identity would be to be guilty of a positivist, dogmatic Marxism. It is in the space of Beckett's stage that subject positions are put into play, rather than fixed in cultural cement.

In the section of the essay below, Bryden focuses on a reading of *Endgame*. Claiming that subject positions in the play are not gender-specific, she goes on, via a comparison of Beckett's Nell with the Dickensian Nell of *The Old Curiosity Shop*, to suggest that it is in *Waiting for Godot* and *Endgame* that Beckett dramatises the 'dissolution of genderised apartheid'.

■ The majority of figures in Beckett's stage and media plays are of discernible gender (though the exceptions, such as the scurrying figures of *Quad* or the djellaba-clad Auditor of *Not I*, should not be overlooked). However, what distinguished the stage women from a great many of those inscribed in Beckett's early fiction is that their gender is relieved of any weight of biologistic essentialism. In other words, though often superficially conventional – witness Nell's lacy cap in *Endgame*, Winnie's lipstick in *Happy Days* – these women are subject to the same suffering, the same incomprehension, the same recurrent unease with their life-occupancy as the males. Both males and females feel the same degeneracy in their bodies which, while degenerate, still play host to a mind painfully aware of its own entrapment. The route is full of setbacks for all, and women struggle with or without men in a hostile environment in which comradeship is sometimes a boon, sometimes a curse.

Nell and Nagg, the bin-bound parents of Hamm in *Endgame*, do seem to demonstrate a solidarity which transcends the metal barriers between them. Moreover, when Nell falls lengthily silent, Nagg is reported by Clov to be silently crying in his can, still clinging to life, like the male bird in *Rough for Theatre II*, who perseveres in singing even when his mate is lying dead in the cage.

Indeed, Nell in *Endgame* is last to speak and first to fall silent. Nevertheless, hers is not a minor part. She shares with Hamm, Clov and Nagg the painful tension between the need for human contact and the consciousness of the inescapable solitude of the individual. When Nell, in her first words, enquires: 'What is it, my pet? [*Pause.*] Time for love?' (*CDW* 99), the only human intercourse available is verbal. Nell and Nagg can no longer touch each other, and can see each other 'hardly' (*CDW* 99). Moreover, even to converse requires that they unseal their bins and expose themselves to a chill air which renders them respectively 'perished' and 'freezing' (*CDW* 100).

What, then, might at first be imagined to be a communion of co-sufferers and even co-comforters in this skull-space turns out in fact to be merely four people oppressed by forces largely beyond their control, and unable to provide salvation for either themselves or others. *Endgame* is not a play about giving comfort, on the part of either males or females, and Beckett saw no need to apologise for the fact. With reference to those who proposed elucidatory readings for these frayed elements, Beckett remarked: 'If people want to have headaches among the overtones, let them. And provide their own aspirin.'

Indeed, for all its heavy pessimism, *Endgame* is not a play which encourages uniform readings. Completely absent from the play is what Claude Lefort refers to as the pervasive 'invisible ideology' which envelops people with an insulating cocoon and which provides (often by means of mass media) 'the constant illusion of a *between-us*, an *entre-nous*'.[60] Thus, by attunement to a common stimulus, whether it be background music, group therapy, radio or television, each person may gain access to 'a hallucination of *nearness* which abolishes a sense of distance, strangeness, imperceptibility, the signs of the outside, of adversity, of otherness'. No such mutual analgesia is available to the *Endgame* players – not even the aspirin which Beckett recommends to the critical constituencies, for there's 'No more pain-killer. You'll never get any more pain-killer' (*CDW* 127). Nell, though gentle, elegiac and seemingly devoid of acrimony, is nevertheless clearsightedly candid about the weariness ensuing from being the continual butt of unhappiness: 'Nothing is funnier than unhappiness, I grant you that . . . And we laugh, we laugh, with a will, in the beginning. But it's always the same thing' (*CDW* 101).

As in *Godot*, recognition of shared adversity, even brave amusement in the face of it, fail to provide a permanent remedy, and both camaraderie and interpersonal conflict can only alternate with that interior angst whose root is deeply personal. It is to deal with this latter turmoil that each character in *Endgame* – and Nell is no exception – clings to remote imaginative spaces or time-spans. While Hamm dreams of running into the woods, Clov of 'a world where all would be silent and still' (*CDW* 120), and Nagg of the day when Hamm will call out to him in need as he did when a small boy, Nell is lost in contemplation of: 'ah yesterday!' (*CDW* 99, 101). While lodged upon a dirty layer of sand, she nevertheless dreams of clear, bright desert sand. Indeed, her last audible word, before being rammed back by

Clov into the darkness of her ashcan is 'Desert!' (*CDW* 103).

In this, Nell can be compared to another Nell, that of Dickens's *The Old Curiosity Shop*,[61] who, fallen upon misfortune, sits 'still and motionless' in the 'cold and gloomy' chamber (*TOCS* 68), but who, rousing to reverie, recalls happier times with her grandfather and envisions a scene akin to that of her Beckettian namesake: 'Sun, and stream, and meadow, and summer days, shone brightly in her view, and there was no dark tint in all the sparkling picture' (*TOCS* 93). Both Nells embark on long journeys in which they damage their legs: Nell in *Endgame* remembers how she and Nagg travelled one behind the other and met with misfortune 'When we crashed on our tandem and lost our shanks' (*CDW* 100), whereas Little Nell's grandfather relates how, with her bare feet cut and bruised by stones, she 'walked behind me . . . that I might not see how lame she was' (*TOCS* 520).

As we have seen, the last we hear of *Endgame*'s Nell is when she is pushed firmly down into her bin. Its lid is then replaced, and Hamm enquires of Clov: 'Have you bottled her?' Receiving an affirmative reply, he recommends: 'Screw down the lids' (*CDW* 103). Dickens' Nell comes to a similar end. Taken to the dark church crypt by the sexton, she terms it: 'A black and dreadful place!' (*TOCS* 402), and is invited to peer into a vault, its lid uplifted. Later, after her death, her body is removed to that same vault, which is then 'covered and the stone fixed down' (*TOCS* 529). Doubt attaches in both cases to the moment of death. It is never established definitively that *Endgame*'s Nell is dead: merely that it 'looks like it' (*CDW* 122). Similarly it is stated of Little Nell that: 'They did not know that she was dead, at first' (*TOCS* 525). However, the presences of both appear to linger after the cessation of their voice. The villagers linger in the snow in *The Old Curiosity Shop*, 'coming to the grave in little knots, and glancing down' (*TOCS* 529), and, long after Nell's silencing, Nagg requests two sugar-plums: 'One for me and one for –' (*CDW* 116), the blank denoting his absent wife whose pulse trace has become a straight line. Then, after hearing from Hamm that there are no more sugar-plums, Nagg perseveres in attending upon Nell's bin-lid, knocking on it and calling her name in hope of a response which, if given, is never heard.

The temporary linkage above of Nell and Little Nell is suggested here in tentative fashion as productive of a few interesting parallels. Beckett is known, moreover, to have read Dickens widely, and not only makes (both veiled and explicit) reference to his work in the early unpublished *Dream of Fair to Middling Women*,[62] but also speaks approvingly in the essay *Dante . . . Bruno. Vico . . . Joyce* of his robustly vivid descriptive powers; 'We hear the ooze squelching all through Dickens's description of the Thames in *Great Expectations*'.[63] In this context, it would be inconceivable that Beckett would be unfamiliar with the character of Little Nell. However, as with all such inter-textual resonances in the case of Beckett, it must eventually be laid aside, for, whereas Dickens leaves the reader with the comforting assurance that: 'Of every tear that sorrowing mortals shed on such green graves, some good is born' (*TOCS* 529), the only solace which results from Nagg's tears is a biscuit to suck in seclusion. Moreover, this crypt contains no 'green graves', for, as Hamm surmises: '. . . we're down in a hole. But beyond the hills? Eh? Perhaps it's still green' (*CDW* 111).

Nevertheless, in a sense, Nell's impulse to brightness retains its powerful association, for Hamm, after hearing of Nell's probable death, commands: 'Bring me under the window. I want to feel the light on my face' (*CDW* 123). After all, as Clov later reminds him in connection with the mysterious Mother Pegg who 'was bonny once, like a flower of the field' (*CDW* 112), the inability to procure lamp oil – the means to induce light – can invite more than darkness: 'You know what she died of, Mother Pegg? Of darkness' (*CDW* 129). It seems probable that the retracted Nagg too will soon succumb to the darkness, for, as Hamm callously observes: 'The dead go fast' (*CDW* 125). In this process, once again, gender membership is of no relevance or influence.

In the final analysis the difficulty in finding an equilibrium between human partnership needs and individual imperatives is never resolved in this play. While, as we have seen, each participant has a memory-refuge and/or a rich fantasy life, the merit of this facility – that it insulates self from other in a flight of enjoyable escapism – is counterbalanced by its penalty of sealing the dreamer off from his/her co-locutors. Thus, Nell, deep in her recollections of the 'so white' lake (*CDW* 103), is oblivious to Nagg's laboriously-told story about the tailor, at the conclusion of which he alone '*breaks into a high forced laugh*' (*CDW* 103). Similarly, Clov misunderstands Nell's lyrical outburst: 'Desert!' and, assuming its meaning to be: 'She told me to go away, into the desert' (*CDW* 103), roughly reseals her into the bin from which she never again emerges.

So no concessions or privileges are observable on grounds of gender in this play. Indeed, though observable, gender membership appears to be not only random but also immaterial, and other instances in *Endgame* compound this impression. When Clov gives various details to the blind Hamm about the toy dog the latter wishes to have placed in front of him, the dog's sexual organs are seemingly regarded as a bothersome detail, on a par with the neck-ribbon, to be added as a finishing touch:

HAMM: You've forgotten the sex.

CLOV: But he isn't finished. The sex goes on at the end. (*CDW* 111)

The important function of the dog is, as Hamm instructs, to be left propped on its three legs 'gazing at me' and 'imploring me' (*CDW* 112). Its denoted sexual capacity is thus subsidiary to its inter-relational potential. As such, it merely adds gender indeterminacy to the imagined sexual sterility it shares with Nagg and Nell, no longer able to reach each other to kiss, and with Clov and Hamm. For the latter, memories of sexual activity are now past, the stuff of nothing more than a 'reminiscent leer' in tribute to Mother Pegg, who was 'bonny once. . . . And a great one for the men!' (*CDW* 112). For Clov, moreover, a human touch is now unthinkable, and he repulses decisively Hamm's appeal for an embrace: 'I won't kiss you anywhere . . . I won't touch you' (*CDW* 125). In a barren, post-sexual world, all he can discern is 'between my legs a little trail of black dust' (*CDW* 132).

In such an environment, where physical and psychic insecurity are high, the need to specify and record gender patterns has already receded. At one point, Hamm describes a desperate man who, on Christmas Eve, 'came crawling towards me, on his belly. Pale, wonderfully pale and thin'. The man raises his face, which is 'black with mingled dirt and tears' and begs for 'bread for his brat' (*CDW* 117). In so doing, he identifies the child's gender in a manner which infuriates Hamm, who recalls venomously: 'My little boy, he said, as if the sex mattered' (*CDW* 117).

An echo of this occurs in the original French *Fin de partie*, when, towards the close of the play, Clov reports picking out through his telescope a small, immobile figure outside. In the English version, the figure is said to resemble 'a small boy' (*CDW* 130), his movement pattern is not mentioned, and the topic is speedily abandoned. The exchange is, however, considerably expanded in the French original, where, apropos of this 'quelqu'un' [somebody], Hamm enquires: 'Sexe?' and receives the reply: 'Quelle importance?' ['What does it matter?'].[64] (Clov's reply, interestingly, is identical to that given by Beckett to the question posed by Ahmad Kamyabi Mask, concerning the suggested female/male substitution in *Godot* productions.) After this displayed indifference to gender identification, Clov goes on in the French version to refer to the object of curiosity as 'un môme' [a kid, brat], and the question of gender is suspended (though Clov thereafter styles the apparition 'il' – the masculine pronoun – presumably for convenience). The figure, upon further examination, appears to be sitting on the ground, leaning against an object. The object, intervenes Hamm, is 'la pierre levée' [the raised stone]. By using the definite article 'la', Hamm makes allusion to the rolled-away stone described in Gospel accounts as a sign of the resurrection of Christ. No such life-renewal will occur in *Endgame*'s landscape, however, for Hamm declares that the figure is perhaps dead, and/or will die eventually in any case. Thus this outer being, unable to procreate, is of no further threat or even interest. Its gender is as immaterial as its doubtful existence, which is itself made subject to that dead-line which Hamm chooses to describe in the reported death-words of Christ: 'C'est fini' ['It is finished'].

To sum up, both *Waiting for Godot* and *Endgame* represent a significant moment in the development of gender inscription in Beckett's writing. Behind them, among the wordier surroundings of Beckett's early prose work, lie a multitude of women who are grounded in alterity, in what is viewed by the central male narrator as awkward divergence. Short stories such as *First Love* or those included in the early collection *More Pricks than Kicks* are prime examples of this. Moreover, the later 'woman-plays' . . . lie many years ahead. It is at this early point in Beckett's writing for the theatre – that stage marked by *Waiting for Godot* and *Endgame* – that the objectified female referent begins to fade. Indeed, gender begins to shed any consistency as a predictor of behaviour or attitude. Such static essentialism becomes in fact the first casualty of a radically transformed self-epiphany.

It would be difficult to sustain such an argument on the evidence of *Waiting for Godot* alone. Indeed, as we have seen, the play is often justifiably under pressure from without when projected as a male preserve rather than as a luckless misadventure. Nonetheless, it is *Godot* which presents one of the most startling images of that deterritorialisation which unsettles all stabilities of expectation. Included in those destabilisations is that of gender. Moreover, as *Endgame* proceeds to demonstrate, that dissolution of genderised apartheid is not so much a function of pressure towards integration as an intense recognition of the mutuality (and yet, in the end, the solitude) attendant upon the life-predicament. That predicament is thus to be avoided, for birth reactivates the weary cycle of pain. Yet women are no longer reviled as the prime culprits in the sin of reproduction, as so often in Beckett's early writing. Pozzo in *Waiting for Godot* undoubtedly makes it clear . . . that birth is a regrettable occurrence in which women are the delivery agents. Nevertheless, they – 'Elles' – do not receive the opprobrium directed at them in Beckett's earlier work. Indeed, in *Endgame*, both parents are regarded by their offspring, Hamm, with equal indifference: 'My father? My mother? My . . . dog?' (*CDW* 93). Furthermore it is his father whom he singles out at one point as his 'accursed progenitor' (*CDW* 96).

What is remarkable about both these plays, therefore, is not any supposed rehabilitation of women, but rather their steady erasure of specificity from gender patterning, such that male and female alike, divorced from any notion of privilege, can be seen to struggle as best they may in a tattered world. In such circumstances, Hamm's bitter gibe: 'As if the sex mattered' (*CDW* 117), begins to seem more apposite than perverse. Of course, in thus experimenting with sexual indifference, Beckett runs the risk of attracting accusations of tolerating that phenomenon of female 'invisibility' with which many women are only too familiar. Yet the visible/invisible dichotomy can only remain functional and convincing if the 'other' sex – male – is contrastingly prominent and pre-eminent. As we have seen, if any seen/unseen dialectic exists, it does not render consistent or fruitful data in association with gender distribution by this stage in Beckett's writing. Moreover, the slackening hold on gender determinism which these plays display points forward to a succession of later drama and prose in which gender as a categoriser retreats, along with other organising categories, to cede to the all-encompassing quest of the fragmenting yet persisting self.[65] □

The focus that Bryden brought to bear on Beckett's work as a space in which the gendered subject is constantly fragmenting and reasserting itself was extremely influential. Since Bryden's and Ben Zvi's groundbreaking work, there have been a number of feminist critics who have developed an increasingly nuanced and subtle approach to the construction of gender in Beckett's writing, which has come a long way from the model of Beckett's man as 'all mankind'. Indeed, there has been an extraordinarily rapid growth in the range of theoretical approaches to Beckett since the early work of Steven Connor, Leslie Hill and Mary Bryden. Throughout the nineties, Beckett's writing has adopted an increasingly central position, as a theoretical discourse capable of approaching the oeuvre has become available. With the work of critics such as Peter Gidal, Simon Critchley, Paul Lawley, and the appearance in 1999 of a monograph entitled *Beckett and Poststructuralism* by Anthony Uhlmann, the gap between Beckett and theory has been gradually closing.[66] To some extent, the emergence of this theoretical discourse in Beckett studies has bridged the gulf that opened in the early days of Beckett criticism between the German, Marxist emphasis on Beckett's negativity, and the British, liberal insistence upon his recuperable affirmativeness.[67] The theoretical approaches to Beckett's work under consideration in this chapter have their roots in a recognition of its negativity, and its consequent transgressive, destabilising capacity. In this they maintain some of the potency of Beckett's writing as disruptive challenge that was emphasised by critics such as Adorno, and defused by critics such as Esslin. At the same time, with the adaptation of a critical discourse with which to articulate Beckett's negativity (a discourse, incidentally, which Derrida has been unable to discover), these critics have been able to bring Beckett's writing into mainstream culture in a way that seemed impossible to Adorno. Beckett's work has been given the central place reserved for it by Martin Esslin, without being reconstructed as an affirming endorsement of the cultural *status quo*.

Whilst this theoretical discourse has provided a means of approaching Beckett's aesthetic negativity, however, it has done so at the expense of some of its critical edge. The gap that opened up in the fifties between Esslin and Adorno was a gap between a reading that saw Beckett as supportive of a Western bourgeois ideology, and one that saw him as offering a *critique* of such an ideology. For the latter, part of the value of Beckett's drama lay in its attack on a specific culture. Beckett's plays were seen as a response to the predicament of post-war European culture – his negativity was a mute reflection of such a culture's disintegration. It is partly for this reason that Beckett's writing resists theoretical or philosophical articulation. The negativity that has been preserved in recent theoretical approaches to Beckett, however, tends not to be so politically engaged. Indeed, the deconstructive approach to Beckett's writing tends towards an abstract universalisation of cultural referents that can be almost as politically disabling as the liberalism that it opposed. Bryden's impatience with those dogmatic Marxists who insist on viewing Beckett's representations of gender as ideologically loaded, for example, stems from her conviction that gender is created as textual effect rather than material reality. If we see Beckett's experiments with gender representation as taking place in an ideologically neutral space, in which he is free to make and remake subject positions which have no essential reality anyway, then it is possible to remove his work from an arena in which a representation of a woman imprisoned with a mound of earth will have an immediate political connotation. We can turn our attention from contingent political realities to the dramatist's exploration of the culturally non-specific mechanics of subject formation. Similarly, Connor's readings of Beckett's experiments with dramatic language are geared towards effects that occur in *all* forms of representation. His monograph on Beckett, for example, includes a subtle and revealing exploration of Beckett's treatment of power, but the theoretical model within which he is working makes it difficult for him to think about power as anything other than an abstract and universally applicable textual effect, rather than as a series of specific relations grounded in material life.[68] Connor's reading of Beckett is revealing about the way in which he reflects upon, in Connor's phrase, the 'paradox of all time', but it is not well adapted to exploring Beckett's treatment of a specific time, or a specific place. For both Connor and Bryden, Beckett's work is released into a space in which political and material realities are cleared away to reveal the universal linguistic mechanics that lie behind and before life in the world.

Such a reading of Beckett's work, revolutionary and rehabilitating as it has in many ways been, has done little to question the prevailing assumption, made originally by Beckett's humanist critics, that he is an apolitical writer. His vision appears as inclusive and universal in the hands of Connor and Bryden as it did in the work of Cohn, Kenner and Michael Robinson, and the problem with talking about everywhere and everytime is that it prevents you from making the commitment to a specific material reality that is the basis of political life. Whilst the continued caricature of Beckett as apolitical has seemed to many critics and readers of Beckett to be inadequate, however, it has proved very difficult to find a means of giving critical expression to the ways in which his writing is actively engaged with the political world. Despite this difficulty, since Adorno's reading of *Endgame* there has been a thin but persistent current of writing that has attempted to approach Beckett's politics. It is to this body of criticism that we turn in the final chapter.

CHAPTER FOUR

Political Criticism

IF POST-STRUCTURALIST criticism came late to Beckett, it would be fair to say that overtly political criticism has yet to make a truly significant impact upon English-speaking Beckett studies. Of the large number of questions that have arisen about Beckett's politics, the majority have remained unaddressed and unanswered. Whilst critics such as Mary Bryden have produced welcome work on Beckett's representations of gender (as we saw in the last chapter), the discourse in which their analyses are couched leads them towards a certain depoliticisation of the question of gender in Beckett.[1] We are still waiting for a sustained exploration of the impact of Beckett's misogyny on his writing, or of the significance and status of his deeply nostalgic treatment of maleness. Similarly, there has been very little work on the political effects of Beckett's representation of Protestantism, Catholicism or Jewishness, of class relations, or of race relations, all of which seem to be required. There has been work that has pointed out the interface between Beckett's writing and the political world – Vivian Mercier's very well-known work *Beckett/Beckett*, for example, places Beckett's work accurately and sensitively in a middle-class Irish Protestant context[2] – but such work almost always shies away from any suggestion that Beckett's writing is in any significant measure *engaged* with such contexts. The interpretive model developed in the early sixties, which insists that Beckett's work treats of a universal predicament that underlies the trivialities and contingencies of social being, is so pervasive that socio-political references in Beckett's work tend to be reduced to the level of cultural seasoning or coffee-table-book curiosity.[3] Jean-Jacques Mayoux, writing in 1961, provides an early example of an attitude to Beckett's relation to the geo-political world that has proved extraordinarily enduring. Mayoux is happy to allow Beckett's writing a degree of geographical location – indeed he is enthusiastic about Beckett's ability to 'internalise' his adopted French in order to 'draw from it a new music that is still Irish, or at least Celtic'.[4] The 'tramps' in the plays and novels are 'lashed by the rain and the gales of Beckett's native heaths, and still smell the peat in the heart of sordid cities'.[5] This specific referentiality, however, in no way undermines Beckett's universality – his Irishness is a surface peculiarity that embroiders his dramatisation of a 'condition' that is not remotely influenced by culture or politics. Rather than telling us about contemporary cultural experience, he tells us a 'truth about humanity – a truth not chosen personally but imposed universally'.[6]

Despite the prevalence of decontextualised, universalist readings of Beckett's work, however, there has, since Adorno's 1958 essay on Endgame, been a small but persistent tradition of largely Marxist criticism that has sought to find ways of understanding Beckett's politics. That the mainstream English-speaking Beckett industry has been so little influenced by this critical tradition is due partly to the fact that almost all political readings of Beckett's work from the fifties to the early nineties have been in German. Whereas in French- and English-speaking critical communities Beckett has been received as an apolitical writer, he has been regarded from the beginning in Germany as a writer whose work has political significance. Responses to Beckett's work in Germany have been structured around questions such as whether it is unashamedly decadent or critical of Western bourgeois decadence, whether it is a symptom of a sociopathic withdrawal from social responsibility or an attack on the cultural conditions that lead to such social alienation.[7] For those critics who regarded Beckett's work as being a radical threat to the status quo, rather than a quiescent supporter of it, the challenge has been to find ways of articulating Beckett's work as a dramatisation of political resistance. From Adorno's defence of Beckett against Lukács' accusations of his moral degeneracy, to the work of writers such as Ernst Fischer in the late sixties and early seventies, the aim of Beckett's sympathetic Marxist critics[8] has been to understand and elaborate the means by which Beckett's work reflects upon and critiques dominant ideological conditions. Since the first performances of Warten auf Godot in West Germany in the fifties, and his growing influence in East Germany since the seventies, this broad approach to the ideological status and role of Beckett's art has been accompanied by a second, more concentrated line of argument. Again confined largely to German-language criticism, there has been an ongoing debate about the relation between Beckett's drama, and the more obviously committed work of Bertolt Brecht. Where there was originally a sharp demarcation between Brecht's politically responsible work, and what was regarded in East Germany as Beckett's morally reprehensible apology for Western bourgeois complacency, this division was increasingly brought into question as Beckett's influence in East Germany grew. From the mid-seventies to the present day, there has been a gradual rethinking of Beckett's drama as a Brechtian epic theatre, with an attendant shift in attitude to the political validity and effectiveness of his art. The space of his stage has moved during this time from appearing as a static representation of Western class relations, masquerading as a timeless image of the human condition, to appearing as a self-reflexive, epic theatrical critique of social life. The self-reflexiveness which for critics such as Kenner, Cohn and Homan emphasised the sheer human presence of Beckett's characters on stage, and for deconstructive critics such as Connor contributed to Beckett's exploration of the slippage between being and representation,[9] functioned for his Marxist critics as a Beckettian version of Brecht's alienation effect.[10]

Whilst these two approaches to the political in Beckett's writing have, at least until very recently, taken place in German and in Germany, there is a third area of political criticism that is just starting to gain some momentum in Anglo-American Beckett studies. As a result partly of an increase in the amount of bibliographical material available to locate geographical references in Beckett's writing, and partly of a widespread theoretical trend in the nineties towards a cultural materialism that tempers the universalising tendencies of post-structuralist criticism, there has been a recent upsurge of interest in Beckett's relationship with Ireland. Where it had become conventional to regard Beckett's work as exemplary of the Irish internationalist-modernist rejection of the nationalist literature and theatre envisaged by writers such as W.B. Yeats and Lady Gregory, this new wave of criticism sees Beckett's work as a postcolonial aesthetic. Theorists of Irish post-coloniality such as Declan Kiberd and David Lloyd[11] draw heavily on the insights of post-structuralism in their analysis of Beckett's deconstructive linguistic practices, but, unlike critics such as Connor and Hill, they insist that Beckett's aesthetic is deeply engaged with an Irish landscape, and with the experience of colonial dispossession. His dramatisation of a barren 'no-man's land' in which all forms of cultural identity and belonging are under threat is not so much an exploration of the timeless, placeless dynamics of language and representation, as a kind of mournful resistance to colonial oppression. As Terry Eagleton comments in *Heathcliff and the Great Hunger*, demonstrating the mixture of geographical specificity and non-specificity as protest that is the cornerstone of this kind of criticism, 'the art of Samuel Beckett, with its starved landscapes that are at once Ireland and anywhere, shows well enough how to be stripped of your particular culture is to become a citizen of the world'.[12]

This final chapter will trace these three modes of political criticism – Beckett's 'art against ideology', Beckett's Brechtian dynamics, and Beckett and Ireland – as they develop from the sixties to the present day, using three extracts as examples. The first extract is drawn, appropriately enough, from Ernst Fischer's 1969 work, *Art Against Ideology*. In his essay *'Endgame* and Ivan Denisovich', collected in *Art Against Ideology*, Fischer draws a speculative but sustained comparison between Beckett's avant-garde modernist play, and Solzhenitsyn's realist novel *One Day in the Life of Ivan Denisovich*.[13] The comparison, whilst seeming to be drawn between two very different writers, is valid, Fischer insists, because 'the problems they deal with are the same'.[14] Both Beckett and Solzhenitsyn are responding to forms of cultural unfreedom, with the specific art forms they have at their disposal – Solzhenitsyn the Socialist Realist novel, Beckett the experimental theatre. That which distinguishes the two writers from each other is not that Solzhenitsyn writes committed literature that talks about the 'outside world' whilst Beckett writes a decadent literature that has no relevance to worldly concerns, but that the modes of expression that each adopts compels them to write about the world in particular ways.

■ What distinguishes the one from the other is obvious. It has nothing to do with the view generally held in the East that Beckett is a 'decadent anti-realist', nor with the one prevalent in the West that Solzhenitsyn is a respectable, though not outstanding, representative of Socialist Realism. Beckett is a great artist in complete control of his means of expression. Solzhenitsyn is a writer of considerable stature in search of a new means of expression commensurate with the almost inexpressible things he has to say. The one is able to assume that his readers are familiar with the outside world from which the characters in his play have come; the other is compelled to reproduce the world of the labour camps not by symbolic imagery but with naturalistic precision. The one inherits all the modern experiments of artistic concentration; the other has to overcome a literary legacy of 'epic' diffuseness where nothing may be left unsaid.[15] □

For Fischer, both Beckett's Clov and Solzhentisyn's Ivan Denisovich are struggling to free themselves from the rule of a tyrannical master (Hamm, Stalin), and both works are structured around the prospect that the oppressed slave will be liberated. The tendency of the literature, and the tendency of Fischer's comparison, is towards a time and a place in which Clov and Ivan can meet, freed from the tyrannical forces that oppress them, freed from the critical prejudices that prevent us from recognising that they have a shared goal.

    In the extract that follows (which forms the introduction to the main essay), Fischer sketches out a Hegelian Marxist approach to the play's master–slave narrative, which focuses on the economic basis of the power relation between Hamm and Clov. Hamm and Clov do not occupy for Fischer an other-worldly place in which the relations between them are governed by abstract rules, but rather live in a worldly place whose rules are dictated by economic relations of production. It is in Hamm's interests as master and exploiter to represent these relations as universal, unchanging, meaningless, but it is just this deception against which Clov struggles. That which is 'taking its course' in *Endgame* is Clov's painful progression towards political consciousness, in which the ideological basis of Hamm's vision of the world will become clear. Hamm has been able to subject Clov, and to carry out his atrocities, because he insists that the *status quo* that has given him power is inevitable, and in its grand senselessness requires no reference to a higher epistemological, ethical or moral source for its validation. The play dramatises Clov's search for a clearer political vision that will allow him to judge Hamm independently from the latter's 'false and falsifying consciousness', and to bring him to account.

■ Master and Servant

Hamm, a wreck of a man, sits crippled and blind in his chair. The fact that he can still keep alive in his bunker, motionless, helpless, a lump of flesh with vague recollections and desires, he owes to Clov, his servant and general factotum. This Clov, a dismal clown, loathes his master more profoundly, more desperately than his tougher ancestors hated their healthier masters: more than Grazioso hated Hidalgo, more than Hanswurst hated the Prince or Doctor Faustus, whose services he entered later.

The game they are both playing is a double one. They are playing at the end of the world – the master not without pathos: 'Can there be misery – [*he yawns*] – loftier than mine?' Clov plays with a laugh of surprise and disgust at whatever still exists, that brief laugh when he looks out of the window, attends to the rubbish bins, contemplates the swollen Hamm. But also they are playing the end-game in the struggle between master and servant: who is going to checkmate whom? or will it be just a stalemate or a draw? Hamm cannot live without Clov. Can Clov live without Hamm?

> HAMM: Get me ready. [CLOV *does not move.*] Go and get the sheet. [CLOV *does not move.*] Clov!
>
> CLOV: Yes.
>
> HAMM: I'll give you nothing more to eat.
>
> CLOV: Then we'll die.
>
> HAMM: I'll give you just enough to keep you from dying. You'll be hungry all the time.
>
> CLOV: Then we shan't die. . . .

HAMM: . . . Why do you stay with me?

CLOV: Why do you keep me?

HAMM: There's no one else.

CLOV: There's nowhere else. (*CDW* 94–95)

The master–servant relationship, too, is touched with decay. In *Waiting for Godot* there was a transposition of roles between Pozzo and Lucky, the revolution that alters none of the essential nature of power. In *Endgame* Clov stays with Hamm, not only because he is paralysed by habit and inaction, but also because he dreads going out in a world which may no longer be there, away from his master's dwindling provisions, into the unknown, into the wreckage of the great disaster.

The World of Having

It is the fashion in both West and East to classify Samuel Beckett's great plays under the heading of 'Theatre of the Absurd'. In it, they say, the riddle of human existence is revealed or suggested outside and beyond all social implications, by images with a multitude of possible meanings. Great imaginative writing always takes the form of images, and these always have many meanings; but neither Hamm nor Clov is a creature from outer space: they come from a society of haves and have-nots, masters and servants, a *world of having*; they are not merely allegorical characters, they also wear disintegrating social masks. It is foolish to trace works of the imagination back to social realities alone, to regard them purely as a 'reflection' of social conditions: but equally it is dogmatic to interpret them solely as the result of an autonomous imaginative process, an internal spectacle independent of the social world.

Hamm has lived a life of prosperity and greed. He tries to hold on to what he once was, now reduced to memories – the land he owned, the grain he stored, the beggar to whom he offered philosophy instead of bread. With the attitude of a writer working on a story he seeks to justify his senseless existence, his still-being-there. He tells the story not without complacency.

The man came crawling towards me, on his belly . . . It was an extra-ordinarily bitter day, I remember, zero by the thermometer. But considering it was Christmas Eve there was nothing . . . extra-ordinary about that . . . [*Pause.*] Well, what ill wind blows you my way? He raised his face to me, black with mingled dirt and tears . . . Come on, man, speak up, what is it you want from me, I have to put up my holly. [*Pause.*] Well to make it short it finally transpired that what he wanted from me was . . . bread for his brat. Bread? But I have no bread, it does not agree with me. Good. Then perhaps a little corn? [*Pause. Normal tone.*] That should do it. [*Narrative tone.*] Corn, yes, I have corn, it's true, in my granaries. But use your head. I give you some corn, a pound, a pound and a half, you bring it back to your child and you make him – if he's still alive – a nice pot of porridge . . . Use your head, can't you, use your head, you're on earth, there's no cure for that! . . . But what in God's name do you imagine? That the earth will awake in spring? That the rivers and seas will run with fish again? That there's manna in heaven for imbeciles like you? . . . In the end he asked me would I consent to take in the child as well – if he were still alive . . . [*Pause. Normal tone.*] I'll soon have finished with that story . . . (*CDW* 116–117)

Clov asks how the story goes on. Isn't it also *his* story that the master is telling? A story for Hamm; the truth for him? Hamm thinks he can remember offering the beggar a job as a gardener. Clov bursts out laughing: 'A job as a gardener!'

HAMM: What is there so funny about that?

CLOV: A job as a gardener!

HAMM: Is that what tickles you?

CLOV: It must be that.

HAMM: It wouldn't be the bread?

CLOV: Or the brat.

[*Pause.*]

HAMM: The whole thing is comical, I grant you that. What about having a good guffaw the two of us together?

CLOV: [*After reflection.*] I couldn't guffaw again today. (*CDW* 121–122)

Was not Clov the child whom the rich man took into his house? And would he not – his hatred asks him – have climbed the trees? Hamm replies coldly: 'All the little odd jobs.' Trees don't grow for the beggar's child. But he – how was it with him?

CLOV: And then he would have grown up.

HAMM: Very likely.

[*Pause.*]

CLOV: Keep going, can't you, keep going!

HAMM: That's all. I stopped there.

[*Pause.*]

CLOV: Do you see how it goes on.

HAMM: More or less.

CLOV: Will it soon be the end?

HAMM: I'm afraid it will. (*CDW* 122)

The world of having is sketched as economically as that. Beckett presumes our knowledge of it. It is present in each concentrated detail. It is introduced into the play only to the extent that it carries the action forward. For inside the simulated standstill there is movement, development. We have learnt to recognise as great a dynamism in the atom as in the universe. Something is going on. Hamm wants Clov to tell him that it is an evening like any other. But Clov refuses to reassure him. Hamm is afraid: 'What's wrong?' And Clov: 'Something is taking its course.'

Something is Taking its Course

What is 'taking its course' is not only time, whose stealthy silence becomes audible, dripping with fear, ticking away into nothingness; not only the irresistible process of decay, but Clov's struggle to liberate himself, to get free from the master to whom he is bound by habit, the power of the father-image, hatred and the larder, the accumulated stores. This is taking its course. It begins with the master's certainty that Clov cannot go free: 'Very well, then go!', and Clov does not move, and Hamm in his chair sits up again, still representing power, although he is blind and crippled: 'I thought I'd told you to go?' and Clov says: 'I'm trying' – and goes to the cupboard and stops: 'Ever since I was born.' This cat-and-mouse game then leads to the sly question to Clov: 'Do you remember when you came here?' and Clov, exasperated by the frozen situation, replying: 'You've asked me these questions millions of times'; then the master's patriarchal hypocrisy: 'It was I was a father to you . . . My house a home for you . . . But for me, no father. But for Hamm, no home.' It begins with this dictum of all rulers, that without them there is no world-father, no home for the little ones, never mind if the home is a bunker and the world a hell. It ends with the discovery that the provisions have been used up. It begins with the question: 'And where were *you*?' It ends with the undisguised insolence of one who always served as a servant, never as a son.

HAMM: I was never there.

CLOV: Lucky for you.

HAMM: Absent, always. It all happened without me. I don't know what's happened . . .

CLOV: When? Where?

HAMM: [*Violently*.] When! What's happened! Use your head, can't you! What's happened?

CLOV: What for Christ's sake does it matter?

[*He looks out of window.*]

HAMM: I don't know.

[*Pause.* CLOV *turns towards* HAMM.]

CLOV: [*Harshly*.] When old Mother Pegg asked you for oil for her lamp and you told her to get out to hell, you knew what was happening then, no? [*Pause.*] You know what she died of, Mother Pegg? Of darkness.

HAMM: [*Feebly*.] I hadn't any.

CLOV: [*As before*.] Yes, you had. (*CDW* 128–129)

Something is taking its course. Hamm reviews his past, toned down by consideration for his own feelings, for the crippled self is hypersensitive. If life has been a dream, he need not be held responsible for it. 'What dreams! . . . Those woods!' The fact that he is losing his hair, his teeth, his earthly possessions, he shares with Clov; but the thing that raises him above Clov, so he boasts, are the lost *ideals* which he tries to smuggle fraudulently into his past. Clov has nothing to lose.

HAMM: Have you not had enough?

CLOV: Yes! [*Pause.*] Of what?

HAMM: Of this . . . this . . . thing.

CLOV: I always had. [*Pause.*] Not you? (*CDW* 94)

Hamm is a gentleman with an ideology, with a false and falsifying consciousness. Clov does not fool himself. For Hamm, cosmic suffering is a way of ennobling his own shoddiness; Clov suffers without self-deception. The words, the symbols at Hamm's command are not without grandeur; in the master's mouth they represent the power of subjugating the servant inwardly as well as outwardly.

CLOV: There's one thing I'll never understand . . . Why I always obey you. Can you explain that to me?

HAMM: No . . . Perhaps it's compassion. [*Pause.*] A kind of great compassion. [*Pause.*] Oh you won't find it easy, you won't find it easy. (*CDW* 129)

The master proves to be a master of psychology. You have to play on the servant's feelings, celebrate his obedience as a kind of great compassion, as Christianity, as humanity, and at the same time appeal to his uncertainties: Poor fellow, you won't find it easy without me! How do you expect to manage in the world without my experience, my intellect, my store of material and spiritual wealth?

If we Mean Something

And so, in order to set himself free, Clov must see through the master's false consciousness. He must prevent Hamm from escaping into the pathos of established ideas and force him to acknowledge his part in what he has done, in what he has known he has done. Hamm, on the other hand, in order to excuse his existence, his doing and not doing and the fact that Mother Pegg died of darkness because of him, must postulate total meaninglessness, the world as Nothing in which we mean nothing. Otherwise they come out of the darkness, encircling him: 'All those I might have helped. [*Pause.*] Helped! [*Pause.*] Saved. [*Pause.*] Saved! [*Pause.*] The place was crawling with them! [*Pause. Violently.*] Use your head, can't you, use your head, you're on earth, there's no cure for that! [*Pause.*] Get out of here and love one another! Lick your neighbour as yourself!'

CLOV: Something is taking its course.

[*Pause.*]

HAMM: Clov!

CLOV: [*Impatiently.*] What is it?

HAMM: We're not beginning to . . . to . . . mean something?

CLOV: Mean something! You and I, mean something! [*Brief laugh.*] Ah that's a good one!

HAMM: I wonder. [*Pause.*] Imagine if a rational being came back to earth, wouldn't he be liable to get ideas into his head if he observed us long enough . . . And without going as far as that, we ourselves . . . [*with emotion*] . . . we ourselves . . . at certain moments . . . [*Vehemently.*] To think perhaps it won't all have been for nothing! (*CDW* 107–108)

If we mean something, if perhaps it won't all have been for nothing, Hamm has lost the end-game. He is then to be *judged*. How can he bear it if it all means something, if the worldlessness of his refuge is only illusory? Was the catastrophe inevitable? Was the cripple always crippled, the blind man always blind? Could he not have done something instead of never being there, when it was a matter of saving or helping? What he *possessed* was there; but he as an 'I', a self, beneath all those *things* and beneath the conventions and institutions relating to them, was never there: so he was without responsibility.

It is the same order, the same powerful domination of *things*, that has also robbed Clov of his capacity to realise his 'I', his self, that is to say to *be there*, to decide in relative freedom.

Beyond the refuge, which is suggestive of Max Weber's 'casing of enslavement', beyond the old wall, a world is – perhaps – being created in which it is possible to *be there* as a human being; possible for Clov, not for Hamm. Hamm lays his hand on the wall: 'Old wall! [*Pause.*] Beyond is the . . . other hell.'[16] □

One of the suggestions implicit in Fischer's argument is that, in order for Clov to free himself from Hamm's control – for him to meet up with Ivan Denisovich in a better world – the nature of his struggle has to be recognised by his critics. The mutual exclusivity between an East European commitment to socialist realism, and a Western emphasis on artistic autonomy and apoliticism, keeps Ivan and Clov locked up in their respective 'shelters' as effectively as do Stalin and Hamm. Fischer's 1966 call for a critical approach that could negotiate between commitment and autonomy, however, was for a long time unanswered in the West. An indicator of the location of Beckett's drama in the critical and ideological battles between East and West has been the attitude towards Beckett's relationship with Brecht, and up to the present day there is a strong contingent in the West that regards the concerns of the two dramatists as diametrically opposed. Rosemary Pountney, for example, writing in 1988, speaks for many critics when she claims that

■ unlike Brecht, who believed that to present a problem on the stage presented also an implied solution, in the desirability of social change, Beckett has no solutions to offer. Nor does he believe that it is the task of the artist to provide any . . . Instead he confronts his audience with the problem, the image of human suffering. This, he says, is 'how it is'.[17] □

As I have already suggested, however, there has been a gradual rapprochement between Beckett and Brecht in the East over the last forty years, which is now beginning to have some influence in the West. Since

Brecht's initial dissatisfaction with the play, and his intention to correct its politics by making the characters and the situation more morally and politically determinate, East European critics and audiences have come to regard Brecht and Beckett both as sharing similar concerns and as adapting related dramatic methods for expressing such concerns. The extract printed below, from an article by Werner Huber entitled 'Godot, Gorba, and Glasnost: Beckett in East Germany', traces this shifting relation between the two writers as it develops over four phases: refutation; rapprochement; recovery; and post-propriation.

■ First Phase: Refutation

Brecht's plans to 'stand *Godot* on its feet' are the first instance of Beckett's reception in the German Democratic Republic and coincide with the German premiere of *Waiting for Godot* in (West) Berlin in 1953.[18] In order to add the necessary socio-historical dimension, Brecht, in his 'Gegenentwurf', intended to specify the social background of Beckett's characters, Estragon becoming a 'proletarian', Vladimir an 'intellectual', Lucky 'an ass or a policeman', and Pozzo, one of the landed gentry. Brecht's other idea was to have films (newsreels) projected against the back of the stage showing the progress of revolutionary movements worldwide, while Vladimir and Estragon would do their waiting in the foreground.

What can be concluded from Brecht's project, which incidentally he never came round to putting into practice, is that, initially, during this first phase, Beckett was generally rejected as a proponent of Western decadence, whose works demonstrated the irresistible retreat of the bourgeois individual. Beckett was blamed for presenting 'alienation' and the Absurd as ontological and historically irreversible conditions. With a view to his booming reception in the West Beckett's work was seen as an apologia for late bourgeois capitalism. What irritated the theorists and propagandists of socialist realism most were his lack of perspective, his pessimism, and his nihilism. In a manner of speaking he had become a class enemy.

This being the time when the cold war extended even to the cultural front, opportunities for critics to engage openly in an ideological battle with Beckett were very rare. One of these instances was provided by *Sinn und Form*, a journal published by the East German Academy of Arts. In 1964 it carried an article by Werner Mittenzwei, in which he took on the 'Abstract ones' together with the Absurdists and demonstrated their lack of social understanding and political responsibility. Mittenzwei polemicized against what he perceived as Beckett's fetish-like idealisation of alienated man, in order to conclude that the Absurd interlude was just that – an interlude – with no chance of a future.[19]

This East–West difference in views on Beckett was cemented at an experimental theatre event which was held at Frankfurt am Main and was organised by the West German Academy for the Performing Arts. It literally pitted Brecht against Beckett. A staging of Brecht's *Messingkauf Dialogues* was contrasted with a number of Beckett dramaticules. This was followed by a panel discussion which saw East Berlin Brechtians (among them, members of the Berlin Ensemble) confront West German Beckett supporters. Naturally, the dialogue and antagonism centred around such predictable dichotomies as social realism/ahistorical abstraction, therapy/diagnosis, agitation/description, optimism/pessimism, with each side holding its ideological ground.[20]

Second Phase: Rapprochement or Subversive Appropriation

Despite the official ban on Beckett, knowledge of his works was introduced and imported into East Germany in a very roundabout way. Beckett plays broadcast on West German television would also have reached East German viewers. Therefore, it is not all too surprising to find a very gradual rapprochement being prepared during this phase, especially by playwrights working with Beckettian echoes through parody, parallelism, allusion, and other intertextual strategies. The first example is Claus Hammel's *Le Fraiseur oder Warten Auf Godeau* (1970). This play, based on the plot of Balzac's comedy *Le Fraiseur*, originally one of the possible inspirations for Beckett's title, concerns a businessman, Mercadet, who tries to save himself from bankruptcy by spreading the rumour that one Godeau, his partner, has absconded with all the money. Working with rumour and counter-rumour and exploiting bourgeois gullibility, Mercadet begins to issue Godeau shares to the general public with immense profit to himself. As can be gathered, Beckett's eponymous play and the 'demagogic' ideologies of imperialism and capitalism become the target of socialist satire.

East German dramatists taking an ambivalent view of the ruling ideology often enough found themselves in confrontation with the powers that be. It became their speciality to work with insinuations and oblique references to the Beckett canon. Heiner Müller's *Nachtstück*, a scene from his play, *Germania Tod in Berlin* (1977), is a radical reworking of Beckett's *Actes sans paroles* with explicit references to Beckett's goad. Müller's *Leben Gundlings Friedrich von Preußen Lessings Schlaf Traum Schrei* (1979) includes a section entitled 'Lessings Schlaf', which in its monologic form and (auto)biographical themes bears a more than obvious resemblance to *Krapp's Last Tape*.

In Volker Braun's *Simplex Deutsch* (1980) we find a scene with a full *Godot* scenario: 'a Beckett tree, two hippies on the ground, presumably

Estragon and Vladimir'. Estragon and Vladimir keep exchanging stereotypes and platitudes while Godot/Beckett appears. He tries very hard to explain himself to them, but they, having waited too long and the times having changed, are no longer interested. An instance where the Beckett model is less obvious was provided by Christophe Hein. His dramatisation of a Chinese story, *Die wahre Geschichte des Ah Q* (1983), has two Chinese anarchists, Ah Q and Wang, waiting for the revolution in 1911. The revolution passes over their heads. Their 'bountiful master', who never appears, becomes their 'revolutionary master' without ever gaining insight into what has happened. All these examples hover between homage and parody. Paradoxically enough, they assume in their intertextual gestures a knowledge of Beckett's works which could not be reasonably expected of the average reader/play-goer at the time, who would never have had the opportunity to see or study the works of this 'banned' writer.

Third Phase: Recovery or Rescue

The year 1985 saw the first production ever of a Beckett play in East Germany.[21] But, as if an evening of pure Beckett would have been too dangerous, Ekkehard Schall, Brecht's son-in-law who played Krapp, followed it up with a musical version of Brecht's *lehrgedicht* 'Die Erziehung der Hirse/The Education of Millet' (1950). This is the successful life story of a nomad turned kolkhoznik in Kasachstan, who found a new and more 'productive' variety of millet, which later became the staple diet of the Red Army. (Schall, by the way, took care to drop the references to Stalin in the poem.) Under the title for this double bill, *Lebensabende*, Schall made it easy for himself to contrast a frustrated life with a productive one. Schall's half-hearted and casual approach to Beckett as expressed in his style of acting and in a subsequent interview seems to suggest that a concession was made here, a final effort to stem the tide of Beckett's growing (underground) popularity.[22] The orthodox party organ *Junge Welt* summarised this Brecht/Beckett encounter in the theatre with outright bluntness: 'Why play Beckett, if you want to show that Brecht is closer to us?'.

The volte-face in East German attitudes towards Beckett and his works came around 1985 and was brought about by the critics. In an article in *Die Weltbühne* by Alfred Dreifuß, a doyen of the East German theatre world, we find *Waiting for Godot* described as a highly topical political parable: it is the result of the Marshall Plan and of a few years of economic boom, its message is *homo homini lupus* and thereby proves the socialist right and the West wrong. For J.C. Trilse,[23] writing in 1986, Beckett's work now exudes a sincere humanism which had been lost in the highly philosophical interpretations of his plays in Western

theatres. Ontological darkness, metaphysical mystification, and decadent culinary attitudes towards 'endgames' had distorted Beckett's
original intentions. The counter-measure would be to underline the
comic potential of Beckett's plays.[24]

According to Trilse, *Waiting for Godot* staged as a carnival event, as a
Punch and Judy show, would set matters right again. This idea of seeing this play and, pars pro toto, Beckett as a clown has a long tradition
in East Germany. Heiner Müller had used the term 'Clownsspiele' in
1975 to defend Beckett's original intentions against Western trends of
mystification.

Enormous mental Houdini acts are performed when it comes to
explaining, now in 1986, the elective affinities between Brecht and
Beckett. Basically, the *verfremdungseffekt* (defamiliarisation) is seen as
being inherent in Beckett's work, whom Trilse is later to call 'the poet
of alienation'. Thus, the difference between Brecht and Beckett
becomes almost insignificant. While Brecht aimed at life processes of
the collective, Beckett, renouncing the bourgeois world of his origins,
had no choice but to concern himself with processes of individual consciousness in a theatre of the inner life.

In the final analysis, Trilse writes, the slow recognition of Beckett's
real greatness is to be blamed on the wrong approach, the wrong
reception attitudes on the part of the audience. Beckett's works require
an epic theatre approach rather than the traditional one of catharsis.
And now that East German audiences have become used to modes of
the grotesque and the parabolic in the theatre by being exposed to the
Polish absurdists, there should no longer be any problem. Another
obstacle had been the label 'decadent', which, Trilse admits, has been
used in a rather indifferent and undistinguishing manner in the wake
of Lukács's early pronouncements.

Some of this aesthetic rationalisation was borne out in the first East
German production of *Waiting for Godot* in Dresden in 1987. The clow-
nesque elements were there in abundance. The scene was 'laid' – if
that is the right phrase to use with any Beckett play – in *Saxony*, an
analogy to the different settings realised in the English, French, and
'West' German versions. The beginning showed Vladimir and
Estragon clambering up through the trap and getting entangled in the
stage curtains which separated the stage as a circus arena from the
auditorium. They were not able to pronounce either the author or the
title of the play they were involved in without much hemming and
hawing. It has been suggested that this was a way of symbolising the
return of the repressed.

As Wolfgang Engel, the director, cautiously pointed out in an interview, his intention was to present the play as a twentieth century
classic and to put the thematic stress on the theme of hope and/or the

futility of hoping. Nevertheless, the audience was left to speculate – not on Western decadence and the collapse of the capitalist system – but on political changes signalled from the East. Lucky, in his monologue, was heard 'thinking' aloud about the rivers Elbe, Oder, and Niesse, the equivalent for the 'Vaucluse/Merdecluse' pun became 'Erzgebrige/Scherzgebrige', and at one point Pozzo was heard mumbling something about an appointment with one Mr. Gorba. . . .

Fourth Phase: Post-propriation

The fourth and final phase of Beckett's reception in East Germany deserves the label 'post-propriation'. This was coined by Heiner Müller and was meant to express regret at the late arrival of Beckett in East Germany. *Waiting for Godot* is now seen as running counter to all the unhealthy ideologemes of the West – which are named as evolutionary euphoria, dreams of omnipotence, an exaggerated ideal of individual self-realisation, a consumer mentality, the all-pervading desire for instant satisfaction. *Waiting for Godot* contradicts the bourgeois assertion that it is the best and the most human of all possible worlds. If we look for it, we find in *Godot* an expression of the solidarity of human beings, an elementary humanism. At this juncture Beckett's reputation reaches a point, where critics unashamedly conclude that Beckett's realism is only possible in socialist theatres.

The story from here on is difficult to predict.[25] A cynic might well suggest the following scenario: next we could have a version of *Waiting for Godot* in which Mr. Gorba . . . is replaced by Chancellor Kohl, in which Vladimir and Estragon are shown waiting for the economic 'upswing' promised to East Germans.[26] □

Huber here betrays an impatience with the growing enthusiasm in Germany for an approach to Beckett's drama as Brechtian epic theatre that has some similarity to Brecht's original problem with *Godot*. Brecht was uncomfortable with the play because, whilst he recognised its critical potential, he felt it was not sufficiently anchored to a specific cultural moment. His instinct was thus, as we have seen, to determine the characters' roles, to ground the play more firmly in a recognisable economic and material reality. Huber's wry suggestion that *Godot* will continue to mutate in order to reflect social changes in the time and place in which it is being performed suggests that he too feels that the play's critical capacity is undermined by its perceived generality – *Godot* begins to appear as a kind of portable, peripatetic critical gesture that will bite with equal effect into any cultural scenario. Under these circumstances, it may seem difficult to grant the play any political coherence or integrity. It becomes a choreographed acting out of alienation that has no say in that from which it is alienated, and thus has no critical content.

It is with this perception that Beckett's drama is unanchored and culturally non-specific that his recent post-colonial critics have taken issue. For critics such as David Lloyd and Declan Kiberd, Beckett's critical faculties are engaged very specifically with the cultural conditions under which he grew up – those of the post-colonial nation. Lloyd claims, in his essay 'Writing in the Shit: Beckett, Nationalism and the Colonial Subject', that Beckett's oeuvre 'stands as the most exhaustive dismantling we have of the logic of identity that at every level structures and maintains the post-colonial moment',[27] and Kiberd anchors Beckett's treatment of the post-colonial predicament more firmly in Ireland, claiming that Beckett is 'the first truly Irish playwright'.[28] For both of these critics, however, Beckett's writing occupies an ambiguous position between location and placelessness – his work corresponds to the simultaneously placed and displaced model of post-colonial writing described earlier by Terry Eagleton. The oeuvre is shot through with references that attach it to Irish culture and an Irish tradition, but it also rids itself of such references in its tendency towards emptiness and cultural alienation. For Kiberd, Beckett's work is undeniably Irish, yet it is located in 'a no-man's land between cultures', it 'sets up shop in the void'. For Lloyd, Beckett's dramatisation of the struggle to write one's national identity is a dramatisation of a vain struggle, as his characters' attempts to achieve a stable national identity end in failure and 'inauthenticity'. But this failure to secure a stable national identity does not free Beckett from Irishness into placeless, anonymous universality, as 'such inauthenticity is equally the perpetual condition of the colonised: dominated, interpreted, mediated by another'.[29] The wide open expanses of empty, indeterminate waste land in Beckett's work are multivalent for these critics. For Kiberd they are the site of a residual but powerful Irishness that has been all but eradicated by a colonising power; in their very emptiness they are a protest against the colonial forces that have erased Irish history from the landscape; but their emptiness is also expressive of the possibility that the post-colonial subject is free to rewrite his/her identity, to re-inscribe his/her history afresh upon the naked space of the stage.

In the extract that follows, Kiberd reads *Waiting for Godot* and *Endgame* as the protests of a colonised people against their colonisers. He draws attention to the attachment of the plays to an Irish cultural and literary tradition, whilst also reading the political significance of their movement away from such tradition. He points out the extent to which the plays are grounded in an Irish context whilst insisting that 'their surroundings seem decontextualised, because they represent a geography which has been deprived of a history'. In his emphasis upon the sparseness of Beckett's stage as a protest against and a retreat from the forces of colonisation,

Kiberd reads the plays as expressive of a nascent, authentic Irish consciousness emerging from the shadow of English rule.

■ A . . . version of [Gaelic] tradition may be found in the figure of the tramp in *Waiting for Godot*. That figure had already featured in the poetry of Yeats as an image of the now-rootless Anglo-Irish, neither Irish nor English, but caught wandering across the no-man's-land between the two cultures. Synge had developed it further, signing letters to his Catholic girlfriend 'your old tramp',[30] and in his essays comparing the artistic son of Protestant families to the youngest son of a farmer who takes to the roads for the want of a better inheritance.[31] The temperament of such men was artistic, he claimed, and they could harmonise more easily with the forces of nature than could any member of the settled community. For Synge, the tramp was a gloriously ambivalent presence, more respectable than the universally despised tinker, but much less compromised than the solid, sedentary citizen: he had his appointed place in the rural economy, as a casual, seasoned labourer or as the bearer of news, but he nonetheless remained a free spirit, a poet who epitomised all that the emerging rural class was busily rejecting in itself.

The ultimate roots of this figure were, of course, in the *spailpín* poets cast out onto the roads after the collapse of the old Gaelic order in the seventeenth and eighteenth centuries. Yeats, for example, read the doom of Anglo-Irish poets into the fate of Aogán Ó Rathaille in 'The Curse of Cromwell': just as the Gaelic bard had been faced with a new philistine middle class, to whom the Muses were 'things of no account',[32] so was he. Ó Rathaille's self-image was aristocratic, haughty, mandarin: he had the learning and the training of a bard, entitled to princely patronage, but in actual life he seemed little better than a mendicant seeking alms. It was this tradition which Beckett evoked at the opening of *Waiting for Godot*, when Didi laments to Gogo that 'we were presentable in those days. Now it's too late' (*CDW* 12). Their dented bowler hats and shabby morning suits proclaim them as men who once had pretensions to gentility and education. 'You should have been a poet', says a sardonic Didi: and his partner, gesturing towards his rags in the manner of an Ó Rathaille, says 'I was . . . Isn't that obvious?' (*CDW* 14). When a friend complained to Beckett that the tramps at times talked as if they possessed doctorates, he shot back 'How do you know they hadn't?'[33] Their self-image is certainly that of an educated class, even if they are leading the life of the hobo.

They are presented as characters without much history, who are driven to locate themselves in the world with reference to geography. But the world in which they live has no overall structure, no formal narrative: instead, it is a dreadful place in which every moment is like the next. Unable to construct a story of the past, the tramps learn nothing from their mistakes, because they can make none of the comparisons which might provide the basis for a confident judgement. Beckett's characters all know the longing to turn their lives into narrative ('it will have been a happy day' (*CDW* 167)) and, by this second look at their history, to free themselves of it; but the trick is not so easily done. Even those who think they 'possess' their past on a tape-recording or on a page find that the present invariably flavours it, emphasising the near-impossibility of entering into a dialogue with their own history.

On the stage of *Waiting for Godot* is enacted the amnesia which afflicts an uprooted people:

VLADIMIR: At the very beginning.

ESTRAGON: The very beginning of WHAT?

VLADIMIR: This evening . . . I was saying . . . I was saying . . .

ESTRAGON: I'm not a historian. (*CDW* 60)

Such lost souls can, paradoxically, be as deadened by habit as by forgetfulness, a recognition sadly voiced by Gogo: 'That's the way it is. Either I forget immediately or I never forget.' Mostly, however, he forgets everything:

ESTRAGON: We came here yesterday.

VLADIMIR: Ah no, there you're mistaken.

ESTRAGON: What did we do yesterday?

VLADIMIR: What did we do yesterday?

ESTRAGON: Yes.

VLADIMIR: Why . . . [*Angrily*.] Nothing is certain when you're about.

ESTRAGON: In my opinion we were here.

VLADIMIR: [*Looking round*.] You recognize the place?

ESTRAGON: I didn't say that. (*CDW* 16)

As a victim of a history which he does not understand, Gogo must deal with every situation as if it were a wholly new event. In the face of that terror, he enacts – as do all people whose pasts have been denied them – the invention of traditions.

Lacking an assured past, the tramps can have no clear sense of their own future. This is one reason why they cannot persist with any one of their chosen activities for very long. They are waiting without hope for a deliverance from a being in whom they do not really believe, in the manner of the *aisling* poets; and they are doomed to repeat the past precisely because they have never allowed themselves, or been allowed, to know it fully. This explains the paradox of persons who seem at once fixated on the past and supremely indifferent to it. Their surroundings seem decontextualised, because they represent a geography which has been deprived of a history. The historian Louis Cullen has spoken of 'the general poverty of tradition in Ireland', which is why the people view their country 'uncertainly and apologetically'. Another scholar, noting the indifference of country folk to local antiquities, likens them to a people condemned to live without a key in a superbly coded environment. The loss of the ancestral heritage was a major contributory factor in this process.

The tramps try as best they can to restore and reconnect memories which have been taken from them, but there are just too many gaps, caused by a life of poverty, migration and constant interruption. The 'dead voices' haunt them with teasing possibilities – they are like leaves, like wings, like sand – but the sheer proliferation of possibilities means that all are annulled, and so they induce only vague feelings of guilt and frustration. The past erupts, again and again, to usurp the present, but never to connect meaningfully with it. Worse still, the forgetfulness is catching, as Pozzo discovers after exposure to the tramps' confusions:

VLADIMIR: We met yesterday. [*Silence.*] Do you not remember?

POZZO: I don't remember having met anyone yesterday. But tomorrow I won't remember having met anyone today. So don't count on me to enlighten you. (*CDW* 82)

Lacking a clear sense of themselves, the tramps invent short-term identities (Let's play Lucky and Pozzo) or counterfeit real emotion (Let's abuse each other). Like the Irish in England, or the black man in New York, they feel constantly 'on'. They become obsessed with the performative element in all exploitative relationships: and their curiosity about Pozzo and Lucky centres on the manner in which the master invents (but seldom deigns to notice) his slave, and in which the slave reciprocates by noticing and thus ratifying his master. Pozzo's absolute need is for such ratification ('Is everybody looking at me?' *CDW* 30), for if he is not perceived, he will not feel certain that he exists. Hegel, in his writings on the master/slave paradigm, had taught that the one who attains recognition without reciprocating becomes the master, while he who recognises but is not recognised becomes the slave. The master thus reduces the slave to a mere instrument of his will, yet in that very victory lurks a longer term defeat. Alienated from human labour, Pozzo loses the means of transforming the world and himself. Moreover, since the slave is no better than an animal in the eyes of his master, Pozzo finds the recognition which he obtains inauthentic, because he is recognised only by someone unworthy. Hence, in the play, Pozzo cannot go for long without seeking the society of his likes (the tramps must be 'human beings none the less ... Of the same species as Pozzo') but, he hastily adds, to be suitable to his purposes such figures must be degradedly different as well ('even when the likeness is an imperfect one'). He seeks a botched metaphor, a strained theatricality: while the tramps want most of all to literalise, to write their own script and produce their own drama, of a kind that will not be abjectly dependent on the audience.

The even deeper paradox lies in the fact that onto the slave the master projects many of the qualities which his mastery dictates that he must suppress in himself. So Lucky, like many subject peoples, has once pleased his master by his powers in the dance and by his uplifting, beautiful ideas: 'But for him, all my thoughts, all my feelings, would have been of common things', or, again, 'He even used to think very prettily once, I could listen to him for hours' (*CDW* 39). Pozzo is a specialist who asks Lucky to live out on his behalf those elements which he must deny in himself; and Lucky, like the traditional clown, is given freedom to speak, but if he says too much, he can be patted on the head (or, as the case may dictate, kicked in the shins).

For here is a servant who will not just do your living, but also your dancing and your philosophy for you, and at the same time connive in his own oppression. The inevitable consequence is that the master becomes enslaved to the limitations and disabilities of his subject: and so the rope on which Pozzo 'leads' Lucky becomes the cord by which Lucky confines his master. The tyranny of the weak over the strong becomes lasting indeed. In a world whose characters constantly seek and deny 'likeness', the final yearning is for an escape from the endless play of metaphor into a pure declarative statement: and beyond that an escape from communication as such. Lucky exercises a strange, spell-binding power, having done just this, but he manages also to belittle the central activity of waiting for Godot with his subversive hint that the existence of a personal God would solve nothing anyway.

The relentless attempt of the tramps to demetaphorise, to stop life turning into literary material, is expressed in their aversion to theatricalisation. They compel Pozzo to scale down his rhetorical excesses, in the manner of a Beckettian prose narrator who knows that *style* is less the expression of self than a means for pursuing the self:

> POZZO: He wants to impress me, so that I'll keep him.
>
> ESTRAGON: What?
>
> POZZO: Perhaps I haven't got it quite right. He wants to mollify me, so that I'll give up the idea of parting with him. No, that's not exactly it either.
>
> VLADIMIR: You want to get rid of him?
>
> POZZO: He wants to cod me, but he won't. (*CDW* 31)

Here, already in Act One, the subservient ones (the tramps, as well as Lucky) are seen to dictate terms to the overlord at a rhetorical level, and this anticipates the second act in which they will also be his physical masters. By then, Pozzo will have been punished for his insincere, metaphorised account of the sunset in Act One by the literal and permanent fall of night over his eyes: the result, it is often said, of his refusal to see his life as it really is. As Pozzo lies prostrate on the ground, Didi will deliver over his body just the kind of insincere rhetoric which Pozzo was guilty of in an earlier scene:

> Let us not waste time in idle discourse! [*Pause. Vehemently.*] Let us do something, while we have the chance! It is not every day that we are needed. Not indeed that we personally are needed. Others would meet the case equally well, if not better. To all mankind they were addressed, those cries for help still ringing in our ears! But at this place, at this moment of time, all mankind is us, whether we like it or not. Let us make the most of it, before it is too late! Let us represent worthily for once the foul brood to which a cruel fate consigned us! (*CDW* 74).

It is a moment of rare poetic justice when such theatricality punishes the theatrical. Pozzo, the landlord who wears the clothing of English gentry, is for the moment at the mercy of mere tramps: and Didi's studied rationalisations might seem to resemble the neutral pose adopted by most Irish in the face of England's crisis at the height of the Second World War. Instead of offering help, Didi makes a pretty speech; instead of taking upon himself the reality of Pozzo's suffering, he becomes a professor of the fact that someone else is suffering. Of course, Pozzo's punishment, like Didi's hypocrisy, is quite undeliberated: it is simply the outcome of a life spent denying the reality of his own partner's pains, which are invariably treated as mere spectacle.

The atomism of life in an oppressed society leads to such a loss of communal feeling and to a disinclination among people to help one another: rather, the protagonist retreats into a posture of idiocy, in the sense of *idiot* as a hopelessly private person. And, ultimately, the overlord joins the underlings in a state of anomie and amnesia, becoming one of the blind from whom the things of time are hidden too.

The *attempt* by each of these protagonists to hold down a role becomes of far more pressing concern to the audience than is any role which each might conceivably play. The feeling which assails the audience is akin to that which might trouble the friends of an amateur cast at a rickety production which is constantly verging on breakdown. It is here that the roots of Beckett's human comedy lie: in the Schopenhauerian will which pushes persons forward regardless of their capacities. Desire is idiotic and the Beckettian protagonist is therefore ludicrous not in repose but in motion: Belacqua on his painful walks with spavined gait, Murphy on the job-hunt, Molloy on the crawl, all of them are fishes out of water. The desire of the tramps has thrust them into a locale where they are patently incongruous, and without clues as to any activity which could be other than pointless. Because they are out of role, because they are caught, indeed, between a role and a self, they are forever watching themselves, monitoring their own performances, as if living life at a remove. Their experiences are thus taken away from them even before they are completed. This is but one further reason why the suffering of Pozzo can only strike them as a distant, even ridiculous, spectacle.

In *Waiting for Godot* the attempt to construct a person, or even a script, is finally abandoned. A stage devoid of props can provide no helpful indications as to how the protagonists might interpret their roles. Institutional behaviour, conditioned by easily visible props, might relieve a person of the task of choosing every single action with agonised deliberation, and without that support the tramps face the bleakness of freedom. But beyond all that, there is a deeper problem. The sheer energy which the tramps invest in constructing a context is one of the factors which prevents them from looking within, from 'having thought', from becoming themselves. The open, undefined nature of a text, whose lines they didn't write and don't understand, alongside the extremely detailed and coercive stage directions, serves only to emphasise their unfreedom.

No sooner is a thesis or a personal attribute established in Act One than it is annulled in Act Two. Within specific scenes, a rudimentary, tentative portrait of a character might be sketched, but this impulse is always defeated by the text as a whole. The implications of this for the actor are clear: one cannot impersonate a self which just is not there. The lines must be played in the most literal sense, with a tone of irony, distance, even pointlessness. This, after all, merely mimics the authorial techniques of one who asks the audience to imagine with him the making of endless 'plays' and their subsequent disruption. In such a context, Pozzo's self-confident bluster, his bravura performances, may create a momentary illusion of personality and presence, but they cannot ultimately conceal his hollowness. Behind the mask there is no face, no authority at all. The tramps, who always suspected this, were willing for a time, as are all dependants, to indulge a superior's prevailing mood; but, in the end, they tire of a man who seems concerned only with the effect he is making. They, at least, are still obsessed with finding a self worth impersonating and, if that is not possible, of scaling down all ridiculous claims:

> VLADIMIR: This is becoming really insignificant.
>
> ESTRAGON: Not enough.
>
> [*Silence.*] (*CDW* 64)

The play, though initially castigated for high pretentiousness, is actually not pretentious at all: it leaves a pure space between contradictory possibilities, which interpreters are wont to fill with their own desires and fore-meanings. It may well be that the safest reading is a merely descriptive account of the workings of a text which is clearly an essay on theatricality: but that will inevitably become an analysis of the power-relations which make theatricalisation possible. Nor is the play a helpless diagnosis, devoid of any hope, for, although Godot fails to come, Didi does manage, very late in the proceedings, to voice his care for the sleeping Gogo and his resolution to wake from his own dream to the sufferings of the world. The speech which begins 'Was I sleeping while the others suffered? Am I sleeping now?' goes on to consider a wider possibility: 'At me too someone is looking, of me too someone is saying, he is sleeping, he knows nothing, let him sleep on' (*CDW* 84–85).

In the image of that couple, bound in a rare moment of solidarity and linked to a wider chain of caring perceptors, Beckett hints at the possibility of a restored community. Yet, within a few moments, the shepherd boy reappears and reactivates Didi's faith in Godot and the entire illusion. Didi regresses and succumbs for the ignoblest of reasons: that if he didn't, he might be punished. This has been read as Beckett's commentary on the malfunction of an old-time religion based on fear, but it is much more than that. It is an indictment of all- isms – religious, colonial, political – which use the illusion of a perfect future to turn them away from suffering in the present.

The critic Vivian Mercier has argued that Pozzo in *Waiting for Godot* is dressed as were wicked landlords in the melodramas of Victorian

Ireland (sporty bowler, riding breeches, cloak-overcoat) and Lucky in the unfastened knee-breeches, bare legs and buckled shoes which 'recall the nineteenth-century Irish peasant of *Punch* cartoons'. He contends that Pozzo's insistence on the goodness of his own heart and the dog-like devotion to him of Lucky are 'as familiar in the mythology of the Irish landlord class as they were in that of the plantation owner in the Old South'.[34] Undeniably, Lucky conspires in his own oppression, yet, by a sort of uncultivated incompetence and foot-dragging, he seems to bring his master down along with him, since even the simplest orders issued by Pozzo take an eternity to perform. Mercier's is a plausible reading, given the well-known aversion among the Irish Protestant middle class to the pretensions of a clapped-out aristocracy.

A fuller treatment of the theme, however, may be found in *Endgame*, whose central figure, the blind Hamm, barks out constant orders while doing nothing himself. He appears the very epitome of a ruling class gone rancid: 'it's time it ended . . . and yet I hesitate, I hesitate to . . . to end' (*CDW* 93). His servant yearns, on the contrary, for a 'terrific' end. Clov speaks at times to Hamm with the ingratitude of a Caliban who knows that his master's language has been the medium in which his yearnings for expressive freedom have been improvised.

What keeps them on-stage, however, is an unfinished script, 'the dialogue' (*CDW* 121). *Endgame* is, in fact, the most extreme example of a repeated revivalist theme: the study of the sufferings of characters who make themselves willing martyrs to an approved text. Hamm, true to his name, is a consummate actor, impersonating the sort of authority he feels he ought to be, and Clov the human nail which is driven in by the force of his master's voice. But doubts nag, and they bother Hamm as much as Clov. Hamm senses acutely enough that the authority which he represents may be non-existent, that he can never centre himself at the exact mid-point of the stage, that he is 'never there' (*CDW* 128). Clov tells him he is lucky, for as a slave he *has* suffered and been there. If both men are marooned between an assumed role and an authentic self, then Hamm has gone far more deeply into the role, while Clov hovers painfully near to those zones in which he might become himself, those moments when he will counter what 'they said to me' with 'I say to myself' and become the subject of his own history.

One of the mysteries of the relationship is why Clov tolerates the tyranny of a man, who is obviously enfeebled and, in any practical sense, powerless. Hamm glories in his remaining control, taunting Clov with the possibility of opening the door to walk towards a free, beautiful landscape beyond their ravaged terrain:

HAMM: Did you ever think of one thing?

CLOV: Never.

HAMM: That we're down in a hole. [*Pause.*] But beyond the hills? Eh? Perhaps it's still green. Eh? [*Pause.*] Flora! Pomona! [*Ecstatically.*] Ceres! [*Pause.*] Perhaps you won't need to go very far. (*CDW* 111)

This sounds like a mischievously-devised test. Earlier in their exchanges, Hamm had established that Clov will obligingly repeat whatever he chooses to decree: that there is no more nature, that there is nothing outside their shelter but a devastated landscape.

Of course, in wearily repeating these platitudes, Clov is very likely doing no more than humouring a cranky and demanding master, whose performance of despair ('Can there be misery' he stifles a yawn, 'loftier than mine?' *CDW* 93) expresses more his illusion of disillusion than the real thing. A man who repeats these truisms, day in day out, may finally come to believe them: or he may not. Hamm wants to know and so he propounds his little test, but Clov doesn't take the hint. Perhaps, like Lucky, he is in love with his own servitude and cannot, at such a late stage, face the rigours of change: or perhaps, with some cunning, he divines that Hamm is testing the fidelity of his partner, employing that ultimate blackmail between lovers, when one tells the other to go, the better to savour that secret hold which ensures that the partner will stay. When servitude is so extreme that the servant cannot contemplate freedom, then the master knows a final form of control: Clov is as in love with his subjection as Hamm is with his gloom. Beckett, like O'Casey, is scandalised by the apparent willingness of men and women to adapt themselves even to disaster and catastrophe. Winnie, in *Happy Days*, is but the most blatant case, buried up to her chest in sand, hating her existence, but not letting on, and thereby upsetting everybody all the more. But the lineaments of the situation were sketched most fully in *Endgame*, where habit has so deadened the servant that his eye can see only what it has been trained to see: or so it seems.

There is, however, in Clov's responses a mindless, automatic quality which suggests that he knows his assigned script far too well. At times he jumbles it as if from over-familiarity, supplying rote-answers to questions which Hamm has not yet fully asked. This could be done out of numbed fatigue. Or it could be done to shut a prattling master up. Or it could be a scathing subversion of a smug system, which asks questions in a form which ensures that the answer has already been provided:

HAMM: Have you not had enough?

CLOV: Yes! [*Pause.*] Of what? (*CDW* 94)

This was the problem which faced the previous generation of Irish writers: they had questions to answer, but, as long as these were asked in forms imposed from without, the answers could only be drearily formulaic. In the play, Clov must unlearn the rhetorical habits of a lifetime in order to look into himself *and* in order to believe in the reality of the boy who suddenly appears at the close, in an apparently destroyed world. *Godot* had ended with the appearance of a boy who distracted the tramps from the task of self-authentication; *Endgame* concludes with the revelation of a boy whose identification confirms Clov's own ability to speak for himself. If the former play was a critique of man's inability to stop hoping against the odds, the latter is a repudiation of those who cannot transcend their own self-induced despair.

Clov is one of those underlings, described by Hegel, who knew more than their rulers, but who cannot often or easily pretend to. The kitchen is his zone, that time-honoured preserve of servants, but the master keeps the key to the cupboard. In theory it contains the means of their deliverance; in all probability it holds nothing. The underling knows exactly what is going on, and yet he must accept an obsolete rhetorical account of the world from the current holder of power, a man who is but a broker in outmoded forms. The Marxian application of Hegel's master/slave paradigm is rehearsed in the exchanges between both men, but with a certain weariness, as if the act is wearing thin:

HAMM: . . . get the sheet. . . . I'll give you nothing more to eat.

CLOV: Then we'll die.

HAMM: I'll give you just enough to keep you from dying. You'll be hungry all the time.

CLOV: Then we shan't die. [*Pause.*] I'll go and get the sheet. (*CDW* 94–95)

So threadbare have these routines become that Hamm sometimes shrewdly hints at their staged inauthenticity, as when he instructs Clov to place a toy dog standing before him in an imploring posture. And Clov's nascent rebellion is clear in the reassuring answer: 'Your *dogs* are here' (*CDW* 111).

That looming rebellion is even more obvious in their exchange about religion. When Hamm suggests that they pray, he evokes Clov's derision, and then proceeds to concur with it by calling down a curse on 'the bastard', who has the audacity not to exist. Clov's simple, subversive answer is 'Not yet' (*CDW* 119). The Irish grudge which he feels against God was summed up by the Gaelic poet Seán Ó Ríordáin, who said in response to the same question 'Bhuel, má tá sé ann, is bastard ceart é' (well if he does exist, he's a proper bastard). What is rejected in *Endgame* is the old religion of fear satirised also at the end of *Godot*; but Clov's 'not yet!' becomes a moving reprimand to those who see prayers as a set of demands rather than a real conversation, as an ultimatum rather than an overture. In his stage directions, Beckett goes to some lengths to mock the 'attitudes of prayer', the mechanical hand-joining and the insincere silence of those on-stage who seek a sign of God's favour. The artist whose motto was 'no symbols where none intended' might have been expected to hate all wicked generations who seek obvious signs; and so the boy whom Clov sees at the end comes unbidden, to one who uttered that tentative, undogmatic phrase 'Not yet!'

What is enacted on-stage in both *Waiting for Godot* and *Endgame* is the bleakness of a freedom from which there will always be numerous mechanisms of escape. Beckett's is a world whose characters are constantly tempted to allow others to do their thinking for them, to resign their wills to a higher authority (often no more than a polite phrase for tyranny).

ESTRAGON: Well? If we gave thanks for our mercies?

VLADIMIR: What is terrible is to *have* thought.

ESTRAGON: But did that ever happen to us? (*CDW* 60)

Freedom from ancient spiritual authorities will be meaningful only if the character is capable of actual thought. Too often, what he calls 'freedom' is actually and only the freedom to be like everybody else. As Erich Fromm has written: 'the right to express our thoughts means something only if we are able to have thoughts of our own.'[35] The problem is that, having cut the cords which connected them to the old authority, the tramps sag like redundant puppets: theirs is the empty freedom of the puppet. Their consequent fear of their own insignificance – joked about because so greatly feared – leads them to make a final surrender to the Old Testament god of fear and loathing, or to a modern variant thereof. All of Beckett's characters worry as to whether or not they have loved or been worthy of love: many assume that this will only be possible on conditions of complete self-surrender. Their attachments to one another are not the free solidarity of equals so much as a sado-masochistic conspiracy of the wounded:

HAMM: Gone from me you'd be dead.

CLOV: And *vice versa*. (*CDW* 126)

The psychology at work here is that which fed the fascist cult. There may well be a link between it and the vengeful deity on which Beckett poured such scorn in his post-war plays. Erich Fromm remarks that 'once man was ready to become nothing but the means for the glory of a God who represented neither justice nor love, he was sufficiently prepared to accept the role of a servant to the economic machine – and eventually a führer'.[36] Clov is tempted, like the tramps, to make himself dependent an a charismatic authority-figure, in whose aura he can bathe, and from whose confidence he can acquire a measure of the strength in which he is lacking. Because Hamm is so closely identified with his role, he is less conflicted than Clov, and more able (like Pozzo) to give a convincing impersonation. Yet in Clov's listlessness, his inability to maintain a role for any length of time, lies his great hope: the assertion of a still defiant self.

Students of the sado-masochistic relation report that, in it, feelings of real love and tenderness only assert themselves at the very moment when the relationship is about to break up. This can also be true of the transactions between entire peoples; but it may also be found in the interplay between individuals too. Near the close of *Endgame*, Hamm suddenly finds in himself the grace to thank the Clov whom he believes to be leaving:

HAMM: I'm obliged to you, Clov. For your services.

CLOV: Ah pardon, it's I am obliged to you.

HAMM: It's we are obliged to each other. (*CDW* 132)

This closing declaration is made against all the odds, and it is one of the most beautiful moments in Beckett's writings.

There is high irony in what follows, as the blind man fixes to die in the belief that Clov has gone. But Clov remains beside him, no longer a speaking servant but a silent partner, aware that there is no need for any rebellion now, because a true freedom never needs to declare or prove itself as such. Having spoken for himself in the first person singular, Clov is free to stay without objection, or to go without cruelty. The compassion, which he finds in himself in these late moments, suggests also that his earlier repetitions of Hamm's platitudes may have been offered as much out of care for a suffering mortal as out of numb acquiescence. This duo, like Didi watching over the sleeping Gogo, take their places alongside all the other couples of O'Casey and Shaw, of Wilde and Synge, as the rudiments from which a real society might yet be built. It may not even take these persons, just a rational being, or, indeed, a flea. For the moment, however, the two wordless men, broken and blasted though they may be, point like shattered signposts on a battlefield towards an uncertain but feasible future.

For his own part, Beckett appears to have believed that the conditions of post-war France, in which he wrote his plays, held vital lessons for Irish people, still nursing their own wounds three decades after British withdrawal from the twenty-six counties. In June 1946, he prepared a broadcast for Radio Éirann on the work of an Irish Red Cross hospital, of which he was storekeeper, at St. Lô, a town which had been bombed almost out of existence in a single night. Now, he was happy to report, it was being rebuilt by a combination of German war-prisoners, Irish technical expertise, and French pluck. In a coded rebuke to Irish neutrality during the war, he ended by suggesting that the Irish doctors, nurses and relief-workers at St. Lô 'got at least as good as they gave . . . got indeed what they could hardly give, a vision and sense of a time-honoured concept of humanity in ruins, and perhaps even an inkling of the terms in which our condition is to be thought again'.[37] The talk was never broadcast. One of the editors at Radio Éireann was Roibeárd Ó Faracháin, a follower of those antiquarian poets whom Beckett had derided in 1934 for their flight from self-perception. In the suppressed broadcast, Beckett clearly stated that the Irish in France were the real inheritors of a national genius for building amid ruins with the shreds and patches, the metal sheeting and the wooden boards, of a shattered society. When asked whether his migration from Dublin, publication in London and domicile in Paris, meant that he was no longer to be considered an Irishman, his reply was laconic enough: 'au contraire'. To the end, Beckett held onto his green passport.

Perhaps, in the contours of a France remaking itself after the devastation wrought by the Nazis, he saw the image of an ideal Ireland of the future.[38] □

Kiberd's reading of Beckett's relationship with Ireland, and his insistence that there is a specific political content to Beckett's aesthetic, is encouraging, and, with the emergence of several other critics who are rethinking Beckett's politics, promises to lead to a richer and subtler understanding of Beckett's cultural status. As the insights of Beckett's post-structuralist readers are adopted and adapted by critics who seek to locate his writing more firmly in relation to what Beckett's *Murphy* describes as 'the big world', Beckett studies seems to be approaching a new stage. The story of this chapter is one of the gradual growth of a culturally engaged criticism, from enclosure within the German language, towards a much broader, international audience. It suggests that soon, those critics who propose a political reading of Beckett's work will no longer be forced into tortured caveats explaining why such an 'apolitical' writer may merit such treatment.

Whilst the critics represented here offer welcome ways of thinking about Beckett's writing, however, they all share assumptions about his drama and its relationship to the world that lead them dangerously close to humanist modes of criticism that Anglo-American post-structuralist Beckett critics have already brought into question. From Ernst Fischer's illuminating but sometimes clumsily literal reading of Clov as a subject trembling on the verge of freedom and revelation, to Kiberd's suggestion that the antidote to alienation in Beckett's post-colonial universe lies in self-knowledge, these critics tend to forsake Beckett's negativity for an insistence on the politically radical nature of his humanist vision. In claiming that Beckett's drama, rather than offering a static and bleak view of an unchanging status quo, points the way to a better future, they have been led to substitute his critical negativity for an affirmative promise or solution. And dangerously for this mode of criticism, the solution often lies in the emancipation and self-validation of the individual – the very category that lies at the heart of the bourgeois, colonial ideologies that Beckett is being read as critiquing, and that critics from Adorno to Connor insist Beckett is most anxious to undermine. Back in 1958, Adorno set a challenge to the theoretical community to produce a critical language that was able to articulate the political promise of Beckett's negative aesthetic, without collapsing it back into the very ideological structures it sought to critique. For such a critical language we are, like Vladimir and Estragon, still waiting. There are signs that, unlike Godot, it may come.

NOTES

INTRODUCTION

1 This spate of writing activity included the stories that eventually comprised the *Four Novellas*, Beckett's novels *Molloy, Malone Dies* and *The Unnamable*, and the plays *Eleutheria* and *Waiting for Godot*. For an account of this period, see James Knowlson's chapter 'A Frenzy of Writing 1946–53', in James Knowlson, *Damned to Fame: The Life of Samuel Beckett* (London: Bloomsbury, 1996), pp. 356–87.

CHAPTER ONE

1 Samuel Beckett, *Happy Days*, in Samuel Beckett, *Complete Dramatic Works* (London: Faber and Faber, 1986), p. 156. All further page references to the *Complete Dramatic Works* will be included in brackets in the text, preceded by the abbreviation *CDW*.

2 Jacques Lemarchand, 'Review of *En attendant Godot*', 17 January 1953, trans. Jean M. Sommermeyer, in *Figaro Littéraire*, reprinted in Lawrence Graver and Raymond Federman, eds., *Samuel Beckett: The Critical Heritage* (London: Routledge & Kegan Paul, 1979), p. 90.

3 Lemarchand, 'Review', p. 90.

4 For an extended analysis of the relationship between dramatic convention and individual plays, see Raymond Williams, *Drama From Ibsen to Brecht* (London: Chatto and Windus, 1968).

5 Lemarchand, 'Review', p. 91.

6 Kenneth Tynan, 'Review of *Waiting for Godot*', in the *Observer*, 7 August 1955, reprinted in Graver, ed., *Beckett*, pp. 95–7.

7 Harold Hobson, 'Review of *Waiting for Godot*' in *Sunday Times*, 7 August 1955, reprinted in Graver, ed., *Beckett*, p. 93.

8 Jean Anouilh, 'Review of *Waiting for Godot*', in *Arts Spectacles*, 27 February– 5 March 1953, reprinted in Graver, ed., *Beckett*, p. 92.

9 Theodor Adorno, 'Trying to Understand *Endgame*', in Theodor Adorno, *Notes To Literature:* Volume One (New York: Columbia University Press, 1991), trans. Shierry Weber Nicholsen, p. 244.

10 Vivian Mercier, 'The Uneventful Event', in *Irish Times*, 18 February 1956, reprinted in Lance St. John Butler, ed., *Critical Essays on Samuel Beckett* (Aldershot: Scolar Press, 1993), p. 29.

11 G.S. Fraser, 'Review of *Waiting for Godot*', in *Times Literary Supplement*, 10 February 1956, reprinted in Graver, ed., *Beckett*, pp. 98–100.

12 For another example of a fifties Christian reading of the play, see Ronald Gray's article, '*Waiting for Godot:* a Christian Interpretation', in *The Listener*, 24 January 1954, reprinted in Butler, ed., *Beckett*, pp. 44–8. For a somewhat more nuanced reading of the theological and Christian content of Beckett's writing, see Richard N. Coe, 'God and Samuel Beckett', in J.D. O'Hara, ed., *Twentieth Century Interpretations of Molloy, Malone Dies and The Unnamable* (New Jersey: Prentice Hall, 1970), pp. 91–113.

13 Kavanagh's contrasting of Beckett's work with O'Casey's is underlined by O'Casey himself, who wrote a damning critique of *Waiting for Godot* in *Encore*, entitled 'Not Waiting for Godot'. See Sean O'Casey, *Blasts and Benedictions* (London: Macmillan, 1967), pp. 51–2.

14 Patrick Kavanagh, 'Some reflections on *Waiting for Godot*', in *Irish Times*, 28 January 1956, reprinted in Butler, ed., *Beckett*, pp. 27–8.

15 *Fin de partie* was first performed at the Royal Court Theatre, London, on 3 April 1957, directed by Roger Blin. *Endgame* was first performed in New York, at the Cherry Lane Theatre, on 28 January 1958, directed by Alan Schneider. The first performance of *Endgame* in London was at the Royal Court Theatre, on 28 October 1958, directed by George Devine.

16 See Kenneth Tynan, 'Review of *Waiting for Godot*', in the *Observer*, 7 August 1955, reprinted in Graver, ed., *Beckett*, pp. 95–7.

17 Beckett's English translation reads 'Clov: He's crying/Hamm: Then he's

living' (CDW 123).

18 In Beckett's translation, 'Something is taking its course' (CDW 98).

19 Kenneth Tynan, 'Review of *Endgame*', in the *Observer*, 7 April 1957, reprinted in Graver, ed., *Beckett*, pp. 164–6.

20 Harold Hobson, 'Review of *Endgame*' in *Sunday Times*, 7 April 1957, reprinted in Graver, ed., *Beckett*, p. 161.

21 The possibility that Beckett's drama was contentless, and that he was having a laugh at the expense of his critics, was noted by several reviewers. Ronald Barker, for example, writes: 'Now that Beckett has made enough money out of pulling both legs of the audience in most European countries, he should sit down and write a real play.' Ronald Barker, '*Waiting for Godot*', *Plays and Players*, September 1955, reprinted in Butler, ed., *Beckett*, p. 23.

22 Martin Esslin, *The Theatre of the Absurd*, 3rd edition (Harmondsworth: Penguin, 1983), p. 28.

23 Esslin, *Absurd*, p. 28.

24 Esslin, *Absurd*, p. 28.

25 Adorno, '*Endgame*', p. 243.

26 Alain Robbe-Grillet, 'Samuel Beckett, or Presence on the Stage', in Alain Robbe-Grillet, *For a New Novel: Essays on Fiction* (Salem: Ayer Company Publishers, 1965), trans. Richard Howard, p. 111.

27 See *Act Without Words I* and *Act Without Words II*. Beckett later wrote a third, perhaps more famous, mime entitled *Quad*. All three are collected in Samuel Beckett, *Complete Dramatic Works*.

28 Esslin, *Absurd*, pp. 85–6.

29 Samuel Beckett, *Proust* (New York: Grove Press, no date), pp. 2–3.

30 Beckett, *Proust*, pp. 4–5.

31 Beckett, *Proust*, p. 13.

32 Samuel Beckett, *En Attendant Godot* (Paris: Les Editions de Minuit, 1952), p. 30.

33 Esslin, *Absurd*, pp. 50–3.

34 See Fraser's 'Review of *Waiting for Godot*', quoted on pp. 14–15, for an example of this kind of argument.

35 Eva Metman, 'Reflections on Samuel Beckett's plays', in *Journal of Analytic Psychology*, London, January 1960, p. 51.

36 Beckett, *Proust*, p. 8. Esslin's italics.

37 Beckett, *Proust*, p. 9.

38 Jean-Paul Sartre, *L'Être et le Néant* (Paris: Gallimard, 1943), p. 111. Esslin, *Absurd*, pp. 56–61.

39 Lionel Abel, 'Joyce the father, Beckett the son', in *The New Leader*, New York, 14 December 1959.

40 Esslin refers here to a famous production of *Waiting for Godot*, performed for the inmates of San Quentin penitentiary on 19 November 1957. The production was a great success. Esslin discusses the production in his introduction to *The Theatre of the Absurd* (pp. 19–22). For an interesting review of the production, written by one of the prisoners, see the article in *San Quentin News* written by 'C.B.', reprinted in Graver, ed., *Samuel Beckett: The Critical Heritage*, pp. 111–13.

41 *Fin de partie* includes an episode, missing in Beckett's English version, in which Clov watches, through his telescope, the boy contemplating his navel. Samuel Beckett, *Fin de partie* (Paris: Les Editions de Minuit, 1957), p. 103.

42 Samuel Beckett, *Malone Dies*, in Samuel Beckett *Molloy/Malone Dies/The Unnamable* (London: John Calder, 1959), p. 193.

43 Samuel Beckett, *Murphy* (1938; London: Picador, 1973), p. 138.

44 Metman, 'Reflections', p. 58.

45 Esslin, *Absurd*, pp. 66–76.

46 Pierre Marcabu, 'Review of *Waiting for Godot*', in *Arts-Spectacles*, 10–16 May 1961, trans. Jean M. Sommermeyer, reprinted in Graver, ed., *Beckett*, p. 113.

47 Esslin draws heavily on Sartre's theorisation of existentialism in his reading of Beckett's drama, but his insistence on the futility of action marks a clear divergence between Sartre's and Esslin's understanding of existentialism. Sartre is emphatic that his view of the value of freedom is heavily dependent upon action. Existentialism is a 'doctrine of action', in which it is proven that 'it is not by turning back upon himself, but always by seeking, beyond himself, an

aim which is one of liberation or of some particular realisation, that man can realise himself as truly human.' For Sartre, art is seen as a powerful tool in the struggle for political freedom. See Jean-Paul Sartre, *Existentialism and Humanism* (London: Methuen, 1966), trans. Philip Mairet, p.56.

48 See, for example, Terry Eagleton, *Heathcliff and the Great Hunger: Studies in Irish Culture* (London: Verso, 1995), where Eagleton describes ideology succinctly as the 'naturalisation of culture', p.4.

49 P.J. Murphy, *Reconstructing Beckett: Language for Being in Samuel Beckett's Fiction* (Toronto: University of Toronto Press, 1990), p.xiii.

50 Adorno, *'Endgame'*, p.250.

51 There is a sustained dialogue between Adorno and Lukács concerning the political and aesthetic validity of Beckett's art, some of which is collected in *Aesthetics and Politics*. Lukács claims that Beckett's work is irresponsible, because it depicts man as a degenerate species that is retreating into subjectivity as a result of a failure to deal with the demands of communal political life. Adorno claims, in response, that Beckett's subjectivism is the only valid response to late capitalist society, and as such the most effective protest against forms of tyranny and control. See Georg Lukács, 'Realism in the Balance', and Theodor Adorno, 'Reconciliation under Duress' and 'Commitment', collected in Ernst Bloch, ed., *Aesthetics and Politics* (London: NLB, 1977).

52 Adorno has commented that an 'apolitical' stance is itself a political standpoint, even if it does not recognise itself as one.

53 Adorno, *'Endgame'*, p.242.

54 Esslin, *Absurd*, p.88.

55 Adorno, *'Endgame'*, p.241.

56 Adorno, *'Endgame'*, p.249.

57 Adorno, *'Endgame'*, p.249.

58 Cf. Theodor Adorno, 'Extorted reconciliation', in Adorno, *Notes to literature*, p.226. This essay is also published, under the title of 'Reconciliation Under Duress' trans. Rodney Livingstone, in Ernst

Bloch, ed., *Aesthetics and Politics* (London: NLB, 1977), pp.151–76.

59 Adorno, *'Endgame'*, pp.241–50.

CHAPTER TWO

1 See, for example, F.R. Leavis, *The Great Tradition* (London: Chatto and Windus, 1948), Q.D. Leavis, *Fiction and the Reading Public* (London: Chatto and Windus, 1932), I.A. Richards, *Practical Criticism* (London: Routledge, 1929).

2 See T.S. Eliot, 'Tradition and the Individual Talent', in T.S. Eliot, *Selected Essays* (London: Faber, 1951). Eliot's critical and political agenda in this essay, which seeks to theorise the relationship between original new poetry and the traditional canon, has several affinities with the pioneering work of Leavis and Richards.

3 See David Hesla, *The Shape of Chaos: An Interpretation of the Art of Samuel Beckett* (Minneapolis: The University of Minnesota Press, 1971), p.v–vi: 'With remarkable perspicacity, Hugh Kenner has touched on nearly every theme, problem or idea worth serious study.'

4 See Ruby Cohn, *Samuel Beckett: The Comic Gamut* (New Jersey: Rutgers University Press, 1962).

5 See Hugh Kennner, 'The Cartesian Centaur', in Hugh Kenner, *Samuel Beckett: A Critical Study* (Berkeley: University of California Press, 1968).

6 See G.C. Barnard, *Samuel Beckett: A New Approach* (New York: Dodd, 1970).

7 For a succinct account of the development of New Criticism, see Terry Eagleton, 'The Rise of English', in Terry Eagleton, *Literary Theory: An Introduction* (Oxford: Blackwell 1983), pp.17–53.

8 For an analysis of the emergence of *Scrutiny* and its subsequent effect on the critical landscape, see Francis Mulhern, *The Moment of Scrutiny* (London: NLB, 1979).

9 I.A. Richards, *Science and Poetry* (London: Kegan Paul, 1926), pp.82–3.

10 Mulhern, *Scrutiny*, p.28, quoting I.A. Richards, *Principles of Literary Criticism*, p.vii.

11 Esslin, 'Introduction', p. 5.

12 For a discussion of Esslin's earlier work on Beckett, see chapter one, pp. 21–38.

13 P. J. Murphy, Werner Huber, Rolf Breuer and Konrad Schoell, *Critique of Beckett Criticism: A Guide to Research in English, French and German* (Columbia: Camden House, 1994), p. 17.

14 Esslin takes this notion of an aesthetic of failure from the 'Three Dialogues', in which Beckett famously asserts that 'to be an artist is to fail, as no other dare fail'; Samuel Beckett, 'Three Dialogues with Georges Duthuit', in Samuel Beckett, *Proust and Three Dialogues with Georges Duthuit* (London: Calder, 1965), p. 125.

15 Esslin, 'Introduction', p. 4.

16 Esslin, 'Introduction', p. 4.

17 For a fictional account of the (vain) search for the 'outline of the main design' of a literary work, which reflects ironically upon Esslin's recommendation here, see Henry James, 'The Figure in the Carpet', in *Henry James, The Figure in the Carpet and Other Stories* (Harmondsworth: Penguin, 1986), edited by Frank Kermode [ed].

18 'To be is to be perceived.' This is taken from Bishop Berkeley, an eighteenth-century idealist Irish philosopher, and is quoted by Beckett as the epigraph to his only film, starring Buster Keaton, entitled *Film*. See Samuel Beckett, *Film*, in Samuel Beckett, *Complete Dramatic Works* [ed].

19 See Günther Anders, 'Being Without Time: On Beckett's Play *Waiting for Godot*', and Eva Metman 'Reflections on Samuel Beckett's Plays', both collected in Martin Esslin, ed., *Samuel Beckett: A Collection of Critical Essays* (New Jersey: Prentice Hall, 1965) [ed].

20 See Samuel Beckett, *Watt* (1953; London: Calder, 1976), p. 247 [ed].

21 Martin Esslin, 'Introduction', in Esslin, ed., *Beckett: A Collection.*

22 Eagleton, *Literary Theory*, p. 42.

23 Theodor Adorno, 'Commitment', in Ernst Bloch, ed., *Aesthetics and Politics* (London: NLB 1977), p. 185.

24 Hugh Kenner, *A Reader's Guide to Samuel Beckett* (London: Thames and Hudson, 1973), pp. 28–9.

25 Kenner, *Reader's Guide*, p. 18.

26 Kenner, *Reader's Guide*, p. 128.

27 Kenner, *Reader's Guide*, p. 126.

28 Kenner, *Reader's Guide*, p. 35.

29 Kenner, *Reader's Guide*, p. 37.

30 Hugh Kenner, *Samuel Beckett: A Critical Study*, second edition (1961; London: University of California Press, 1968), p. 142.

31 This quotation in taken from a chapter called 'The Cartesian Centaur', in which Kenner suggests that the typical Beckettian image of a man on a bicycle is representative of the possibility of perfect structural harmony between mind and body, between knowledge and movement. See Kenner, *Critical Study*, pp. 117–32.

32 Kenner, *Critical Study*, p. 132.

33 The Tannhäuser legend, subject of an opera by Wagner, tells the story of Tannhäuser's plea for forgiveness from the Pope. The Pope tells Tannhäuser, who has been engaged in seven years of revelry ensconced in a grotto with Venus, that it is as impossible for Tannhäuser to be granted absolution as it is for the Pope's staff to bloom again. Tannhäuser leaves in despair, and shortly after the Pope's staff blossoms [ed].

34 This quote is taken from a letter from Samuel Beckett to Alan Schneider, printed in Samuel Beckett, *Disjecta: Miscellaneous Writings and a Dramatic Fragment* (London: Calder, 1983), edited by Ruby Cohn, p. 109 [ed].

35 See Christopher Marlow, *Tamburlaine the Great*, a drama in blank verse published in 1590. The drama concerns Tamburlaine's rise to power in Persia, and his conquests in Babylon. The phrase 'papered jades of Asia' is quoted by Pistol in Shakespeare's *2 Henry IV*, 2.4.161 [ed].

36 'Do you know what he calls it? . . . The Net. He thinks he is entangled in a net.' Compare the words Miscio Ito spoke, 'with perfect precision', to Ezra Pound:

'Japanese dance all time overcoat.' The one stable item of Noh décor is painted on the back of the stage: 'a pine tree, symbol of the unchanging.'

37 Cf. James Joyce, *Finnegans Wake* (London: Faber and Faber, 1939) p. 508: 'I am sorry to have to tell you, hullo and evoe, they were coming down from off him. – How curious an epiphany!'

38 Kenner, *Critical Study*, pp. 133–9.

39 See John Peter, *Vladimir's Carrot: Modern Drama and the Modern Imagination* (London: André Deutsch, 1987), pp. 6–7: 'The point about Vladimir's carrot is how little it tells us. It comes out of his pocket and Estragon eats it; but it tells us nothing about the two men and their world. . . . Like all objects in the play – hats, boots, belts, basket, rope – the carrot is there for no other reason than to fulfil (or fail to fulfil) its most basic function.'

40 *How It Is* is geometrically divided into a series of journeys through a bleak muddy landscape, each followed by a rest. The journeying character carries his supplies with him in a jute sack as he crawls through the mud. See Samuel Beckett, *How It Is* (1964; London: Calder, 1996) [ed].

41 Malone, the narrator of Beckett's novel *Malone Dies*, spends the entire novel preparing to draw up an inventory of the objects that he still has in his possession, which he hopes to complete before his death. See Samuel Beckett, *Malone Dies*, in Samuel Beckett, *The Beckett Trilogy* (1959; London: Picador, 1979) [ed].

42 Kenner is here quoting from Beckett's French short story *La fin*, which Beckett published in an English translation as *The End*. In this translation, the passage Kenner quotes reads 'without the courage to end or the strength to go on'. Samuel Beckett, *The End*, in Samuel Beckett, *The Expelled and Other Novellas* (Harmondsworth: Penguin, 1980), p. 93 [ed].

43 See Samuel Beckett, *Molloy*, in Beckett, *The Beckett Trilogy*. Moran's narration of his journey with his son constitutes the second section of this two-part novel [ed].

44 See Abbot Payson *Usher, A History of Mechanical Inventions*, chap. xii, p. 313.

45 Kenner, *Critical Study*, pp. 153–5.

46 Kenner very influentially draws attention to the preponderance of mathematical equations and theories that run through Beckett's oeuvre, and particularly to the prominence of the figure of the 'surd'. See Hugh Kenner, 'The Rational Domain', in Kenner, *Critical Study*, pp. 79–115.

47 Kenner, *Reader's Guide*, p. 32.

48 Kenner, *Reader's Guide*, p. 35.

49 This admirable phrase is Mr Roy Walker's, in the December 1958 *Twentieth Century*.

50 Kenner is referring here to *The Tempest*, and to Prospero's famous speech, in which he says the line 'Our revels now are ended'. William Shakespeare, *The Tempest*, 4.1.148 [ed].

51 Or always win. 'One of the thieves was saved. It's a reasonable percentage.'

52 Samuel Beckett, *Murphy* (1938; London: Picador, 1973), p. 137.

53 Samuel Beckett, *Fin de partie*, (Paris: Les Éditions de Minuit, 1957) p. 103.

54 Kenner, *Critical Study*, pp. 155–60.

55 Kenner, *Reader's Guide*, p. 121.

56 For readings of the impact of theatrical self-reflexivity that differ widely from Kenner's, see, for example, Antonin Artaud, *The Theatre and its Double* (London: Calder, 1970), and Bertolt Brecht, *Brecht on Theatre* (London: Methuen, 1964). The next two chapters will explore different ways in which Beckett's self-reflexivity has been understood by his critics.

57 Kenner, *Reader's Guide*, p. 121.

58 Kenner, *Critical Study*, p. 138.

59 I owe this suggestion to Mr Walker's article.

60 The Lord Chamberlain, a less subtle (or less orthodox) theologian, required that for performances on the English stage 'bastard' should be altered to swine.

61 Kenner, *Critical Study*, pp. 160–5.

62 Cohn, *Comic Gamut*, p. 228.

63 Cohn, *Comic Gamut*, p. 6.
64 Cohn, *Comic Gamut*, p. 5.
65 Cohn, *Comic Gamut*, p. 5.
66 See chapter one, pp. 13–16, where some Christian interpretations of the play are explored [ed].
67 Cohn, *Comic Gamut*, pp. 220–5.
68 Cohn, *Comic Gamut*, pp. 229–32
69 Cohn's reading of *Endgame* as a mourning for an earlier, pre-Cartesian age in which mind is in efficient harmony with body, recalls Kenner's work, particularly in 'The Cartesian Centaur'. See pp. 65–6 above, and p. 171, note 31.
70 Cohn, *Comic Gamut*, pp. 239–42

CHAPTER THREE

1 For an introduction to post-structuralist theory, see Eagleton, *Literary Theory*, pp. 127–50. For more detailed introductions to deconstruction, see Christopher Norris, *Derrida* (London: Fontana, 1987), and Rodolphe Gasché, *Inventions of Difference: On Jacques Derrida* (Cambridge: Harvard University Press, 1994).
2 Important exceptions to this rule are Theodor Adorno and Georg Lukács, for whom Beckett's writing is a centre of critical debate. For a discussion of these critics' response to Beckett, see chapter one, pp. 38–50.
3 See Michel Foucault, 'What is an Author', in Paul Rabinow, ed., *The Foucault Reader* (Harmondsworth: Penguin, 1986), p. 101: 'Beckett nicely formulates the theme with which I would like to begin: "What does it matter who is speaking," someone said, "what does it matter who is speaking." In this indifference appears one of the fundamental ethical principles of contemporary writing (*écriture*). I say "ethical" because this indifference is not really a trait characterising the manner in which one speaks and writes, but rather a kind of immanent rule, taken up over and over again, never fully applied, not designating writing as something completed, but dominating it as a practice.' For a full reading of the significance of Beckett's indifference, that relies heavily on Maurice Blanchot rather than

Foucault, see Leslie Hill, *Beckett's Fiction: In Different Words* (Cambridge: Cambridge University Press, 1990).
4 See Julia Kristeva, 'The Father, Love and Banishment', in Julia Kristeva, *Desire In Language: A Semiotic Approach to Literature and Art* (Oxford: Blackwell, 1981), ed. Leon S. Roudiez, trans. Thomas Gora, Alice Jardine, Leon S. Roudiez.
5 See, for example, Maurice Blanchot, 'Where Now? Who Now?', in *Evergreen Review* 2, 1953, pp. 222–9, and 'Oh tout finir', *Critique* 46, 1990, pp. 635–7.
6 See Colin MacCabe, *James Joyce and the Revolution of the Word* (Basingstoke: Macmillan, 1979).
7 It is worth pointing out here that it is problematic to describe Beckett either as a modernist, or as Joyce's natural successor.
8 For a critical evaluation of MacCabe's (and others') reading of Joyce as abandoning nationalist commitment in favour of an internationalist aestheticism, see Emer Nolan, *James Joyce and Nationalism* (London: Routledge, 1995).
9 Israel Schenker, 'A Portrait of Samuel Beckett, the Author of the Puzzling *Waiting for Godot*', *New York Times*, May 6, 1956, section 2, pp. 1, 3. For further commentary on this 'interview', and a selection of essays that consider the relationship between Beckett and Joyce, see Bernard Benstock, ed., *The Seventh of Joyce* (Bloomington: Indiana University Press, 1982), pp. 25–44.
10 Beckett, *Molloy*, p. 14.
11 For an unusually explicit commentary by Beckett on his own tendency to use words to deconstruct words, see the German letter of 1937: 'It is indeed becoming more and more difficult, even senseless, for me to write an official English. And more and more my own language appears to me like a veil that must be torn apart to get at the things (or the Nothingness) behind it.' Cohn, ed., *Disjecta*, p. 171.
12 Jacques Derrida, *Acts of Literature* (London: Routledge, 1999), ed. Derek Attridge, pp. 60–1.

13 For a brief discussion of Derrida's 'background' as a Jewish Algerian, see Chris Norris's 'Introduction' to *Derrida*.

14 Derrida, *Acts*, p. 61.

15 Derrida, *Acts*, pp. 61–2.

16 Wolfgang Iser, *The Implied Reader: Patterns of Communication in Prose Fiction from Bunyan to Beckett* (Baltimore: Johns Hopkins University Press, 1974), p. 261.

17 For a discussion of Robbe-Grillet's reading of *Waiting for Godot*, see chapter one, pp. 22–3. For a discussion of Esslin's reading of *Waiting for Godot* and *Endgame*, see chapter one, pp. 22–38.

18 Iser is using Saussurian terminology here, where paradigmatic denotes 'a whole class of signs which may stand in for one another', and syntagmatic denotes signs which 'are coupled together with each other in a "chain"' (Eagleton, *Literary Theory*, p. 101). For a definition of syntagmatic and paradigmatic relations, see Ferdinand de Saussure, *Course in General Linguistics* (London: Peter Owen Ltd, 1960), trans. Wade Baskin, ed. Charles Bally and Albert Sechehaye, pp. 122–34. For an introduction to semiotics, and its importance to structuralist literary analysis, see Eagleton, *Literary Theory*, pp. 91–126 [ed].

19 Wolfgang Iser, 'Counter-sensical Comedy and Audience Response in Beckett's *Waiting for Godot*', in Steven Connor, ed., *'Waiting for Godot' and 'Endgame'* (Basingstoke: Macmillan 1992), pp. 55–6. This essay originally appeared in German in 1979, and was reprinted in English translation in *Gestos* in 1987.

20 See Ruby Cohn, *Back to Beckett* (Princeton, 1973), p. 130; Ruby Cohn, *Samuel Beckett: The Comic Gamut* (New Jersey: Rutgers University Press, 1962), p. 211; Beryl Fletcher, John Fletcher *et al.*, *A Student's Guide to the Plays of Samuel Beckett* (London: Faber, 1978), pp. 38, 45; Geneviève Surreau, 'Beckett's Clowns', in *Casebook on Waiting for Godot: The Impact of Beckett's Modern Classic: Reviews, Reflections and Interpretations*, ed. Ruby Cohn (New York: Grove Press, 1967), pp. 171–5.

21 Joachim Ritter, 'Über das Lachen', *Blätter für deutsche Philosophie*, 14 (1940/41), p. 14.

22 Sigmund Freud, *Jokes and Their Relation to the Unconscious*, Pelican Freud Library, vol. 6, trans. James Strachey (Harmondsworth: Pelican, 1976), p. 255.

23 See Martin Esslin, *The Theatre of the Absurd*, p. 12, where he quotes Beckett's reply to a question asked by the American director Alan Schneider.

24 For a more detailed discussion of this point, see Iser's essay 'Samuel Beckett's Dramatic Language', *Modern Drama*, 9 (1966), p. 251–9.

25 See Martin Esslin, 'Godot at San Quentin', in Ruby Cohn, ed., *Casebook on Waiting for Godot*, pp. 83–5.

26 See the material collected in *Casebook on Waiting for Godot*, as well as the following: Anon., 'They Also Serve', *TLS* (10 February 1956), p. 84 and readers' letters from J. M. S. Tompkins, *TLS* (24 February 1956), p. 117, Katherine M. Wilson, *TLS* (2 March 1956), p. 133, J. S. Walsh, *TLS* (9 March 1956), p. 149, Philip H. Bagby, *TLS* (23 March 1956), p. 181, William Empson, *TLS* (30 March 1956), p. 195, John J. O'Meara, *TLS* (6 April 1956), p. 207; and the leading article, *TLS* (13 April 1956), p. 221. See also Friedrich Hansen-Löve's essay 'Samuel Beckett oder die Einübung ins Nichts', *Hochland*, 50 (1957/8) pp. 36ff. Günther Anders, *Die Antiquiertheit des Menschen* (Munich, 1956), p. 123, was one of the first to express basic doubts concerning any religious interpretation of this play shortly after its first publication.

27 Helmuth Plessner, *Lachen und Weinen: Eine Untersuchung nach den Grenzen menschlichen Verhaltens* (Bern, 1950), pp. 111f. and 121.

28 One of Ritter's fundamental definitions of comedy, in 'Über das Lachen', pp. 9f.

29 See Kenner, *Beckett*, p. 165.

30 The degree to which the comic is always directed towards the totality of existence is dealt with more thoroughly by Ritter, 'Über das Lachen', pp. 7, 9.

31 Freud, *Jokes*, p. 300.

32 Iser, 'Counter-sensical Comedy', pp. 56–63.

33 Ritter, 'Über', p. 15.

34 Plessner, *Lachen*, p. 89.

35 Plessner, *Lachen*, p. 90.

36 Freud, *Jokes*, p. 228, n. 1.

37 Samuel Beckett, *Watt* (1953; London: Calder, 1976), pp. 46–7.

38 Iser, 'Counter-sensical Comedy', pp. 63–8.

39 See, for example, Steven Connor, *Samuel Beckett: Repetition, Theory and Text* (Oxford: Blackwell, 1988), Mary Bryden, *Women in Samuel Beckett's Prose and Drama* (Basingstoke: Macmillan, 1993), Leslie Hill, *Beckett's Fiction: In Different Words* (Cambridge: Cambridge University Press, 1990), and Carla Locatelli, *Unwording the World: Samuel Beckett's Prose Works after the Nobel Prize* (Philadelphia: University of Pennsylvania Press, 1990).

40 'Moody Man of Letters', *New York Times*, Sunday 6 May 1956, section 2, p. 3.

41 Michael Robinson, *The Long Sonata of the Dead: A Study of Samuel Beckett* (London: Rupert Hart-Davis, 1969), p. 230.

42 Quoted in *Materialen zu Becketts 'Endspiel'*, ed. Michael Haerdter (Frankfurt, 1968), p. 88. [Connor's translation – ed.]

43 Robbe-Grillet, 'Presence', p. 119. For a discussion of Robbe-Grillet's approach to presence on Beckett's stage, in relation to Esslin's reading of the plays, see chapter one, pp. 22–3. References to this essay are hereafter included in the text, preceded by the abbreviation *P* [ed.].

44 See the discussion in Bruce Morrissette, 'Robbe-Grillet as a Critic of Samuel Beckett', in *Samuel Beckett Now: New Critical Approaches to the Novels, Poetry and Plays*, 2nd edn, ed. Melvin J. Fiedman (Chicago: University of Chicago Press, 1970), pp. 59–72.

45 This critical manoeuvre, in which self-reflexivity is taken to consolidate rather than undermine the presence of actors on the stage, can be found in many of the critics represented in chapter two. See, for example, p. 66 [ed.].

46 William Worthen, 'Beckett's Actor', *Modern Drama*, 26 (1983), p. 420.

47 Sidney Homan, *Beckett's Theatres: Interpretations for Performance* (Lewisburg: Bucknell University Press, 1984), p. 49.

48 Beckett, in a letter to Alan Schneider, 29 December 1957, in *Disjecta*, p. 109.

49 See the discussion of drama and art in general as historical 'play' in Hans-Georg Gadamer, *Truth and Method* (London: Sheed and Ward, 1981), pp. 104–7.

50 Antonin Artaud, 'Production and Metaphysics', in *The Theatre and its Double* (London, 1970), trans. Victor Corti, p. 7. Page references to *The Theatre and its Double* are hereafter included in the text, preceded by the abbreviation *TD*.

51 Steven Connor, 'The Doubling of Presence in *Waiting for Godot* and *Endgame*', in Connor, ed., *'Waiting for Godot'*, pp. 128–31.

52 Vivian Mercier, 'The Uneventful Event', *Irish Times*, 18 February 1956, p. 6. For a discussion of this review, see chapter one, p. 13 [ed.].

53 Lewis Carroll, *The Complete Works of Lewis Carroll* (London, 1939), p. 680.

54 Quoted in Haerdter, *Materialen*, p. 46.

55 Jacques Derrida, 'The Theatre of Cruelty or the Closure of Represent-ation', in *Writing and Difference* (London: Routledge, 1978), trans. Alan Bass, p. 248.

56 Connor, 'Doubling', pp. 131–8.

57 See Bryden, *Women in Samuel Beckett*, and Linda Ben Zvi, *Women in Beckett: Performance and Critical Perspectives* (Urbana: University of Illinois Press, 1990).

58 Mary Bryden, 'Gender in Transition: *Waiting for Godot* and *Endgame*', in Connor, ed., *'Waiting for Godot'*, p. 153.

59 Bryden, 'Gender', p. 155.

60 Claude Lefort, 'Outline of the Genesis of Ideology in Modern Societies', trans. John B. Thompson, in John B. Thompson ed., *The Political Forms of Modern Society: Bureaucracy, Democracy, Totalitarianism* (Cambridge: Polity, 1986), p. 228.

61 Charles Dickens, *The Old Curiosity Shop* (London, 1907). Page references to this text will be hereafter included in brackets in the main text, preceded by the abbreviation *TOCS*.

62 *Dream of Fair to Middling Women* has since been published both in America and in Britain. See Samuel Beckett, *Dream of Fair to Middling Women* (London: Calder, 1993).

63 Beckett, *Disjecta*, p. 28.

64 See Samuel Beckett, *Fin de partie* (Paris: Les Editions de Minuit, 1957), pp. 103–5.

65 Bryden, 'Gender', pp. 156–63.

66 See Peter Gidal, *Understanding Beckett: A Study of Monologue and Gesture in the Works of Samuel Beckett* (London: Macmillan, 1986), Simon Critchley, *Very Little . . . Almost Nothing: Death, Philosophy, Literature* (London: Routledge, 1997), Paul Lawley, 'Adoption in *Endgame*', *Modern Drama*, 31.4, 1988, pp. 529–35, Anthony Uhlmann, *Beckett and Poststructuralism* (Cambridge: Cambridge University Press, 1999).

67 For a discussion of the early relation between German and English Beckett criticism, see chapter one.

68 See Steven Connor, *Repetition*, pp. 170–201.

CHAPTER FOUR

1 For a discussion of Bryden's approach to Beckett's representation of gender, see chapter three, pp. 127–36.

2 See Vivian Mercier, *Beckett/Beckett* (Oxford: Oxford University Press, 1977).

3 Perhaps the best example of criticism that traces Beckett's geographical references, without questioning the universal placelessness of his work, is Eion O'Brien's *The Beckett Country: Samuel Beckett's Ireland* (Dublin: The Black Cat Press, 1986). The book, which has a certain coffee-table quality, is remarkably thorough and useful, and has earned itself a strange respectful notoriety.

4 Jean-Jacques Mayoux, 'Samuel Beckett and Universal Parody' in Martin Esslin, ed., *Samuel Beckett: A Collection of Critical Essays* (New Jersey: Prentice Hall, 1965), p. 91.

5 Mayoux, 'Beckett', p. 91.

6 Mayoux, 'Beckett', p. 91.

7 See, for example, the debate between Adorno and Lukács concerning Beckett's work in Ernst Bloch, ed., *Aesthetics and Politics* (London: NLB, 1977), and the discussion about the relation between Lukács and Adorno in chapter one, pp. 38–50.

8 The Marxist critics sympathetic to Beckett have been outnumbered by those who reject his work out of hand, as the official party line on Beckett was that he was a decadent bourgeois.

9 For the changing critical responses to Beckett's self-reflexivity, see chapter two, p. 66, and chapter three, p. 117.

10 For an introduction to Brecht's alienation effect, and its importance to his political aesthetic, see Bertolt Brecht, *Brecht on Theatre: The Development of an Aesthetic* (London: Methuen, 1978), ed. John Willett.

11 See Declan Kiberd, *Inventing Ireland* (London: Jonathan Cape, 1995), and David Lloyd, *Anomalous States: Irish Writing and the Postcolonial Moment* (Dublin: The Lilliput Press, 1993). For other work that focuses on Beckett's work in an Irish context, see Seamus Deane, *Celtic Revivals: Essays in Modern Irish Literature 1880–1980* (London: Faber and Faber, 1985), Chapter 9; Richard Kearney, *Transitions: Narratives in Modern Irish Culture* (Manchester: Manchester University Press, 1988), Chapter 3; W. J. MacCormack, *From Burke to Beckett: Ascendancy, Tradition and Betrayal in Literary History* (Cork: Cork University Press, 1995), Chapter 11; and Terry Eagleton, *Crazy John and the Bishop* (Cork: Cork University Press, 1988).

12 Terry Eagleton, *Heathcliff and the Great Hunger: Studies in Irish Culture* (London: Verso, 1995), pp. 281–282.

13 See Alexander Solzhenitsyn, *One Day in the Life of Ivan Denisovich* (St. Albans: Triad, 1978), trans. Gillon Aitken.

14 Fischer, *Art Against Ideology* (London: Allen Lane the Penguin Press, 1969), trans. Anna Bostock, p. 15.

15 Fischer, *Art*, p. 15.

16 Fischer, *Art*, pp. 7–13.

17 Rosemary Pountney, *Theatre of Shadows: Samuel Beckett's Drama 1956–76* (Gerrards Cross: Colin Smythe, 1988), p. 194.

18 For an account of Brecht's intention to write a counter-play to *Waiting for Godot*, see Clas Zilliacus, 'Three Times Godot: Beckett, Brecht, Bulatovic', in *Comparative Drama*, 4 (1970), pp. 3–17.

19 In 1978, Mittenzwei struck a more conciliatory tone in *Kampf der Richtungen* (Werner Mittenzwei, 'Endspiele der Absurden: Zum Problem des Figurenaufbaus', in *Sinn und Form* 16 (1964), pp. 329–37). Here he acknowledged the dramatic excellence and aesthetic radicalism of *Waiting for Godot*. Nevertheless, Mittenzwei did not refrain from including excerpts from a panel discussion on *Waiting for Godot*, organised by the East German Academy of Arts in 1976, in which Peter Hacks, a leading East German playwright, condemned Beckett outright: 'A Craving for Beckett signals sickness in the head' (Mittenzwei, 'Endspiele', pp. 335–7).

20 For reports on this event from the respective points of view, see Liane Pfelling, 'Experimenta 1', in *Theatre der Zeit*, 21.14 (1966), p. iv, and Henning Rischbieter, 'Experimenta: Theater und Publikum neu definiert', in *Theater heute* (1966), pp. 8–17.

21 Further instances of an incipient Beckett reception in East Germany are the publication of Elmar Tophoven's translation of 'Le Concentrisme' alongside Trilse's 1986 essay in *Sinn und Form*, a Berlin Ensemble production of *Play* as a chamber oratorio with music by Paul-Heinz Dittrich in 1987, and what appears to be the first East German doctoral dissertation on Beckett by Renate Sandberg.

22 Jonathan Kalb, *Beckett in Performance* (Cambridge: Cambridge University Press, 1989), pp. 74–5, 212–19. In the interview with Kalb, Schall remained strikingly non-committal and evasive on the early impact of Beckett's works in East Germany: 'I don't think at all about playing Brecht off Beckett or Beckett off Brecht, using them that way. . . . The confrontation in the theatre of socialism/capitalism doesn't interest me' (p. 215).

23 It seems that Trilse first formulated his main ideas about Beckett in an 'afterword' to a selection of Beckett's plays, *Spiele*, which was not published until 1988. The afterword is dated March 1980. From it are derived Trilse's essays in *Sinn und Form* (1986) and *Deutschunterricht* (1991).

24 Trilse here points to George Tabori's unorthodox production of *Waiting for Godot* as a rehearsal (Munich 1984) and his other highly controversial Beckett evenings, which, most unusual for Beckett, seem to have had his blessing more as a sign of his personal friendship with Tabori than for artistic considerations (Kalb, *Performance*, pp. 91–2, 252–4).

25 Shortly before the demise of the German Democratic Republic, selections of Beckett's plays (*Spiele*, 1988) and stories (*Ausgewählte Erzählungen*, 1990) were published. In 1990 *Sinn und Form* printed excerpts from a new translation of the 'Proust' essay, once considered the manifesto of Beckett's decadence.

26 Werner Huber, 'Godot, Gorba, and Glasnost: Beckett in East Germany', in Marius Buning and Lois Oppenhein, eds., *Beckett in the 1990s: Selected Papers from the Second International Beckett Symposium* (Amsterdam: Editions Rodopi, 1993), pp. 50–4.

27 David Lloyd, 'Writing in the Shit: Beckett, Nationalism and the Colonial Subject', in Lloyd, *Anomalous States*, p. 56.

28 Kiberd, *Inventing Ireland*, p. 531.

29 Lloyd, 'Writing in the Shit', p. 54.

30 See Anne Saddlemyer ed., *Letters to Molly: John M. Synge to Maire O'Neill* (Harvard: Belknap Press, 1971).

31 J. M. Synge, *Prose* (Oxford: Oxford University Press, 1968), p. 202

32 W. B. Yeats, *Collected Poems* (Basingstoke: Macmillan, 1950), p. 350.

33 Mercier, *Beckett*, p. 46.

34 Mercier, *Beckett*, p. 53.

35 Erich Fromm, *The Fear of Freedom* (London: Routledge, 1984), p. 207.

36 Fromm, *Fear*, p. 96.

37 The text is reproduced in O'Brien, *Beckett Country*, p. 337.

38 Kiberd, *Inventing Ireland*, pp. 537–50.

SELECT BIBLIOGRAPHY

1. Works by Samuel Beckett

Poetry

Whoroscope (Paris: The Hours Press, 1930).
Echo's Bones and Other Precipitates (Paris: Europa Press, 1935).
Collected Poems in English and French (London: Calder, 1977).
Anthology of Mexican Poetry (Bloomington: Indiana University Press, 1958),
    trans. Samuel Beckett.

Fiction

Dream of Fair to Middling Women (London: Calder, 1993).
Murphy (1938; London: Picador, 1973).
Watt (1953; London: Calder, 1976).
Mercier and Camier (London: Calder and Boyars, 1974).
Molloy (1955), *Malone Dies* (1956), *The Unnamable* (1958), published as *The*
    Beckett Trilogy (1959; London: Picador, 1979).
Novellas and Texts for Nothing in No's Knife (London: Calder and Boyars, 1967).
From an Abandoned Work in No's Knife (London: Calder and Boyars, 1967).
How It Is (London: Calder, 1964).
Imagination Dead Imagine (London: Calder and Boyars, 1967).
Enough, in No's Knife (London: Calder and Boyars, 1967).
No's Knife: Collected Shorter Prose 1945–1966 (London: Calder and Boyars, 1967).
The Lost Ones (London: Calder and Boyars, 1972).
For to End Again and Other Fizzles (London: Calder, 1976).
The Expelled and Other Novellas (Harmondsworth: Penguin, 1980).
Company (1980), *Ill Seen Ill Said* (1981), *Worstward Ho* (1983), published as
    Nohow On (London: Calder, 1989).
Stirrings Still (London: Calder, 1988).
As The Story was Told: Uncollected and Late Prose (London: Calder, 1990).

Drama

Eleutheria (London: Faber, 1996).
Waiting for Godot (London: Faber and Faber, 1956).
Endgame (London: Faber and Faber, 1958).
Happy Days (London: Faber and Faber, 1962).
All That Fall (London: Faber and Faber, 1957).
Act Without Words I (London: Faber and Faber 1958).
Act Without Words II (London: Faber and Faber, 1967).
Krapp's Last Tape (London: Faber and Faber, 1959).
Rough for Theatre I (London: Faber and Faber, 1977).
Rough for Theatre II (London: Faber and Faber, 1977).
Embers (London: Faber and Faber, 1959).
Rough for Radio I (London: Faber and Faber, 1977).

Rough for Radio II (London: Faber and Faber, 1977).
Words and Music (London: Faber and Faber, 1964).
Cascando (London: Faber and Faber, 1964).
Play (London: Faber and Faber, 1964) .
Film (London: Faber and Faber, 1967).
The Old Tune (London: Calder, 1963).
Come and Go (London: Calder and Boyars, 1967).
Eh Joe (London: Faber and Faber, 1967).
Breath (London: Faber and Faber, 1972).
Not I (London: Faber and Faber, 1973).
That Time (New York: Faber and Faber, 1976).
Footfalls (London: Faber and Faber, 1976).
Ghost Trio (London: Faber and Faber, 1977).
. . . but the clouds . . . (London: Faber, 1977).
A Piece of Monologue (New York: Grove Press, 1981).
Rockaby (New York: Grove Press, 1981).
Ohio Impromptu (New York: Grove Press, 1981).
Quad (London: Faber and Faber, 1984).
Catastrophe (London: Faber and Faber, 1984).
Nacht und Träume (London: Faber and Faber, 1984).
What Where (New York: Grove Press, 1983).
All the above plays, with the exception of *Eleutheria,* are collected in
   Complete Dramatic Works (London: Faber and Faber, 1986).

Essays and Criticism
'Dante . . . Bruno. Vico . . . Joyce', in Samuel Beckett *et al., Our*
   Exagmination Round His Factification for Incamination of Work in Progress
   (Paris: Shakespeare and Co., 1929).
Proust (London: Chatto and Windus, 1931).
Three Dialogues with Georges Duthuit (London: Calder, 1965).
Disjecta (London: Calder, 1983), ed. Ruby Cohn.

2. Biographies
Bair, Dierdre, *Samuel Beckett: A Bibliography* (London: Jonathan Cape, 1978).
Brater, Enoch, *Why Beckett* (London: Thames and Hudson, 1989).
Cronin, Anthony, *Samuel Beckett: The Last Modernist* (London: HarperCollins, 1996).
Knowlson, James, *Damned to Fame: The Life of Samuel Beckett* (London: Bloomsbury, 1996).

3. General Critical and Theoretical Works Cited
Adorno, Theodor, 'Commitment', in Ernst Bloch, ed., *Aesthetics and Politics* (London: NLB, 1977).
Artaud, Antonin, *The Theatre and its Double* (London: Calder, 1970), trans. Victor Corti.
Artaud, Antonin, 'Production and Metaphysics', in *The Theatre and its Double* (London: Calder, 1970), trans. Victor Corti.

Benstock, Bernard, ed., *The Seventh of Joyce* (Bloomington: Indiana University Press, 1982).

Bloch, Ernst, ed., *Aesthetics and Politics* (London: NLB, 1977).

Brecht, Bertolt, *Brecht on Theatre* (London: Methuen, 1964).

Critchley, Simon, *Very Little . . . Almost Nothing: Death, Philosophy, Literature* (London: Routledge, 1997).

Deane, Seamus, *Celtic Revivals: Essays in Modern Irish Literature 1880–1980* (London: Faber and Faber, 1985).

Derrida, Jacques, *Acts of Literature* (London: Routledge, 1999), ed. Derek Attridge.

Derrida, Jacques, 'The Theatre of Cruelty or the Closure of Representation', in *Writing and Difference* (London: Routledge, 1978), trans. Alan Bass.

Eagleton, Terry, *Crazy John and the Bishop* (Cork: Cork University Press, 1988).

Eagleton, Terry, *Heathcliff and the Great Hunger* (London: Verso, 1995).

Eagleton, Terry, *Literary Theory: An Introduction* (Oxford: Blackwell, 1983).

Eliot, T. S. 'Tradition and the Individual Talent', in T. S. Eliot, *Selected Essays* (London: Faber, 1951).

Esslin, Martin, *The Theatre of the Absurd*, 3rd edition (Harmondsworth: Penguin, 1983).

Fischer, Ernst, *Art Against Ideology* (London: Allen Lane the Penguin Press, 1969), trans. Anna Bostock.

Foucault, Michel, 'What is an Author', in Paul Rabinow, ed., *The Foucault Reader* (New York: Pantheon, 1984).

Freud, Sigmund, *Jokes and Their Relation to the Unconscious*, Pelican Freud Library, vol. 6, trans. James Strachey (Harmondsworth: Penguin, 1976).

Fromm, Erich, *The Fear of Freedom* (London: Routledge, 1984).

Gasché, Rodolphe, *Inventions of Difference: On Jacques Derrida* (Cambridge: Harvard University Press, 1994).

Iser, Wolfgang, *The Implied Reader: Patterns of Communication in Prose Fiction from Bunyan to Beckett* (Baltimore: Johns Hopkins University Press, 1974).

Kearney, Richard, *Transitions: Narratives in Modern Irish Culture* (Manchester: Manchester University Press, 1988).

Kiberd, Declan, *Inventing Ireland* (London: Jonathan Cape, 1995).

Leavis, F. R., *The Great Tradition* (London: Chatto and Windus, 1948).

Leavis, Q. D., *Fiction and the Reading Public* (London: Chatto and Windus, 1932).

Lefort, Claude, 'Outline of the Genesis of Ideology in Modern Societies', trans. John B. Thompson, in John B. Thompson ed., *The Political Forms of Modern Society: Bureaucracy, Democracy, Totalitarianism* (Cambridge: Polity, 1986).

Lloyd, David, *Anomalous States: Irish Writing and the Postcolonial Moment* (Dublin: The Lilliput Press, 1993).

MacCabe, Colin, *James Joyce and the Revolution of the Word* (Basingstoke: Macmillan, 1979).

MacCormack, W. J., *From Burke to Beckett: Ascendancy, Tradition and Betrayal in Literary History* (Cork: Cork University Press, 1995).

Mulhern, Francis, *The Moment of Scrutiny* (London: NLB, 1979).

Nolan, Emer, *James Joyce and Nationalism* (London: Routledge, 1995).

Norris, Christopher, *Derrida* (London: Fontana, 1987).

O'Casey, Sean, *Blasts and Benedictions* (London: Macmillan, 1967).

Peter, John, *Vladimir's Carrot: Modern Drama and the Modern Imagination* (London: André Deutsch, 1987).

Richards, I. A., *Practical Criticism* (London: Routledge, 1929).

Richards, I. A., *Science and Poetry* (London: Kegan Paul, 1926).

Saddlemyer, Anne, ed., *Letters to Molly: John M. Synge to Maire O'Neill* (Harvard: Belknap Press, 1971).

Sartre, Jean-Paul, *L'Être et le Néant* (Paris: Gallimard, 1943).

Sartre, Jean-Paul, *Existentialism and Humanism* (London: Methuen, 1966), trans. Philip Mairet.

Saussure, Ferdinand de, *Course in General Linguistics* (London: Peter Owen Ltd, 1960), trans. Wade Baskin, eds. Charles Bally and Albert Sechehaye.

Synge, J. M., *Prose* (Oxford: Oxford University Press, 1968).

Williams, Raymond, *Drama From Ibsen to Brecht* (London: Chatto and Windus, 1968).

4. General Critical Work on Beckett

Abel, Lionel, 'Joyce the father, Beckett the son', in *The New Leader*, New York, 14 December 1959.

Barnard, G. C., *Samuel Beckett: A New Approach* (New York: Dodd, 1970).

Ben Zvi, Linda, *Women in Beckett: Performance and Critical Perspectives* (Urbana: University of Illinois Press, 1990).

Blanchot, Maurice, 'Where Now? Who Now?', in *Evergreen Review* 2, 1953.

Blanchot, Maurice, 'Oh tout finir', *Critique* 46, 1990.

Bryden, Mary, *Women in Samuel Beckett's Prose and Drama* (Basingstoke: Macmillan, 1993).

Cohn, Ruby, *Samuel Beckett: The Comic Gamut* (New Jersey: Rutgers University Press, 1962).

Cohn, Ruby, ed., *Samuel Beckett: A Collection of Criticism* (New York: McGraw Hill, 1962).

Cohn, Ruby, *Back to Beckett* (New Jersey: Princeton University Press, 1973).

Connor, Steven, *Samuel Beckett: Repetition, Theory and Text* (Oxford: Blackwell, 1988).

Esslin, Martin, 'Introduction', in Martin Esslin, ed., *Samuel Beckett: A Collection of Critical Essays* (New Jersey: Prentice Hall, 1965).

Fletcher, Beryl, John Fletcher et al., *A Student's Guide to the Plays of Samuel Beckett* (London: Faber and Faber, 1978).

Fletcher, John, and John Spurling, *Beckett: A Study of his Plays* (London: Methuen, 1972).

Hesla, David, *The Shape of Chaos: An Interpretation of the Art of Samuel Beckett* (Minneapolis: The University of Minnesota Press, 1971).

Gidal, Peter, *Understanding Beckett: A Study of Monologue and Gesture in the Works of Samuel Beckett* (London: Macmillan, 1986).

Hill, Leslie, *Beckett's Fiction: In Different Words* (Cambridge: Cambridge University Press, 1990).

Homan, Sidney, *Beckett's Theatres: Interpretations for Performance* (Lewisburg: Bucknell University Press, 1984).

Iser, Wolfgang, 'Samuel Beckett's Dramatic Language', *Modern Drama* 9, 1966.

Kalb, Jonathan, *Beckett in Performance* (Cambridge: Cambridge University Press, 1989).

Kenner, Hugh, *Samuel Beckett: A Critical Study* (Berkeley: University of California Press, 1968).

Kenner, Hugh, *A Reader's Guide to Samuel Beckett* (London: Thames and Hudson, 1973).

Knowlson, James, and John Pilling, *Frescoes of the Skull: The Recent Prose and Drama of Samuel Beckett* (London: Calder, 1979)

Kristeva, Julia, 'The Father, Love and Banishment', in Julia Kristeva, *Desire In Language: A Semiotic Approach to Literature and Art* (Oxford: Blackwell, 1981), ed. Leon S. Roudiez, trans. Thomas Gora, Alice Jardine, Leon S. Roudiez.

Levy, Shimon, *Samuel Beckett's Self-Referential Drama: The Three I's* (Basingstoke: Macmillan, 1990).

Lloyd, David, 'Writing in the Shit: Beckett, Nationalism and the Colonial Subject', in David Lloyd, *Anomalous States: Irish Writing and the Postcolonial Moment* (Dublin: The Lilliput Press, 1993).

Locatelli, Carla, *Unwording the World: Samuel Beckett's Prose Works after the Nobel Prize* (Philadelphia: University of Pennsylvania Press, 1990).

Mayoux, Jean-Jacques, 'Samuel Beckett and Universal Parody' in Martin Esslin, ed., *Samuel Beckett: A Collection of Critical Essays* (New Jersey: Prentice Hall, 1965).

Mercier, Vivian, *Beckett/Beckett* (Oxford: Oxford University Press, 1977).

Metman, Eva, 'Reflections on Samuel Beckett's plays', in *Journal of Analytic Psychology*, London, January 1960.

Metman, Eva, 'Reflections on Samuel Beckett's Plays', in Martin Esslin, ed., *Samuel Beckett: A Collection of Critical Essays* (New Jersey: Prentice Hall, 1965).

Mittenzwei, Werner, 'Endspiele der Absurden: Zum Problem des Figurenaufbaus', in *Sinn und Form* 16, 1964.

Murphy, P.J., Werner Huber, Rolf Breuer and Konrad Schoell, *Critique of Beckett Criticism: A Guide to Research in English, French and German* (Columbia: Camden House, 1994).

Murphy, P.J., *Reconstructing Beckett: Language for Being in Samuel Beckett's Fiction* (Toronto: University of Toronto Press, 1990).

O'Brien, Eion, *The Beckett Country: Samuel Beckett's Ireland* (Dublin: The Black Cat Press, 1986).

Pilling, John, *Samuel Beckett* (London: Routledge and Kegan Paul, 1976).

Pilling, John, ed., *The Cambridge Companion to Beckett* (Cambridge: Cambridge University Press, 1994).

Pountney, Rosemary, *Theatre of Shadows: Samuel Beckett's Drama 1956–76* (Gerrards Cross: Colin Smythe, 1988).

Ritter, Joachim, 'Über das Lachen', *Blätter für deutsche Philosophie* 14, 1940/41.

Robbe-Grillet, Alain, 'Samuel Beckett, or Presence on the Stage', in Alain Robbe-Grillet, *For a New Novel: Essays on Fiction* (Salem: Ayer Company Publishers, 1965), trans. Richard Howard.

Robinson, Michael, *The Long Sonata of the Dead: A Study of Samuel Beckett* (London: Rupert Hart-Davis, 1969).

Schenker, Israel, 'A Portrait of Samuel Beckett, the Author of the Puzzling Waiting for Godot', *New York Times*, 6 May 1956, section 2.

Uhlmann, Anthony, *Beckett and Poststructuralism* (Cambridge: Cambridge University Press, 1999).

Worthen, William, 'Beckett's Actor', *Modern Drama* 26, 1983.

5. Critical Work on *Godot* and *Endgame*

Adorno, Theodor, 'Trying to Understand *Endgame*', in Theodor Adorno, *Notes To Literature:* Volume One (New York: Columbia University Press, 1991), trans. Shierry Weber Nicholsen.

Anders, Günther, 'Being Without Time: On Beckett's Play *Waiting for Godot*', in Martin Esslin, ed., *Samuel Beckett: A Collection of Critical Essays* (New Jersey: Prentice Hall, 1965).

Anouilh, Jean, 'Review of *Waiting for Godot*', in *Arts Spectacles*, 27 February–5 March 1953, reprinted in Lawrence Graver and Raymond Federman, eds., *Samuel Beckett: The Critical Heritage* (London: Routledge & Kegan Paul, 1979).

Bryden, Mary, 'Gender in Transition: *Waiting for Godot* and *Endgame*', in Steven Connor, ed., *'Waiting for Godot' and 'Endgame'* (Basingstoke: Macmillan, 1992).

Coe, Richard N., 'God and Samuel Beckett', in J.D. O'Hara, ed., *Twentieth Century Interpretations of Molloy, Malone Dies and The Unnamable* (New Jersey: Prentice Hall, 1970).

Cohn, Ruby, ed., *Casebook on Waiting for Godot* (New York: Grove Press, 1967).

Cohn, Ruby, ed., *Casebook on Waiting for Godot* (London: Macmillan, 1987).

Connor, Steven, 'The Doubling of Presence in *Waiting for Godot* and *Endgame*', in Steven Connor, ed., *'Waiting for Godot' and 'Endgame'* (Basingstoke: Macmillan, 1992).

Esslin, Martin, 'Godot at San Quentin', in Ruby Cohn, ed., *Casebook on Waiting for Godot* (New York: Grove Press, 1967).

Fischer, Ernst, '*Endgame* and Ivan Denisovich', in Ernst Fischer, *Art Against Ideology* (London: Allen Lane the Penguin Press, 1969), trans. Anna Bostock.

Fraser, G.S. 'Review of *Waiting for Godot*, in *Times Literary Supplement*, 10 February 1956, reprinted in Lawrence Graver and Raymond Federman, eds., *Samuel Beckett: The Critical Heritage* (London: Routledge & Kegan Paul, 1979).

Gray, Ronald, '*Waiting for Godot*: a Christian Interpretation', in *The Listener*, 24 January 1954, reprinted in Lance St. John Butler, ed., *Critical Essays on Samuel Beckett* (Aldershot: Scolar Press, 1993).

Hobson, Harold, 'Review of *Endgame*' in the *Sunday Times*, 7 April 1957, reprinted in Lawrence Graver and Raymond Federman, eds., *Samuel*

Beckett: The Critical Heritage (London: Routledge & Kegan Paul, 1979).

Hobson, Harold, 'Review of *Waiting for Godot*' in the *Sunday Times*, 7 August 1955, reprinted in Lawrence Graver and Raymond Federman, eds., *Samuel Beckett: The Critical Heritage* (London: Routledge & Kegan Paul, 1979).

Huber, Werner, 'Godot, Gorba, and Glasnost: Beckett in East Germany', in Marius Buning and Lois Oppenhein, eds., *Beckett in the 1990s: Selected Papers from the Second International Beckett Symposium* (Amsterdam: Editions Rodopi, 1993).

Iser, Wolfgang, 'Counter-sensical Comedy and Audience Response in Beckett's *Waiting for Godot*', in Steven Connor, ed., *'Waiting for Godot' and 'Endgame'* (Basingstoke: Macmillan, 1992).

Kavanagh, Patrick, 'Some reflections on *Waiting for Godot*', in *The Irish Times*, 28 January 1956, reprinted in Lance St. John Butler, ed., *Critical Essays on Samuel Beckett* (Aldershot: Scolar Press, 1993).

Lawley, Paul, 'Adoption in *Endgame*', *Modern Drama* 31.4, 1988.

Lemarchand, Jacques 'Review of *En attendant Godot*', 17 January 1953, trans. Jean M. Sommermeyer, in *Figaro Littéraire*, reprinted in Lawrence Graver and Raymond Federman, eds., *Samuel Beckett: The Critical Heritage* (London: Routledge & Kegan Paul, 1979).

Marcabu, Pierre, 'Review of *Waiting for Godot*', in *Arts-Spectacles*, 10–16 May 1961, trans. Jean M. Sommermeyer, reprinted in Lawrence Graver and Raymond Federman, eds., *Samuel Beckett: The Critical Heritage* (London: Routledge & Kegan Paul, 1979).

Mercier, Vivian, 'The Uneventful Event', in *The Irish Times*, 18 February 1956, reprinted in Lance St. John Butler, ed., *Critical Essays on Samuel Beckett* (Aldershot: Scolar Press, 1993).

Surreau, Geneviève, 'Beckett's Clowns', in Ruby Cohn, ed., *Casebook on Waiting for Godot* (New York: Grove Press, 1967).

Tynan, Kenneth 'Review of *Waiting for Godot*', in the *Observer*, 7 August 1955, reprinted in Lawrence Graver and Raymond Federman, eds., *Samuel Beckett: The Critical Heritage* (London: Routledge & Kegan Paul, 1979).

Tynan, Kenneth, 'Review of *Endgame*', in the *Observer*, 7 April 1957, reprinted in Lawrence Graver and Raymond Federman, eds., *Samuel Beckett: The Critical Heritage* (London: Routledge & Kegan Paul, 1979).

Zilliacus, Clas, 'Three Times Godot: Beckett, Brecht, Bulatovic', in *Comparative Drama* 4, 1970.

ACKNOWLEDGEMENTS

The editor and publisher wish to thank the following for their permission to reprint copyright material: Routledge (for material from 'Review of *En attendant Godot*', 'Review of *Waiting for Godot*', and 'Review of *Endgame*', in *Samuel Beckett: The Critical Heritage;* and *Acts of Literature*); Scolar Press (for material from 'Some reflections on *Waiting for Godot*', in *Critical Essays on Samuel Beckett*); Ayer Company Publishers (for material from 'Samuel Beckett, or Presence on the Stage', in *For a New Novel: Essays on Fiction*); Penguin (for material from *The Theatre of the Absurd;* and '*Endgame* and Ivan Denisovich', in *Art Against Ideology*); Columbia University Press (for material from 'Trying to Understand *Endgame*', in *Theodor Adorno, Notes to Literature: Volume 1*); Prentice Hall (for material from the 'Introduction' to *Samuel Beckett: A Collection of Critical Essays*); University of California Press (for material from *Samuel Beckett: A Critical Study*); Rutgers University Press (for material from *Samuel Beckett: The Comic Gamut*); New York Times (for material from 'A Portrait of Samuel Beckett, the Author of the Puzzling *Waiting for Godot*'); Johns Hopkins University Press (for material from *The Implied Reader: Patterns of Communication in Prose Fiction from Bunyan to Beckett*); Macmillan (for material from 'Counter-sensical Comedy and Audience Response in Beckett's *Waiting for Godot*', 'The Doubling of Presence in *Waiting for Godot* and *Endgame*', and 'Gender in Transition: *Waiting for Godot* and *Endgame*', in *'Waiting for Godot' and 'Endgame'*); Editions Rodopi (for material from 'Godot, Gorba, and Glasnost: Beckett in East Germany', in *Beckett in the 1990s: Selected Papers from the Second International Beckett Symposium*); Jonathan Cape (for material from *Inventing Ireland*).

There are instances where we have been unable to trace or contact copyright holders before our printing deadline. If notified, the publisher will be pleased to acknowledge the use of copyright material.

Peter Boxall is a lecturer in English Literature in the School of English and American Studies at the University of Sussex. As well as lecturing at Sussex University, he has taught at the universities of Gothenburg and New York. He has published a number of articles on aesthetics and politics in twentieth-century literature, and is currently editing a collection of essays for *Samuel Beckett Today*, entitled *Beckett/Aesthetics/Politics*. He is also completing a monograph on Beckett's writing, entitled *Samuel Beckett: Cultural Politics and the Space of Writing*.

INDEX

Abel, Lionel 32–3
absurdity 7, 10, 12, 27, 81, 148
action 24, 72, 84, 106–7, 108
Adorno, Theodor
    Endgame 38–50, 138
    individual 40
    Marxist reading 6, 8, 51, 134, 138
    negativity 13, 22
    validity of Beckett's art 170 n51
aesthetic
    of failure 56, 171 n14
    negativity 12–13, 22, 38
Anders, Günther 61
Anglo-American criticism 51, 52
Anouilh, Jean 12, 14
art 21, 52, 55
Artaud, Antonin 97–8, 117, 119, 120,
    125–6
Attridge, Derek 97–9
audience 126, 127
authenticity 54, 56

bad faith 26, 30
Bair, Deirdre 92
Barker, Ronald 169 n21
Barnard, G.C. 52
Barthes, Roland 54, 93, 95
Beckett, Samuel 56–7, 59, 65–6, 136,
    151, 166
    audience 126, 127
    and Brecht 48, 138–9, 147–8
    critics 8, 9, 21, 51–2, 63, 169 n21
    culture 41–2, 55
    and Joyce 14, 31
    language 23, 96–7, 98–9, 173 n11
    liberal humanist approach 63–4, 99
    misogyny 127, 137
    on Proust 24, 29, 32
    Schenker interview 96, 117
    stage 7, 24, 59, 66, 117
being there 24, 121
    Heidegger 39, 101, 118
Ben Zvi, Linda 127, 134
Berkeley, George 171 n18
biblical quotes 85, 105
bicycle motif 52
Blanchot, Maurice 95, 98, 173 n3

Blin, Roger 10, 18, 19
boy
    Endgame 34–5, 77, 132, 163
    Waiting for Godot 25, 67, 87, 121–2
Braun, Volker 149–50
Brecht, Bertolt 48, 63, 138–9, 147–8
Bryden, Mary 7, 116–17, 127–34, 137

carnival effect 102–3, 107, 151
Carroll, Lewis 123
catharsis 34, 61–2, 112–13
changes, Waiting for Godot 72–3
chess, Endgame 75–8, 141
Chevigny, Bell Gale 51
Christian approach 13–16, 26–7, 84–5,
    88–90
circular song, Waiting for Godot 122
close reading 53–4
Clov
    habit 144–5
    and Hamm 132, 140–1
    as intellect 31, 35
    liberty 34
    and Nell 129–30, 131
    power 19–20, 162, 163–4
    waking up metaphor 75
    see also master–slave relationship
clown 104, 105, 107
Cohn, Ruby 51, 52, 117
    Endgame 88–92
    Waiting for Godot 83–8
comedy 23
    Cohn 52, 83–92
    Estragon 85, 102, 103–4
    human condition 110
    spectator 108–9
    unhappiness 91, 112–13, 114
    Vladimir 102, 103–4
    see also clown; laughter; vaudeville
        effects
communication 23, 43, 63, 116
Connor, Steven 7, 116–17, 135, 139
    Endgame 123–7
    Waiting for Godot 120–3
counter-sense 108, 109–10
Critchley, Simon 134
criticism 8, 9, 21, 63, 169 n21
    assumptions 52–3
    Endgame 5–6, 9–13, 51–2
    function 10, 52, 54, 59–60
    gender 116–17

Iser's influence 114–16
mystical experience 61
Waiting for Godot 5–6, 9–13, 51–2
cross-talk 29–30
Cullen, Louis 156
culture 40–2, 44–5, 55, 135

deconstructive approach 7, 117, 173 n11
dégoût 43
Democritus the Aberdite 34
depressive state 33–4
Derrida, Jacques 93, 95, 97–9, 125–6
Descartes, René 65–6
Devine, George 18, 19
differentiatedness 48
discourse approach 93
Dostoevski, Fyodor 46
drama
    conventions 5–6, 11
    meaning 38–9, 42
    negativity 42, 51
    spectator 103, 127
    universal truth 83
    see also theatre
Dreifuß, Alfred 150

Eagleton, Terry 37, 139, 153
eidetic intuition 46
Eleutheria 32
Eliot, T. S. 51–2, 52, 53
Endgame 5, 18–19, 31–2, 41
    absurdity 81
    Adorno 38–50, 138
    as autobiography 32–3
    boy 34–5, 77, 132, 163
    as chess game 75–8, 141
    Cohn 88–92
    Connor 123–7
    critical response 5–6, 9–13, 51–2
    Esslin 31–6
    existentialism 39–40, 41
    gender 131–2, 133
    human condition 35, 50, 77–8
    Iser 110–14
    Kenner 74–83
    master–slave relationship 144–6,
        161–2
    power complex 19–20
    repetition 124–6
    resurrection 90–2
    salvation 90

self-reflexivity 78–81, 125
sickness as permanence 18
Tynan 55
vaudeville effects 82
    see also Fin de partie
Engel, Wolfgang 151–2
Esslin, Martin 36, 51, 59–60, 134
    collection of essays on Beckett 55–64
    Endgame 31–6
    language 23
    liberal humanist criticism 6–7, 21–2,
        37–8, 62–3
    redemption 102
    Waiting for Godot 24–30
    see also The Theatre of the Absurd
Estragon
    comedy 85, 102, 103–4
    contemplative life 15
    essential truth 36
    hope 26
    meaning of waiting 12
    as poet 84
    as proletarian 148
    self-image 28, 154–5
Europe, post-war bleakness 14
events/situations 35
existentialism 12, 22, 23
    Endgame 39–40, 41
    freedom 36
    history 44, 46–7
    literature 60
    ontology 46
    Sartre, Jean-Paul 12, 30, 36,
        169–70 n47
    Waiting for Godot 107–8
experience 62, 115

failure
    action 108
    as aesthetic 56, 171 n14
    communication 116
    to learn from mistakes 155–6
    memory 87, 121, 156
false consciousness 146
feminist approach 7, 127–34
La fin 172 n42
Fin de partie 18–20, 132, 169 n41
    see also Endgame
Finnegans Wake (Joyce) 70–1, 95,
    96
First Love 133

Fischer, Ernst 8, 138, 139–47, 167
Fletcher, John 51, 92
formalist criticism 52, 54, 99
Foucault, Michel 93, 95, 173 n3
Fraser, G.S. 13–16
freedom 34, 36, 49, 118, 164
Freud, Sigmund 109, 111
Fromm, Erich 164–5

Gadamer, Hans-Georg 100, 119
gender 131–4
    Beckett's plays 127–8
    criticism 116–17
    Endgame 131–2, 133
    Waiting for Godot 133
German language criticism 51, 138
Germany, Beckett 148–52
Gidal, Peter 134
God and the Irish 164–5
Godot as character 24
Gontarski, Stanley 92

habit 27–8, 28–9, 142, 144–5
Hall, Peter 18–19
Hamm
    as actor 75–6, 79–80, 126
    beggar story 82–3, 142–4
    blindness 31–2, 91
    as chess King 75–6
    and Clov 140–1, 165
    as Godot 18
    and Ham, son of Noah 88–9
    as Joyce 20, 32–3
    Nell 130
    power 19–20, 89
    self-contemplation 82
    solitude 127
    see also master–slave relationship
Hammel, Claus 149
Happy Days, Winnie 9, 128, 162
Hegel, G.W.F. 140, 163
Heidegger, Martin 23, 39, 98, 101, 118
Hein, Christophe 150
Hesla, David 52
Hill, Leslie 116, 134
Hirsch, E.D. 100
history 44, 46–7, 48
Hobson, Harold 11–12, 20
Homan, Sidney 117, 118
How It Is 59, 172 n40
Huber, Werner 148–53

human condition
    comedy 110
    counter-sense 109–10
    Endgame 35, 50, 77–8
    Heidegger 23
    Vladimir 28–9
    Waiting for Godot 15, 16, 17, 28–9, 35, 50
humanism: *see* liberal humanist
    approach
Huxley, T.H. 81

identity, post-colonial 153
ideology 37, 63, 129
idiocy/oppression 159
individual 37, 40, 49
interdependence, mutual 32
intuition 30, 34, 46
Irishness 138, 153, 164–5, 166
Iser, Wolfgang 7, 102
    counter-sense 108, 109–10
    Endgame 110–14
    influence on criticism 114–16
    negativity 100–1
    Waiting for Godot 101–8
isolation/laughter 110, 111

journeying 71, 74
Joyce, James
    and Beckett 14, 31
    Derrida on 98
    Finnegans Wake 70–1, 95, 96
    Hamm 20, 32–3

kaputt 40–1, 44–5
Kavanagh, Patrick 16–18
Kenner, Hugh 51, 52
    Endgame 74–83
    liberal humanism 64–5, 83
    man on bicycle 171 n31
    Waiting for Godot 64–74
Kern, Edith 92
Kibérd, Declan 8, 139, 153–66
Kierkegaard, Søren 46, 60, 61
Knowlson, James 51, 92
Kristeva, Julia 95

language
    Beckett 23, 96–7, 98–9, 173 n11
    communication/thought 23, 43
    Esslin 23
    post-structuralism 139

laughter 103–5, 110–12, 113
Lawley, Paul 116, 134
Lawrence, D. H. 63
Leavis, F. R. and Q. D. 51, 52, 53
Lefort, Claude 129
Lemarchand, Jacques 10, 11
Lévi-Strauss, Claude 54
liberal humanist approach 37, 51
  Beckett 63–4, 99
  Brecht 63
  Esslin 6–7, 21–2, 37–8, 62–3
  ideology 54
  Kenner 64–5, 83
  and Marxism 6–7
literary allusions 57–8
literature
  authenticity 54, 56
  as cultural guardian 53–4
  emotional impact 61–2
  existentialism 60
  quality of experience 62
Lloyd, David 139, 153
Locatelli, Carla 116
Lucky
  as ass/policeman 148
  as Beckett 32–3
  journeying 15, 71, 74
  master–slave relationship 156–7
  oppression 161
  recognition failure 25
  speech 69, 73
  supposed death 85
Lukács, Georg 38, 43, 47, 138, 170 n51

MacCabe, Colin 95
Malone Dies 34, 71–2, 84–5, 172 n41
Marcabu, Pierre 36
Marxist approach 6, 51, 138, 140–1,
    176 n8
  see also Adorno
Mask, Ahmad Kamyabi 132
master–slave relationship 140–2, 163
  Endgame 144–6, 161–2
  Waiting for Godot 142, 156–7
Mayoux, Jean-Jacques 89–90, 137–8,
    176 n4
meaning
  contrasts 111
  drama 38–9, 42
  in meaninglessness 9–10, 13, 42
  universal 39

meaninglessness 7, 9–10, 13, 42
memory failure 87, 121, 156
Mercier, Vivian 13, 72, 120, 137, 160–1
Mercier et Camier 71, 84
Metman, Eva 28, 35, 61
millet heap 124
mime-plays 23
misogyny 127, 137
Mittenzwei, Werner 148, 177 n19
Molloy 84, 96
monodrama, Endgame 31
More Pricks than Kicks 59, 133
Morrissette, Bruce 118
Mulhern, Francis 53–4
Müller, Heiner 149, 151, 152
Murphy 76, 84, 166
Murphy, Murphy 34
Murphy, P. J. 38, 55
mystery plays 35

Nagg
  accident 91
  and Nell 19, 128–9, 131
  as pawn 76
  trouser story 82
naïveté of clown 104, 105
nature, end of 45
negativity 7, 20–1
  aesthetic 12–13, 22, 38
  cultural disintegration 135
  dramatic 42, 51
  of historical age 48
  Iser 100–1
  political radicalism 167
  positivity 13, 18
  silent 41
  Waiting for Godot 11–12
Nell
  death 19, 130
  gender 128
  and Nagg 128–9, 131
  as pawn 76
  unhappiness 91, 114, 129
Nell (The Old Curiosity Shop) 130
New Criticism 51, 52, 53, 56
nihilism 34, 36, 37, 98
  see also negativity
non-play 67–8
nonsense 103
Not I 123
nuclear threat 47–8

O'Brien, Eion 176 n3
O'Casey, Sean 17, 162
Ó Faracháin, Roibeárd 166
Ó Rathaille, Aogán 154
Ó Ríordáin, Seán 163–4
objectivity/subjectivity 39
objects 71–2, 172 n39
The Old Curiosity Shop (Dickens) 130
One Day in the Life of Ivan Denisovich
   (Solzhenitsyn) 140
ontology 43–4, 46
oppression 159, 161

parody 43–4, 46
Peter, John 71
phallocentrism 127
Pilling, John 51, 92
Play 118, 123
Plessner, Helmuth 108, 111
political criticism 137–8
political radicalism 167
positivity from negativity 13, 18
post-colonial approach 8, 139, 153–4
post-structural feminism 127–34
post-structuralist approach 94–6, 139
post-war bleakness 14
Pountney, Rosemary 92, 147
power relations 19–20, 135, 140–1, 162,
   163–4
   see also master–slave relationship
Pozzo
   diminished 122
   helped by tramps 84
   journeying 15, 71, 74
   as landowner 148, 158, 160–1
   and Lucky 32
   master–slave relationship 156–7
   recognition failure 25, 156
   self-centred 28
   sight 72–3
   theatricality 69, 157–8
   time 26
Practical Criticism 51
presentation 41–2, 80
Proust, Marcel 24, 29, 32
psychological approach 61

reader response theory 100, 101–2, 115
reading 53, 100
recognition failure 25, 87, 156
redemption 102, 123

reflection and presentation 41–2
repetition
   ad infinitum 35–6
   with decrease 122–3
   Derrida 126
   Endgame 124–6
   Waiting for Godot 121–3
representations of women 127–8
resurrection, *Endgame* 90–2
Richards, I. A. 52, 53–4, 55
Ritter, Joachim 103, 110
Robbe-Grillet, Alain
   existentialism 22, 39
   present 125
   redemption 102
   self-reflexivity 66
   stage presence 39, 67, 117–18, 120
   stage space 71, 117
Robinson, Michael 51, 117
Rockaby 123

sado-masochistic relations 165
salvation
   clowning 107
   Endgame 90
   Waiting for Godot 16, 26, 30
San Quentin performance of *Waiting for
   Godot* 34, 107, 169 n40
Sartre, Jean-Paul
   absurdity 12
   bad faith 26, 30
   existentialism 12, 30, 36, 169–70 n47
   freedom 49, 118
   Huis Clos 124
Schall, Ekkehard 150
Schenker, Israel 96, 117
schizophrenia 52
Schneider, Alan 18, 19, 83
Schopenhauer, Arthur 19, 159
Science and Poetry 53
Scrutiny periodical 52
self-knowledge 86, 167
self/other 127
self-reflexivity 176 n9
   Connor 117, 139
   Endgame 78–81, 125
   Homan 118
   Waiting for Godot 66
Sextus Empiricus 124
silence 23, 41
situations/events 35

skull imagery 75
socialist realism 38, 49–50, 147, 152
sociological approach 61
Solzhenitsyn, Alexander 140
spailpín poets 154
spectator
    comedy 108–9
    drama 103, 127
    expectations 107–8
    Robbe-Grillet 71, 117
    text/performance 119–20
Spurling, John 51, 92
stage
    Beckett 7, 24, 59, 66, 117
    as inside of skull 75
    Iser 102
    symmetry 7, 66
stage presence 39, 67, 117–18, 120–1
States, Bert O. 92
structuralism 54, 115
subjection 162
subjectivity 39, 49–50, 60
suicide, *Waiting for Godot* 27, 28, 73, 85–6
Sunday Times 20
surds and absurdity 81, 172 n46
surrealism 58
Synge, J.M. 154

Tannhäuser legend 171 n33
text/performance 119–20
theatre
    organic evolution 119
    physicality 119
    quintessential 69
    as spectacle 126
    universal 16–18
    see also drama; stage
Theatre of Cruelty 119, 120, 125–6
The Theatre of the Absurd 7, 21–2, 36, 38,
    51, 142
thinking 23, 29–30, 43, 60
time 25–6, 46–7, 86–7
totalitarianism 43
tragicomedy 87–8
tree, *Waiting for Godot* 66–7, 86
Trilse, J.C. 150–1
truth
    essential 13, 36
    universal 50, 55–6, 64, 83
Tynan, Kenneth 11, 19–21, 38, 55

Uhlmann, Anthony 134
unhappiness 91, 112–13, 114, 129
The Unnamable 69–70, 125
urination 84, 85

value/valuelessness 36, 37
vaudeville effects
    Endgame 82
    Waiting for Godot 67–8, 70–1
victims, freedom 49
Vladimir
    biblical quotes 85
    carrot 172 n39
    comedy 102, 103–4
    contemplative life 15
    essential truth 36
    and Estragon 32
    hope 26
    human condition 28–9
    as intellectual 148
    meaning of waiting 12
    self-image 28, 154–5
    urination 84, 85

waiting
    and action 84
    and existence 86
    journeying 71, 74
    meaning 12
    as objective 28
    sanctified 73–4
    as subject of play 24–6
Waiting for Godot 5, 10–11, 15, 17, 24,
    69–70, 159–60
    biblical references 85, 105
    boy 25, 67, 87, 121–2
    Brecht 148
    carnivalesque 151
    Christian interpretation 13–16, 26–7,
        84–5, 88–90
    circular song 122
    Cohn 83–8
    Connor 120–3
    critical response 5–6, 9–13, 51–2
    East German production 151–2
    Esslin 24–30
    existentialism 107–8
    gender 133
    human condition 15, 16, 17, 35, 50
    Iser 101–8
    Kenner 64–74

Waiting for Godot (cont.)
    master–servant relationship 142,
        156–7
    negativity 11–12
    overall plot-line 105, 107
    repetition 121–3
    salvation 16, 26, 30
    San Quentin performance 34, 107,
        169 n40
    self-reflexivity 66
    suicide 27, 28, 73, 85–6
    time 86–7

tree 66–7, 86
    vaudeville effects 67–8, 70–1
Watt 62, 111
Weber, Max 147
Whitelaw, Billie 126
Winnie, *Happy Days* 9, 122, 128, 162
Wolfskehl, Karl 48
women, representations 127–8
Worth, Katharine 92
Worthen, William 118

Yeats, W.B. 154